The Ganja Complex

The Ganja Complex

Rastafari and Marijuana

by
Ansley Hamid

LEXINGTON BOOKS
Lanham • Boulder • New York • Oxford

LEXINGTON BOOKS

Published in the United States of America
by Lexington Books
An Imprint of the Rowman & Littlefield Publishing Group
4720 Boston Way, Lanham, Maryland 20706

12 Hid's Copse Road
Cumnor Hill, Oxford OX2 9JJ, England

British Library Cataloguing in Publication Information Available

Library of Congress Cataloging-in-Publication Data Available

ISBN 0-7391-0360-1 (cloth: alk. paper)
Library of Congress Control Number: 2002004715

Printed in the United States of America

∞™ The paper used in this publication meets the minimum requirements of American National Standard for Information Sciences—Permanence of Paper for Printed Library Materials, ANSI/NISO Z.39.48-1992.

Contents

Acknowledgments

This book incorporates material from my doctoral dissertation, for which I conducted fieldwork in Trinidad and Tobago in 1975, 1976, 1977, and 1978–1979 and which I completed writing at Teachers College, Columbia University, in New York City in 1980. It also contains additions, revisions, and reflections which I inserted in 2000. Accordingly, two rounds of acknowledgments are due.

First, the cooperation and goodwill of the Trinidadian informants during the periods of field research were indispensable in carrying out this research, especially when the presence of an outsider renders dangerously conspicuous gatherings, events, and purposes for which the penalties are stiff fines and sometimes up to life in prison.

Two exploratory stages of this research, carried out in the summers of 1975 and 1976, were funded by the Institute of Latin American and Iberian Studies, Columbia University. The major stage of fieldwork in Trinidad in the summer of 1977 and for fourteen months in 1978 and 1979, and of write-up in New York City for eight months from 1979 to 1980, were funded by the National Institutes of Mental Health (now the National Institute on Drug Abuse). A generous scholarship from the Ford Foundation supplemented this support.

Without the sponsorship, advice, and encouragement of Professor Lambros Comitas of Teachers College, Columbia University, my graduate studies in anthropology would not have begun, nor would they have been completed. The debt of seminal ideas utilized in this report is owed to him and to Dr. George Bond, also of Columbia University.

During the period of write-up, the facilities of Teachers College, Columbia University, and of the Research Institute for the Study of Man, directed by Dr. Vera Rubin, were made available to me.

My sister Sponse has always been enthusiastic about my studies, giving me both encouragement and generous financial support. She was especially helpful during this research. My sons, Rahul and Jyotin, accompanied me on all the field trips to Trinidad: their presence eased my entry into many situations and gained me enduring friendships. During my fieldwork in New York my daughters, Deshana and Alecia performed the same roles.

A second round of acknowledgments are owed for 2000. Professors Comitas and Bond, my teachers at Teachers College, Columbia University, maintained the encouragement and friendship I have always received from them. My experience as a professor of anthropology at the John Jay College of Criminal Justice, my interaction with thousands of students in the fifteen years after my return from the field, and professional engagements enriched my understanding of drugs and their relation to culture and society. Additionally, funding from several sources, including the National Institute on Drug Abuse, the Harry Frank Guggenheim Foundation, and the Professional Staff Congress of the City University of New York, assisted me in furthering my research on drugs. I particularly wish to thank Ms. Karen Colvard of the Harry Frank Guggenheim Foundation for her unflagging enthusiasm for my work.

In research projects on cocaine during the 1990s, I emphasized the contrasts between the cocaine-smoking epidemic of that decade and the regime of marijuana which had preceded it and which forms the topic of this book. Two major grants from the National Institute on Drug Abuse, entitled "Heroin in the 21st Century" (1996) and "International Drug Markets Convergence" (1997), broadened my perspective by enabling me to investigate new situations and different drugs. I was also able to renew contact with study participants in New York and Trinidad and to learn how marijuana, cocaine, and other drugs had affected them in drug-using (or drug-avoiding) careers which had extended over some twenty years.

Preface

I have tried to combine several distinct but related themes in this book. It will help the reader to be introduced briefly to them at the start.

First, the book is about a plant, cannabis or marijuana, its effects upon men, and some of the political battles which have been engaged for and against it. This plant is an excessively luxuriant, weedy annual which sometimes towers to a height of over eighteen feet. Since it thrives best in the worked, nitrogen-rich soils near human habitations, it has followed human settlement far beyond its original ranges. Indeed, given its near-universal popularity today, it could well be among the first cultivens of the planet earth which scientists and astronauts will introduce (albeit clandestinely and maybe illegally) to outer space. The plant is dioecious: the weaker male or staminate plant is differentiated from the female or pistillate plant. On the latter, pistillate flowers grow in the leaf axils. A resin produced in these flowers and their adjacent leaves and stems contains intoxicating chemical compounds (Abel 1980).

A plant of considerable antiquity, native to India and China and reputedly the first to be cultivated by settled human communities, it was eventually diffused widely throughout the Old World (Abel 1980; Bennett et al. 1995). Asians, Europeans, Arabs, and Africans developed multiple household, industrial, medicinal, religious, and ritual uses for its various preparations. While some Old World political regimes proscribed them, or tolerated them begrudgingly, they were mostly embraced enthusiastically.

While botanists have disagreed about the family to which the plant belongs, sometimes classifying it among the fig or mulberry family (*Moraceae*) or the nettle family (*Urticaceae*), it is now regarded, together with the hop plant (*Humulus*), as belonging to a distinct family (*Cannabaceae*). Following Linnaeus, two varieties of the plant, *cannabis sativa* and *cannabis indica*, are commonly recognized. This classification, however, has been challenged. Problems of plant collection in Linnaeus's time probably limited the identification of other variants. Recognizing the need for investigating wild cannabis in its native habitats, Richard E. Schultes, the renowned Harvard ethnobotanist, has completely revised cannabis taxonomy. Informed by his own field studies, the work of Lamarck, and the observations of Soviet botanists, Schultes introduced a polytypic classification (Schultes 1975).

Many organic chemical compounds have been isolated in cannabis, only some of them having narcotic properties, such as cannabidiolic acids, precursors of the tetrahydrocannabinols, cannabinol, cannabidiol, tetrahydrocannabinol-carboxylic acid, stereoisimers of tetrahydrocannabinol, and cannabichromene. It has been demonstrated that the main psychoactive effects are attributable to delta-1-tetrahydrocannabinol, a nonnitrogenous organic compound derived from terpenes.[1]

Of the two commonly recognized varieties, *cannabis indica* is the smaller plant which thrives in cooler climates, such as are found in the upper slopes of mountains. Selection for narcotic properties, especially in India, has yielded many subvarieties. The potent modern *sinsemilla* varietals (literally, "without seed," or intensively cultivated marijuana requiring advanced techniques such as hydroponics and careful tending, such as the separation of female plants) are grown from strains of *cannabis indica*.

Cannabis sativa is a tall, bushy lowland plant, better adapted to tropical heat and rain. Subvarieties of *cannabis sativa* have been developed principally to improve fiber and oil content. *Cannabis sativa* was introduced to the New World by Spanish conquistadors in the fifteenth century. Until the twentieth century, it was apparently grown in America for hempen fibers, cloths, and seeds. Americans for the most part were ignorant of the tinctures, gums, and other medicinal preparations of the plant described in Old World pharmacopeias. Marijuana smoking for recreational purposes or as a religious sacrament and its use as a food were brought in the mid-1840s to the Americas via the Caribbean by Indian laborers, who had been indentured to replace emancipated African labor in the region's sugarcane plantations (Hamid 1980, 1997a; Weller 1972; Morton 1916). They were bearers of the original "ganja complex" whose modern manifestation I describe in this book. Mexican, Jamaican, and African American laboring populations quickly appreciated the value of this psychotrope; by the 1880s, it had also acquired a following among European Americans.

Marijuana in the Americas had escaped prohibition in 1914, when international conventions outlawed the use and cultivation of many psychotropic substances. It was criminalized in 1937, however, mostly at the instigation of Commissioner Harry Anslinger of the Federal Bureau of Narcotics. A failed career diplomat, Anslinger used the marijuana issue to revive his fortunes in governmental service. Under his direction, an official picture of marijuana was drawn, in which the drug was held responsible for the poverty and moral apathy of native peoples, such as Mexican farm laborers, and posed a threat to American users. Anslinger encouraged the making of *Reefer Madness*, a film showing how an upright European American youth embarked on a life of rape and crime after a single puff of marijuana. Now a cult classic, it is still shown regularly at 3:00 A.M. on some television networks, along with Japanese monster movies. Occurring simultaneously with the rise of xenophobic sentiments against Mexican migrant workers, Anslinger's campaign resulted in severe penalties against the possession, use, and cultivation of marijuana.

The increase in marijuana use during the late 1960s and early 1970s raised hopes that the sanctions against marijuana would be reversed. Several publications proved that the drug's dangers had been previously exaggerated, and advocated that the country's marijuana laws be made more lenient (Solomon 1966; Kaplan 1970; Grinspoon 1971; Brecher 1972). In Canada and the United Kingdom, governmental commissions also favored reform of marijuana laws. In the United States, three presidential commissions—the Prettyman Commission appointed by President Kennedy in 1963, the Katzenbach Commission appointed by President Johnson in 1966, and the Shafer Commission appointed by President Nixon in 1972—recommended abandonment of a strict prohibitionist policy against what they considered a relatively safe mind-altering drug. Heeding them, the federal government and many states reduced the penalties for marijuana possession in the 1970s. Alaska fully decriminalized possession, and in many jurisdictions around the country, de facto decriminalization existed.

Several important anthropological studies of the effects of marijuana in natural settings, pioneering the social-scientific approach in drug research, strengthened the antiprohibitionist cause. The first and most renowned of these was *Ganja in Jamaica*, in which anthropologists not only studied marijuana cultivation, distribution, use, and effects in six distinct rural communities in Jamaica, but also referred their informants to the University of the West Indies Medical School, where exhaustive tests were performed to assess their physiological and neurological functioning (Rubin and Comitas 1975). Students of Vera Rubin and Lambros Comitas, the anthropologists who directed the Jamaican study, subsequently wrote stellar ethnographies of marijuana use in Costa Rica and Greece. Their conclusions echoed those of the Indian Hemp Drugs Commission (1894) that long-term marijuana use was a boon in the lives of laborers in the many parts of India where its members had conducted investigations. The commission specifically refuted claims that marijuana use was associated with an "amotivational syndrome" which robbed men of ambition and prevented them from working. Indeed, members of the commission reported quite the opposite effects. This anthropological report about marijuana cultivation, distribution, and use in Trinidad and Tobago is the most recent descendant of the Indian Hemp Drugs Commission and *Ganja in Jamaica*, the author having been a grateful student of both Professors Comitas and Rubin.

The Reagan administration of the 1980s demolished these expectations. The "war on drugs" was engaged with redoubled energy and money. Crop substitution and eradication programs were initiated in marijuana-growing countries abroad, while full-scale military assaults were conducted against domestic growers in California and Hawaii. Spurred by Nancy Reagan's "Just Say No" campaign and her intransigent attitudes against marijuana, antidrug citizens'organizations proliferated.

At the same time, however, marijuana cultivators worldwide, and especially in the Americas and the Caribbean, significantly improved their horticultural and entrepreneurial skills and succeeded in bringing to market a more potent, better-preserved product, including the sinsemillas and other variants of *cannabis indica* mentioned above. An international fair is still convened annually in Amsterdam, where seeds and techniques are exchanged.

Since the 1990s, hopes have revived again that the prohibition against marijuana in the United States will soon be modified or revoked. Californian voters supported a "medical marijuana" initiative in 1996. Subsequently, the Drug Medicalization, Prevention, and Control Act, which was supported by 65 percent of the Arizona electorate in 1997, actually sought to "medicalize" that state's drug policy. Disallowing further incarceration of nonviolent drug offenders, it mandated drug treatment and probation instead and permitted doctors to prescribe marijuana for the relief of a wide range of health problems, including AIDS, cancer, and glaucoma.

On August 13, 1998, the Oakland City Council named the operators of the Oakland Cannabis Buyers Club (CBC) "officers of the city." This title was intended to give them immunity from federal prosecution under the Controlled Substances Act because they would be "agents of law enforcement" overseeing the distribution of medical marijuana, according to 21 USC 885 (d). The Council also voted to increase the amount of medical marijuana that patients can possess to an amount twenty-four times the maximum that had been established by California attorney general Dan Lundgren in 1996. The decision allowed patients who live in Oakland and use medical marijuana to possess up to one and a half pounds of marijuana, an amount which the FDA considers a three-month supply. Lundgren's limit had permitted possession of up to one ounce. If patients grow their own marijuana, they are permitted to have up to six pounds of marijuana. The City Council decided that in addition to this a patient can grow as many as forty-eight flowering plants and ninety-six nonflowering plants indoors, or thirty flowering plants and sixty nonflowering plants outdoors.[2]

Other states, such as Ohio and Connecticut, may revise their laws in light of the actions of these ordinary American citizens in California and Arizona. Medical marijuana initiatives are on the ballot in the District of Columbia, Nevada, Oregon, and Washington State. In Hawaii, a federal court judge is considering whether Rastafari is a bona fide religion, of which marijuana use and cultivation are cornerstones, and whether the case against a female Rastafari for cultivating a few marijuana plants for personal use should be dismissed according to the Restoration of Religious Freedoms Act of 1995.[3] The struggle to decriminalize or legalize marijuana has been championed by influential private citizens nationwide.[4]

At the same time, supporters of the "war on drugs" have not been idle. Both drug czar Barry McCaffrey and former Drug Enforcement Administration administrator Thomas Constantine have warned doctors who attempt to comply with the sentiments of Arizonans and Californians that they would face charges under the federal laws governing cultivation and sale of marijuana and the DEA regulations which guide them in prescribing controlled substances. They reminded potential offenders that based on the 1988 U.N. Convention Against Illicit Traffic in Narcotic Drugs and Psychotropic Substances, the International Narcotics Control Board (INCB) claims that all nations are obliged to enact laws that prohibit inciting or inducing people "by any means" to "use narcotic drugs or psychotropic substances illicitly." According to the INCB's report, offenders include anyone who "shows illicit use in a favorable light" or who advocates "a change in the drug law."

They noted that the INCB's report criticizes "reputable medical journals" for "favoring the 'medical' use of cannabis," since "such information . . . tends to generate an overall climate of acceptance that is favorable to" illegal drug use. The report also attacks the marketing of nonpsychoactive hemp products, such as clothing and foodstuffs, for "contributing to the overall promotion of illicit drugs."

The new director of the U.N. Drug Control Program, Pino Arlacchi, declared in 1997 that he was determined to make the world "drug-free in ten years." He has begun by attacking advocates of drug policy reform.[5]

The subject matter of this book should interest partisans on both sides. In the late 1960s and during the 1970s, desperate young Trinidadian Africans, both on the islands and in immigrant communities abroad, had been stalemated by the frustrations of exclusion from the educational system and job training, unemployment in an increasingly consumerist society, high rates of inflation, migration, and disarrayed families. They had responded by committing petty crimes and misusing alcohol and eventually by rioting and an attempted overthrow of the government. Then they discovered marijuana. Smoking it in communal settings utterly transformed them. They metamorphosed into prudent, ambitious businessmen, self-employed artisans, and responsible paterfamilias, who delighted in reading the Bible, scholarly books, and the newspapers and philosophizing about what they learned by cross-referencing them. Furthermore, they translated their revolutionary sentiments into a program of community betterment, in which they reinvested marijuana revenues to foster self-sufficiency or independence from mainstream institutions.

Whether, in the twenty-first century, the United States will remain a nation in which respectable, productive, otherwise law-abiding adults can face the risk of arrest, public humiliation, imprisonment, loss of employment, family distress, and asset forfeiture for possessing small amounts of marijuana, or for growing a single marijuana plant, now appears to be not a foregone conclusion but a matter of widening public debate. I hope that my demonstration of how marijuana fortified men leading embattled lives will help promote the needed reappraisal of the nation's drug policy.

Second, a related goal of the book, of course, will be to illuminate how drugs, in this case a mere handful of dried twigs, can possibly have those "magical" effects it appeared to have had in successive human populations, such as the young Caribbean Africans to be discussed particularly in this book. The claims of both those who approve or tolerate marijuana use and those who condemn it—if they take the form of "marijuana turned them into demons" or "marijuana turned them into angels"—are equally implausible to social scientists, who as a rule eschew monocausal (and plainly fantastical!) explanations for complex human behaviors.

Working within the anthropological paradigm, I place the emphasis in the human–drug interaction not on the drug, but on the human. For the most part, groups create the effects drugs have on their members. Thus in this book I illustrate the view that drugs affect humans for better or for worse, not primarily as pharmacological substances but rather as symbols, as meanings or parts of meaningful lifestyles, as the medium of exchange in informal economies, and as icons into which are packed the social-organizational energies of those involved in their production, distribution, and consumption. Accordingly, I identify a "ganja complex," one which I later contrast with other marijuana use-complexes in Trinidad (for example "madi-juana" use: see chapter 7), as responsible for the benign effects I report, and explain how its charters for belief, cognition, and action were transferred cross-culturally across the globe, to be nurtured in contexts quite foreign to the one where it originated.

Thus, after exhaustively describing in the first six chapters how the different outgrowths of the ganja complex broke ground in Trinidad and the Caribbean of the 1970s, I shall have the evidence to argue in chapter 8 that marijuana had had perceptible effects on young islanders as a concentrate of ongoing social and economic dynamisms. They had provided the needed nourishment for the ganja complex to take root in the first place.

Third, in attempting to reach the first two goals, the book alludes to key anthropological issues. It documents the survival and diffusion of a cultural pattern across time and nations. Originating some 5,000 years ago in Northern India, a distinctive ganja complex was established throughout the Indian subcontinent. Over several succeeding centuries, associated with the spread of other Indian cultural products such as Hinduism and Buddhism, it took root elsewhere in southeast Asia. Next, it was carried, from 1838 to 1917, to the Americas when Indian laborers were indentured to the British Caribbean to replace emancipated African labor on the sugarcane plantations. In most of the Caribbean colonies to which the Indians were introduced, such as Trinidad, Suriname and Guyana, the ganja complex withered within a few decades, and the use and cultivation of marijuana virtually disappeared. In Jamaica, however, the ganja complex rapidly became endemic, not only among its Indian bearers but, more remarkably, among rural and urban Africans, who had tenaciously maintained their own African traditions, sometimes syncretized or camouflaged with elements of the Judeo-Christian symbology, throughout more than four centuries of slavery and social marginalization. Adapting the ganja complex to concordance with their ancestral folkways, including traditions of millenarianism and messianism, they have subscribed faithfully and continuously to it for over 150 years to the present day.

The saga of this ancient Asian ganja complex was refueled in the 1960s. By this time, Caribbean immigrant communities had been established in many urban centers in the United States, Canada, and Europe, such as New York, Montreal, London, Paris, and Amsterdam. Young Caribbean Africans in Caribbean nations other than Jamaica, including Trinidad, Guyana, and Suriname, as well as their peers in the Caribbean immigrant populations, now welcomed it. They in turn planted it among their local neighbors, such as African Americans, Latinos, Canadians, the British, and Northern Europeans.

In a final twist, the ganja complex has even returned home. It has been rediffused recently to young fifth-generation Indians from Trinidad, Suriname and Guyana, some living in the Caribbean immigrant communities abroad, whose great-grandparents and grandparents had spurned it after debarking from India.

Fourth, the focus on the ganja complex, or on the drug in its cultural–psychological–political–socioeconomic context rather than on marijuana, the pharmacological substance, marks a major preoccupation. The study of the diffusion of a cultural pattern, and of its evolutionary forms in the diverse contexts in which it was cultivated, provides comparative insight of the social, economic, cultural, and political conditions in which psychological and pharmacological agents interact and combine to produce drug-related effects in humans. It thus supplies an anthropological corrective to the prevailing psychopharmacological paradigm in drug studies.

The revision of this psychopharmacological paradigm, which has provided the scientific justification for the "war on drugs," has been long overdue. In the case of marijuana, it has cluttered the public consciousness with a fearsome melange of half-truths and outright falsehoods. Beginning in the 1930s with the deliberate and opportunistic lies of Harry Anslinger, the campaign has included the pseudoscientific studies of Nahas (1975), which linked marijuana smoking to chromosomal loss and organic brain damage; of Kolanski and Moore (1971), who identified a "cannabis psychosis"; and the Chopras (1968), who, in the midst of the Vietnam War, frightened Americans with the intensity of the disaffection, rebellion, and the "amotivational syndrome" which they claimed to have discovered among American marijuana smokers traveling in India as "hippies" and "flower children."

Fifth, as it is anthropological and based on extensive ethnographic fieldwork, the book is concerned with Trinidad, Caribbean Africans, Asians in the Caribbean, interethnic relations in Caribbean society, Caribbean migration to New York City, and the present status of these island communities in the modern world system. Several considerations are due in this regard:

Thus, while Trinidad and Tobago, the site of this ethnographic research and the islands specifically studied, are Caribbean societies, participating in the same common history of plantation slavery as the other islands, they are in some respects quite unique. For example, the sovereignty of Trinidad and Tobago had changed hands more frequently than the other islands, and thus exhibits the legacy of British, French, and Spanish not only in the cosmopolitan composition of the population, but in enduring customs and quasi-legal institutions. While most other Caribbean islands, such as Haiti, the Bahamas, Barbados, Antigua, Dominica, or the French and Dutch islands, have homogeneous African populations, the advent of large numbers of Asians, both Chinese and Indians, has also given Trinidad and Tobago the sort of atmosphere of such territories as Mauritius, Reunion, Fiji, or the Philippines. Indeed, lessons drawn from Trinidad and Tobago are more readily applicable to the multicultural United States of America than to the other Caribbean islands.

What all these peripheral territories of Africa, Asia, Latin America, and the Caribbean share, however, are informal economies which coexist with the formal, corporate economy, subsidizing the latter with important values, goods, and services. In the 1960s, researchers in Latin America, Asia, and Africa reported these sectors of urban economic enterprise which participated in the overall economy, but were at the same time distinct from it. For example, in Trinidad and Tobago and Rio de Janeiro, a small army of workers are mobilized, for at least six months in the year, to produce their world-famous carnivals. Indeed, the Trinidad carnival has been integrated with fledgling ones on the other islands and in Caribbean African communities throughout North America and Europe, and provides year-round employment (Hamid 1983a). Independently of banks and other official institutions, the carnival personnel provide the financial and fiduciary services, researchers, a clerkdom and the many types of artisans, costumers, and musicians to produce the event, which may last from a single day to a week. In other Catholic capitals in Latin America, year-long employment is provided for food vendors, manufacturers of religious relics, and ritual specialists who cater to the feast days of several saints. Hindu India employs a similar labor force to celebrate a bursting calendar of national, regional, and religious holidays. In Southeast Asia, the kitchens and kitchen gardens of city homeowners are factories where bean curd, condiments, pickles, and other foodstuffs are prepared for local and international markets.

Sidewalks along streets in major third-world cities are thronged with unlicensed vendors selling goods of every description, and the trend extends to New York City, where over 10,000 sidewalk vendors operate throughout the year. They congregate especially in midtown, in Chinatown, and at Africa Square (125th Street and Lenox Avenue) in Harlem. On Labor Day, or Caribbean American Day, thousands more line Eastern Parkway in Brooklyn. More recently, Mexicans and Central Americans have installed curbside taquerías in midtown Manhattan and in the city's Latino communities. In the cities of the third world, many necessities of life—food, shelter, clothing, medical care, spiritual and mental therapy, education, entertainment—are completely satisfied by self-made tinkers, tailors, cooks, builders, artists, "quacks," or other service providers.

Some theorists, relying on a broad definition of informal sector activity, include the "criminal" or underground economy as part of this sector (e.g., Mattera 1985; Gaughan and Ferman 1987), while others reserve the term to apply properly only to "income-generating activities that take place outside the framework of public regulation, where similar activities are regulated"

(Sassen-Koob 1991, 89). For example, a great many enterprises in the informal economic sector are illegal and carry the disability for their proprietors of being unceremoniously removed from the place of business, goods and all, by the police. Technically, the sale of goods offered by street vendors and the services provided by doctors or dentists who practice without licenses, or the religious services rendered by ritual specialists whom the state has not recognized, could be undertaken in the formal economy. Criminal activities, however, including the distribution of drugs, are differentiated by their exclusion from other economic sectors. This study adopts the first, more inclusive definition of informal-sector activity; especially in regard to the features described below, there is little to choose between selling drugs or selling peanuts at a street corner in Harlem or Flatbush.

Thus, several features of this sector distinguish it from the formal or corporate capitalist economic sector. Enterprises in the informal sector tend to be small and locally based, usually employing fewer than fifteen workers. Several economic indices distinguish such businesses from similarly sized, small-scale capitalist enterprise. They are modestly capitalized. Wages are adjusted to provide bare self-sufficiency for workers. Many exchanges are by barter rather than by cash. Access to labor is furnished by appeal to folk culture, or by kinship and ethnic ideologies. Redistribution of wealth, or capital redeployment, is regulated by the same informal contracts which bind labor.

Some enterprises, however, bring affluence and political clout to their proprietors. In Ghana and Nigeria, market women are sources of substantial credit and sponsor youth groups or other voluntary associations which sometimes assume overt political functions. In South Africa and Angola, "shebeens," or "yards" where women brew and sell beer, and where the beer is consumed nightly by crowds of males, have also been the centers of political activism in the two countries. In Jamaica, "higglers," or itinerant female vendors who link kitchen gardens in the remote countryside with urban households, also transfer politically sensitive information and serve as creditors in a mixed portfolio of rural and urban business undertakings (Katzin 1959).

In Italy, where estimates suggest that the informal economy represents about 30 percent of GNP (Mattera 1985), Sicily hosts an informal economic sector sufficiently large to support a "development elite," which controls large voting blocs, agricultural holdings, and entrepreneurial concerns. The "development elite" is opposed to the "modernization elite," which recruits from urban professionals and administrators. While the former approves economic programs for Sicily which emphasize indigenous wealth, talents, and skills, the latter believe that economic growth means greater reliance upon foreign capital and management (Schneider, Schneider, and Hansen 1972).

In Bolivia, where 80 percent of the entire economy is based on the production and export of coca, the informal economy has surpassed the formal economy and dominates economic and political life (Craig 1990). Coca cultivation and cocaine production have penetrated and bolstered existing informal economic-sector activities to the point where the size of illegal transactions is equivalent to the balance of trade (Jiminez 1989).

In the United States, estimates of the size of the informal economy vary from $42 billion to $369 billion (Guttman 1977; Feige 1979; Mattera 1985; McCrohan and Smith 1986). A recent survey of the cash exchange component of the informal economy (which ignored drug distribution and sales and other criminal activities) estimated informal expenditures at $42 billion, suggesting that the informal economy accounts for approximately 11.5 percent of all domestic transactions (McCrohan and Smith 1986). While these estimates are generally regarded as unreliable (Portes and Sassen-Koob 1987), a growing body of research indicates that informal-sector activities in major cities in the United States have expanded considerably over the last decade (Sassen-Koob 1989). Although illegal or the object of various forms of official suppression, the informal economic sector abides in a symbiotic relation with the formal sector (Henry 1988). Poorly paid workers in the latter survive from day to day, and are deterred from labor unrest, because the informal-economic sector provides them with cheap or affordable goods and services. Retired workers are heavily reliant on them to make ends meet. And meantime, in the preparation of goods and services, manpower is trained and developed, without costing government training programs or educational resources, and capital is accumulated which may eventually be incorporated into the formal sector.

On the other side of the coin, the availability of capital through sources other than the legally recognized ones, and of labor earning less than the minimum legal wage (if necessary) is an important prerequisite, when the entrepreneur is uncouth, without creditworthiness, and lacking in accredited business and managerial skills, for that thrust into the mainstream world. An immigrant especially must first use cousins, coreligionists, or his ethnic ties in order to become later an employer who uses employees (Ianni 1972; Light 1972).

The coexistence of capitalist enterprise with other forms of economic activity originates in the thirteenth and fourteenth centuries, when the former was being established. When capitalist entrepreneurs were initiating such capitalist forms of enterprise as cattle herding and the urban economies in Western Europe, Eastern Europe experienced its "second feudalism." To supply Western Europe with grain and other foodstuffs made scarce by the capitalist novelties in land use, feudal arrangements in Eastern Europe were doubly enforced (and with unprecedented cruelty) in a drive to increase agricultural production (Malowist 1972).

The reciprocal relationship has continued between the formal corporate sector of the economy and informal economies as capitalist forms of enterprise took root throughout the world. (Meillassoux 1981; Long 1984). In the Americas, the informal economic system has had a special significance for the African population, among whom it originated in the plot of land planters ceded to slaves four centuries ago. Although the planters intended to reduce their operating costs by prodding slaves to feed themselves, the latter cherished the land as a free space, where African traditions could be revived. They also built a complex internal marketing system by exchanging their agricultural produce. This backbone still supports local trade and rural–urban exchanges in contemporary Haiti and Jamaica.

In the United States, the shift to informalization has necessitated a restructuring of relationships between core and periphery workers. Much agricultural production now utilizes the mix of labor provided by illegal immigrants, homeless populations, and drug users. Recently in New York, a famous fashion designer was arrested for maintaining a sweatshop of Latino seamstresses in the Bronx who were undocumented aliens. To produce her prize-winning fashions, therefore, this designer depended upon the labor of her distributors like Bloomingdale's and upon unionized garment workers and truckers. But the profit margins of the whole enterprise rested upon "unfree," "noncompeting" labor in the informal sector. Much of agricultural production in the United States also utilizes this mix of labor. Indeed, the candidacies of two persons for high governmental offices in the Clinton administration were disqualified because their housekeepers belonged to this category of workers.

Today, both the formal and informal economic sectors are integrated internationally and respond to global cycles of expansion and depression (Wallerstein 1974). Corporate, capitalist enterprise is an international entity in which multinational corporations perform crucial functions. Entities such as the World Bank and the International Monetary Fund unite them formally. The bloc of nations in which it is represented now includes the republics of former Soviet Russia and the Eastern European nations. In these latter countries, conditions are ripe for the growth of local segments of the informal economy, which has also become an international entity. One of its main pillars, the drug trade, which orchestrates the efforts of growers in rural parts of the world, those of processors and importers in several countries, and finally those of distributors in capital cities, exemplifies its transnational, multicultural character.

On a global level, the trend toward informalization has been accelerated by economic recession and the transition to a postindustrial service economy (Sassen-Koob 1989). Global multinational corporations utilize workers in the third world to produce their products at subsistence wages while workers in the West are forced into low-paying service jobs and the informal economy (Portes and Sassen-Koob 1987). However, while many different kinds of activities are suited to informalization, it is the boundaries of state regulation that determine informalization rather than the characteristics of particular activities: the informal economy "is a highly opportunistic process with changing boundaries" that can only be understood by reference to "the basic dynamics that induce informalization" (Sassen-Koob 1991, 89).

It was boosted tremendously in value in the 1980s by the cocaine economy originating in the Andean nations of South America. These drug economies offer a fruitful arena for future investigations of the phases of informal economies and their relation to the corporate world.

Finally, migration and U.S.–Caribbean interconnections and relationships are critical to an understanding of the marijuana economy and to the uses to which Caribbean peoples put the drug. A nodal point of contemporary Caribbean culture and society is Brooklyn, which many claim as the "largest Caribbean territory" rather than part of the American polity. Here Jamaicans, Haitians, Trinidadians, and immigrants from every other territory share neighborhoods; cooperate or compete for employment, housing, and privileges; interact interpersonally; and are forging a contemporary regional identity which will resonate substantially in the political spectrum of New York City. No contemporary consideration of Trinidad and Tobago or of the Caribbean Basin and Circum-Caribbean region is possible, therefore, unless they are placed in the hemispheric context, dominated by the United States, and in the even broader perspective of global society, economics, and politics. What a drug cultivator in Trinidad and Tobago does may be determined by what persons he knows in Brooklyn do, and their actions in turn are those of Americans contending in a global community.

An important (and sinister) aspect of these U.S.–Caribbean interconnections concerns law enforcement and the establishment of a global police regime (Nadelmann 1990). The "war on drugs" waged by the United States has furthered the careers of questionable policies and persons abroad. The murders described in chapter 5 are a gory outcome.

In this book, the reader will be taken back and forth between the Caribbean and the mainland United States. While potentially confusing, these passages portray the reality. I have tried to develop my skills as a writer so that these movements and the several themes they engage are harmoniously blended.

Methods

In April 1977, the National Institute on Drug Abuse funded a research application I had submitted, entitled "Synchronic and Diachronic Variations in

Cannabis Use Among East Indians in Trinidad" (Grant No. DA 01838). The objectives of this study were twofold: (1) to investigate the conditions which led to the virtual abandonment of cannabis use among Indians in Trinidad at the turn of the century, even though they had introduced their long-established knowledge and use of the substance only fifty years earlier; and (2) to describe and account for the present-day readoption of cannabis use in Trinidad by several categories of younger Indians.

To reach these objectives, two major research components were visualized: (1) archival research on early Indian cannabis or ganja usage utilizing the extensive documents housed in the Parliamentary Library, the West Indian Reference Library, and the Law Library in Port-of-Spain, the capital of Trinidad and Tobago, and those more recently collected in San Fernando, the second-largest city of the nation and the most important Christian mission to Trinidadian Indians, by the Presbyterian Church; and (2) social anthropological investigations of contemporary Indian cannabis use. The latter theme was to entail (a) the measurement of the extent of cannabis use; (b) the delineation of users' networks, particularly with respect to buying, selling, and consumption of ganja and of differentiations among these networks; (c) the recording of beliefs, rituals, and justifications related to ganja use among the various categories of Indian users; and (d) the selection of informants, users, and non-users from whose accounts life histories and case studies could be constructed.

During the course of the NIDA-funded research and two earlier exploratory field sessions sponsored by the Institute of Latin American and Iberian Studies, Columbia University, all of these research goals plus a number of others were reached and a rich body of pertinent data was amassed.

A short natural history of the Trinidad project is as follows:

During a three-month period in 1975, I carried out a detailed study of a rural village, with the pseudonym of Raw Deal. This community contains a population almost equally divided between Indians and Africans. A thorough household census of Raw Deal yielded data on differential patterns of social stratification, land tenure, and economic levels. I carefully investigated patterns of cannabis production, distribution, and consumption. This initial, community-wide research provided a substantial basis for hypothesis construction and for planning the overall design and methodology of the research that followed.

During a three-month period in 1976, I undertook fieldwork in a more diversified, more urban site than that afforded in Raw Deal. In this locale, Princes Town, a community in South Trinidad rapidly emerging from its rural roots, I identified networks of cannabis users and studied and recorded patterns of cannabis trade and consumption. I singled out two geographical sections of Princes Town for detailed scrutiny:

(1) an enclave of Indian sugar workers living on the outskirts of the community which also included a quasi-segregated group of Indian landed proprietors who cultivate sugarcane on contract for multinational sugar estates; (2) a neighborhood in the heart of Princes Town inhabited by an ethnically diverse population which was also sharply stratified socioeconomically.

By the end of these two field sessions in Raw Deal and Princes Town, or a total of six months of fieldwork, I had achieved a relatively clear comprehension of the context of ganja use in both rural and urban settings in Trinidad.

During an eleven-month period straddling 1977 and 1978, the fieldwork focus shifted to San Fernando, not only the second-largest city but also the "industrial capital" of Trinidad. I selected this city primarily because of the large concentration of Indians who had been settling there since the earliest days of the Indian indenture. It is also my birthplace. For the first four months, research was carried out in San Fernando which paralleled that completed in Raw Deal and Princes Town in order to provide the project with essential data on urban cannabis patterns. With the completion of this phase, the gross parameters in Trinidadian ganja use in rural and urban settings had been identified. I then devoted the remaining seven months in the field to understanding the complexity and dynamics of the Trinidadian ganja phenomenon through the intensive study of the origins and consequences of marijuana use and distribution among San Fernandian users by focusing on the operation of key networks of urban users and distributors.

To add a necessary dimension to the overall study, I spent several weeks in 1975, 1976, and 1978 in residence in a cannabis-growing village close to the rain forests in South Trinidad and made many daylong expeditions to this locale in the company of urban ganja dealers who had traveled there from San Fernando to buy marijuana wholesale. During these visits, I interviewed the leading local growers and dealers, observed and discussed various aspects of growing and marketing, and investigated village patterns of use.

Attention should be drawn here to the peculiar demands of participant observation—the most distinguishably anthropological of the field methods employed in this study—in researching ganja in Trinidad, where use is sensitive politically and heavily proscribed. Throughout the entire period of fieldwork, absolute discretion was required in locating users and traffickers and in tracing out the networks between them, while at the same time maintaining contact and collecting data among nonusers. During the seven months of research in San Fernando, key informants selected for interviews on various aspects of ganja trafficking (including the police involvement) and for the collection of life histories, were persuaded to allow these data to be tape-recorded. The success of this operation relied heavily on my credentials as a San Fernandian and as an age-mate, neighbor, and friend.

These tape-recorded conversations, rich in relevant detail and conveying some of the ambiance of the field, are given a prominent place in this book. Eventually forty ninety-minute tapes were considered for inclusion: these were transcribed by myself and a Trinidadian assistant. It should be noted that our familiarity with the language spoken in the tapes adds to the accuracy of the transcripts.

As time permitted during the entire field research period, I completed archival research in Port-of-Spain and San Fernando. Pertinent documents related to cannabis were reproduced or hand-copied, newspaper files were carefully combed, and special attention was paid to the collection of materials dealing with the legal status of cannabis in Trinidad from 1863 to the present. These diverse documents proved exceptionally useful during the analytic phase of the project.

Analysis of the Trinidad data commenced in September 1978 in the offices of the Joint Program of Applied Anthropology at Teachers College, Columbia University. During this phase, I made extensive use of the facilities of the university as well as the excellent Caribbean and drug-related library collections of the Research Institute for the Study of Man, New York City. Write-up of the project commenced in March 1979 and was completed by September 1979.

This book goes beyond the original definition of the problem and sets forth theoretical considerations and includes significant data not anticipated in the original design. This, it is felt, is an unexpected dividend of the research and adds testimony to the value of the holistic approach of anthropology. In this regard, early analysis of field data strongly suggested the pivotal role of young Trinidadian Africans, rather than Indians, in creating and continuing the present-day ganja phenomenon in Trinidad. Equally striking were the energies which the ganja traffic, organized chiefly by the African users, lent to this role. In Raw Deal, for example, Africans were the earliest and most numerous ganja users, and the traffic in the substance was controlled entirely by them. In Princes Town, both using and trading networks of several categories of Indian users were tracked back to using and trading networks of the African residents in the town center. Similar observations were made early in the fieldwork in San Fernando. In the cannabis-growing village, an arresting discovery was that middle-aged Indians, who had only recently become growers, were nonusers of the substance and strongly disapproved of use among their adolescent sons. The latter had been taught to use the ganja their fathers grew by the handful of young Trinidadian Africans living in this predominantly Indian countryside. Thus, a full description of the social characteristics of ganja use in Trinidad depended on a thorough collection of data on African users, a fact that had not been completely anticipated in the original design.

Again, in this regard, I quickly discovered that different populations were reporting different effects on behavior as a consequence of regular daily use (approximately five to ten joints daily). A ganja complex, reminiscent of that described in *Ganja in Jamaica*, in which religiopolitical elements predominated, was being differentiated from a madi-juana complex, which featured polydrug use and recreational settings. These differences seemed to be expressed in the segregations and distinctions arising in urban ganja markets, which were dominated by Africans. It appeared again, therefore, that in any serious discussion of effects, a logically early step in the research had to be the collection of data on all aspects of African use. Furthermore, the picture of the ganja traffic that began to emerge in the preliminary analysis and of its place among the economic strategies of the lower-class or unemployed Trinidadian Africans who were the chief users bore a remarkable resemblance to the picture suggested by accounts of early Indian use and trafficking in Trinidad, when income generated from ganja was one very effective form of leverage out of the despised status of "indentured Indian agricultural laborer."

Finally, at the same time that I was acknowledging the importance of African use, the Trinidadian public also realized it. The beliefs, opinions, attitudes, and justifications about the drug and the traffic which Trinidadian African ganja users espoused had deepened into a form of Rastafarianism, an ideological system which provided a biblical stamp of approval for both use and trafficking, at the same time that the media and the police had grown increasingly hostile toward it. The ensuing confrontation divided the citizenry, claimed fatalities, and encroached increasingly on national politics. The significance of ganja as a source of the material production of value, in the context of persistently high rates of unemployment, migration, and inflation, stimulated urgent public discussion.

The charge of irrelevance, often leveled at scholarly endeavors, could not have been avoided in the case of this project if I had not taken steps to broaden the original scope of the research. The final report was drafted, therefore, as much in awareness of the practical and applied uses this study may have in regard to matters of such topical importance as in deference to the logical and theoretical priorities described above. At the same time, it must be noted that full advantage was taken in formulating this manuscript of those absolutely necessary and happily abundant materials collected on the Trinidadian Indians. Moreover, this procedure had an arresting effect in the investigation as it flagged unforeseen complexities of the ganja phenomenon in Trinidad; for example, when the "Indians" cited in this document come to identify themselves through the agency of ganja and through their involvement in the ganja traffic as "Africans" and Rastafari.

This study, while focusing on the ganja phenomenon, addresses itself to several key problems of Trinidadian and Caribbean sociology. The issue of race and ethnicity is raised in the dramatic fashion already suggested. Beyond that, the type of socioeconomic formation Trinidad is, the kinds of social classes participating in it, and the sort of change it is likely to undergo are questions whose usual formulation is unsettled by the emergence of a large unemployed population which has adopted the unique social organizational features, cultural initiatives, and economic functioning to be described in these pages.

The emergence of similar complexes in other populations around the globe, and their increasing politicization in this decade, enhances the plausibility of the world systems approach to be argued in this study. In this approach, Trinidad is viewed as a peripheral-capitalist socioeconomic formation within the capitalist world system. This study seeks to contribute to an understanding of the actual economic life of such societies, and specifically to illuminate the relationship between the corporate, capitalist sector and the informal economy.

This book has also benefited from my continuing research on drugs, specifically cocaine in the 1980s and heroin in the 1990s. These studies have confirmed the notion that in the array of drugs currently available to American users, marijuana distinguishes itself as a prescription for responsible behavior. It appears that its use is rallying yet another disheartened population in the late 1990s. After the much-publicized ravages of cocaine smoking during the 1980s, drug users in American inner cities are restricting themselves to marijuana, which features in what might thus be called an indigenous harm reduction program. For example, they are showing the same caution and circumspection by which they have chosen marijuana over cocaine and heroin in the other areas of their lives. Despite the proliferation of guns and gangs, most young persons in minority, low-income neighborhoods in New York City seem freshly committed to strive for good grades and to complete their education and job training, are concerned about neighborhood revitalization and public health issues, and pursue wholesome activities in sports and the arts (Hamid 1998). As a result, the city has recently benefited from a precipitous decline of criminal offending in all categories. If they are to be furthered in this wholesome direction, the current drug laws, and marijuana laws in particular, should be urgently reviewed. The example of countries such as the Netherlands, which tolerates marijuana use, could be followed.

NOTES

1. Only a few types of chemical compounds are hallucinogenic. In plants, only organic compounds, or those containing carbon, are hallucinogenic. Inorganic compounds, such as minerals, are nonhallucinogenic. Most hallucinogenic compounds are alkaloids

which also contain nitrogen in their structure. The active principles of marijuana, terpenophenolic compounds classed as dibenzopirans and called cannabinols—in particular, tetrahydrocannabinol—are among the few which lack nitrogen (Emboden 1972; Schultes 1975).

2. Christopher Wren, "A Bid to Shield Medical Sales of Marijuana," *New York Times*, 14 August 1998, A15; V. Dion Haynes, "Marijuana Club Given Official Role in Oakland," *Chicago Tribune*, 14 August 1998, 1.

3. The Restoration of Religious Freedoms Act, signed into law by President Clinton in 1997, protects religious practices from state interference, unless government can justify it by showing "a compelling interest."

4. Since the 1990s, wealthy Americans like the philanthropist Ray Smart and the financier George Soros have invested substantial sums in the debate to reform drug policy. Their contributions support the Lindesmith Center in New York and San Francisco, which is headed by Ethan Nadelmann and Marsha Rosenbaum. Prominent supporters of marijuana and drug policy reform include federal judge Robert Sweet; Kurt Schmoke, the mayor of Baltimore; Pat Murphy, the former New York City Commissioner of Police; and Milton Friedman, the Nobel prize–winning, economist at the University of Chicago. Drs. Andrew Weil, Lester Grinspoon, Harry Levine, John Morgan, Lynn Zimmer, Stanton Peele, and Alexander Shulgin are other academics who support reform.

5. Phillip O. Coffin, "A Duty to Censor: U.N. Officials Want to Crackdown on Drug War Protesters," *Reason*, vol. 30, no. 4 (August/September 1998), 54–55.

Introduction: Use-Complexes and the Ganja Complex

The gifts of cannabis to man include hemp fiber, edible fruit, edible seeds, industrial oil, industrial wax, medicine, and a narcotic. Different human populations have valued it for these several uses or have concentrated exclusively on one alone. In the study of all its uses, however, and especially as a narcotic or psychoactive, the concept of use-complexes will aid the reader to understand how the sociocultural and economic processes in human groups predominate in human–drug (or–plant) interactions, rather than merely biochemistry or pharmacology. As the ganja complex, its components as well as its cross-cultural, transnational, and transhistorical diffusion, forms the particular focus of this study, its differentiation from other use-complexes needs to be appreciated.

Marijuana use and cultivation were not prohibited by international agreement until the 1930s, on the insistence of the government of the United States. Since prehistoric times, however, it had been used freely by many peoples of the Old World and was regarded mostly as a benign plant, an unambiguous boon of nature. Its use, however, was interwoven into broader tapestries of cultural practices and traditions which provided a consistent system of beliefs, attitudes, justifications, rituals, and behaviors to regulate it. The term "use-complex" refers to the insertion of the tasks of marijuana cultivation, distribution, and consumption into these regulatory systems which then determined how individuals valued and experienced them.

Use-complexes explain the broad variation in psychosomatic effects and psychosocial outcomes which different societies have reported about marijuana use in different historical periods. Thus, because such use-complexes have mediated the human–drug encounter, it is difficult to assert confidently or meaningfully that Chinese, Assyrian, Hindu, Muslim, Jew,

European, Greek, Turk, and modern-day American "used marijuana": the practice conveyed such unique, sometimes contradictory meanings to these diverse peoples as to be a completely new phenomenon from age to age and from culture to culture. Some users (and those who opposed or persecuted them) felt that marijuana had made them assassins, others were stimulated by pacificism, and yet others by rebellion or heightened nationalism. Many more were affected by little more than a hunger attack or a spell of dreamy sleep. Others restricted use of the plant to its industrial uses, such as the production of oils, waxes, and fiber, and experienced no psychoactive effects at all. In some use-complexes, *cannabis sativa* was used exclusively; in others, mostly *cannabis indica* and its variants.

MARIJUANA USE-COMPLEXES IN HISTORY

A review of some of the diverse relations humans have maintained with marijuana illustrates this variation:

Neolithic

While the exact place has not yet been determined, the cannabis plant is generally believed to have originated in Central Asia, and the earliest recorded references to it are in the ancient literature of China. The earliest tangible evidence of hemp in the world, in the form of hemp cloths and fabric-marked pots, has been recovered in Neolithic sites (circa 4000 B.C.) in north-central China, eastern Siberia, Taiwan, Hong Kong, Kansu, and Chinese Turkestan. Similar deposits have been unearthed in other Neolithic sites in Austria, Romania, Switzerland, and Germany. Neolithic humans harvested wild *cannabis sativa* to make clothing, rope, fishnets, and pottery mats. They may have also eaten the nutrient-rich seeds (Li 1975).

Chinese

In some Chinese languages, the words for "marijuana" and "plant" are one, leading historians to conclude that marijuana had been the first plant these Chinese cultivated. They prized *cannabis sativa* trees for their long stem fibers, and increased fiber production by planting them in dense thickets to enable them to attain their greatest height. Such plantations also yielded abundant harvests of the nutritious seeds. The Chinese use-complex, however, also recognized the medical and therapeutic properties of the plant. The first medical uses of cannabis were documented in China, in a herbal text of the second century A.D. Flowers and stems were steeped in wine to produce medicines and an anaesthetic used by Chinese surgeons. These preparations were also integrated into shamanistic and healing traditions (Bennett et al. 1995).

Southeast Asian and Near Eastern

Elsewhere in the ancient world, other use-complexes, again centered around harvests of wild and cultivated *cannabis sativa*, have been recorded in Persia, Assyria, Babylon, and Palestine. The Persian Avesta reports that the Zoroastrian heroes Gustasp and Ardu Viraf attained wisdom through imbibing a beverage prepared of *cannabis sativa*, while Hvovi, the wife of Zoroaster, prayed that the One God, Ahura Mazda, bless her with gifts of the beverage, so as to keep her god-fearing.

Herodotus, the Greek traveler credited with being the "father of history," reported his sojourn among marijuana users in the fifth century B.C. He describes their funeral rites as follows:

> After a burial, those involved have to purify themselves, which they do in this way. First they soap and wash their heads, then to cleanse their bodies they make a little tent, fixing three sticks in the ground, tied together and tightly covered with felt. Inside a dish is placed, with red-hot stones and some hemp seeds.
>
> There is in that country *cannabis* growing, both wild and cultivated. Fuller and taller than flax, the Thracians use it to make garments very like linen. Unless one were a Master of Hemp, one could not tell which it was—those who have never seen hemp would think it was linen.
>
> The Scythians take *cannabis* seed, creep in under the felts, and throw it under on the red-hot stones. It smoulders and sends up such billows of steam-smoke that no Greek vapor-bath can surpass it. The Scythians howl with joy in these vapor-baths, which serve them instead of bathing, for they never wash their bodies with water (Herodotus 515 BC/1954, IV: 73).

Describing the funeral of a king, he records some variations of these practices among the Scythian nomads originating in Central Asia who inhabited areas near the Black and Caspian Seas.

The Greeks and Romans also valued the medicinal uses of *cannabis sativa.* The famous physicians Dioscorides and Galen prescribed it for earaches and indigestion or as an appetite stimulant. They cautioned, however, that it suppressed sexual appetites. The Romans also used the fiber extensively to make sail cloth.

Jewish and Muslim

In the Old Testament, *kanbus*, *kanabos,* or *kaneh bosm* (Talmudic terms for hemp) was recorded as being put to a very different use. While the Jewish law permitted intoxicants, it reserved marijuana for specific sacred and secular purposes, such as the making the ropes of Solomon's temple and the robes of the priests (Rubin 1975). In Exodus 30:23, God commands Moses to make holy oil for anointing kings and priests out of myrrh, sweet cinnamon, *kaneh bosm,* and cassia. Among neighboring Muslims, who were forbidden all intoxicating substances, marijuana nevertheless was tolerated in multiple cultural patterns. In Egypt, it fueled a "cafe society," which celebrated erotic imagery, jokes, puns, and clever sayings (Levy 1957). In Persia, the Thousand and One Nights were saturated with the odor of hashish (Andrews and Vinkenoog 1967). In the mixed Arab–Berber empire of Morocco, "the "Learned of the Faithful" strictly applied the prohibitions of the Koran against intoxicants, yet permitted the eating and smoking of hashish or *kif* by tribal groups of the Atlas Mountains (Palgi 1975). Marijuana and tobacco smoking also flourished in Turkey from an early age.

Ibn Khaldun, the Arabic historian, also took a keen interest in marijuana and hashish. Suspicious of intoxication, the Koran had warned strictly and explicitly against all alcohol use, but because *cannabis* had long been cultivated in the Middle East, the birthplace of Islam, the eating or smoking of hashish and marijuana was usually tolerated, although not encouraged, throughout the Arab world. Ibn Khaldun commented on the customs and mores of this extensive Muslim demimonde, centered around coffeehouses and pleasure gardens, where wits gathered to recite poetry and enjoy the company of courtesans.

In the thirteenth century, Marco Polo, the Venetian whose family had opened trade routes between Italy and China, drew attention to the relationship between drugs, crime, and violence. Apparently sensationalizing some accounts of his travels, he wrote of the threat posed by "hashishiyya," or thugs who robbed and killed under the influence of cannabis (Abel 1980).

Sub-Saharan African

After establishing Middle Eastern styles of use (together with coffee and tobacco) in Egypt, Morocco, and Algeria, Muslim and Arab expansionism and colonialism introduced the plant, or *dagga*, to central and southern Africa, where distinct *dagga* use-complexes emerged among herders, hunters, and warriors (Du Toit 1975). Mixed with indigenous herbs into powders and pastes for eating, inhaling, and smoking, the drug bred aggressivity during battle and efficiency at work. In Rwanda, the Twa, a vassal lineage of the erstwhile ruling minority caste, the Tutsi, constructed a reputation for extraordinary strength, rowdiness, bestiality, unflinching loyalty to their lords, and unbridled vengefulness around their consumption of the drug (Codere 1975).

Arab traders also introduced cannabis smoking to native peoples in Zanzibar and East Africa. Calling it *mbange* or *lubange*, Bantu- and Swahili-speaking tribes treasured it as a panacea, especially effective in the treatment of malaria, blood poisoning, and snakebite. In South Africa, Zulus smoked it from gourd water pipes as a "war medicine." (Rubin 1975).

Ethiopian

While marijuana was eaten in many traditions, it was mostly smoked among the Christian ascetics of Ethiopia, where ornamental water pipes dating from the thirteenth to fourteenth centuries have been found to contain cannabinoid residues (Dombrowski 1971; van der Merwe 1975). Ethiopians are believed to have invented the water pipe. The drug supplied the fortitude and endurance the stylites, dendrites, and cave-dwelling monks needed to persevere in fasts, bodily mortifications, and vigils.

European

The plant was introduced to European societies in the early thirteenth century, and quickly became a widely prescribed medicine. Early herbals recommended preparations to alleviate coughs, jaundice, ague, fluxes, colic, worms, and inflammations. It was also added to belladonna, henbane, aconite, and opium in the practice of witchcraft. During the Age of Discovery, however, as European nations competed to dominate the seas and overseas territories, it was of critical and strategic importance for the manufacture of cloth, rope, and sail cloth. Both English and French farmers were required by their monarchs, on pain of stiff fines, to apportion a certain stipulated acreage to its cultivation.

In the eighteenth century, European literary and artistic circles were enraptured by cannabis, and works extolling it poured from luminaries like Baudelaire, Rimbaud, Coleridge, and De Quincey. A use-complex was fashioned from their taste for the decadent and their passion to explore both sensuality and spirituality. Meanwhile, physicians continued their inquiry into the plant's therapeutic values. The French physician Louis-Aubert Roche tested it as a cure for plague, while his countryman Jacques-Joseph Moreau de Tours experimented with it as an aid in the diagnosis and treatment of mental illness. William B. O'Shaughnessy, the Scottish physican, treated his rheumatic patients with tinctures of cannabis and successfully quelled muscle spasms of tetanus and rabies with them.

American

In the fifteenth century, during the ages of European exploration and conquest, marijuana was among the many species of plants and animals which were transferred from their countries of origin to far-flung corners of the earth. Leaving Asia, marijuana finally thrived everywhere: by the 1970s, in addition to plantations in five continents, it was being cultivated on the fire escapes or in the living rooms of many apartments in New York City, in barns in Vermont, and in hothouses in Alaska's subzero temperatures.

After its introduction to the Americas by the Spaniards in the 1500s, a use-complex focusing on the commercial value of the *cannabis sativa* variety of the plant formed, and it was cultivated extensively for its fiber, with which hempen cloths and rope were manufactured. Although colonial Americans had been familiar with the medicinal and therapeutic uses of the drug and had used it accordingly, in tinctures and tisanes, it was apparently not used for intoxication or recreation.

In the late 1800s, influenced by European Romantics like Coleridge, De Quincey, Baudelaire, and Rimbaud, American literati adopted cannabis smoking. Fitz Hugh Ludlow popularized the practice in *The Hasheesh Eater* (1857). By 1876, hashish smoking and hookahs were prominently showcased at the Turkish Bazaar at the Centennial Exposition in Philadelphia. In 1883, H. H. Kane described an opulent hashish house in New York, with light shows, ornate fixtures, and sumptuous furnishings, where fashionable men and women smoked from hookahs and ate sweetmeats made of hashish. In his *Essay on Hasheesh* (1912), Victor Robinson described out-of-body experiences such users had enjoyed. Fresh life was blown into this use-complex during the Jazz Age by Louis Armstrong, Cab Calloway, and many other musicians.

In the 1960s, yet another, distinct indigenous American use-complex sprouted among young African Americans and European Americans, which drew on such countercultural currents as opposition to the war in Vietnam, the civil rights struggle against racial inequality, the possibility of revolutionary success in Western industrialized societies, and attempts to challenge the legitimation of mainstream sexual mores and culture generally. Marijuana use became a litmus paper for differentiating between supporters of the socio-economic, political, and cultural status quo and middle-class mores and those who opposed them. The psychoactive properties of the experience were therefore emphasized. This use-complex proved enormously influential and was transplanted worldwide. "Westernized" youths in every country embraced and it and their experiences enriched it.

The Ganja Use-Complex

Some of the cultural patterns associated with marijuana have been remarkably durable and long-lived. The subject of this book is the ganja complex, one of the most distinctive and long-lasting. Originating in Northern India some 5,000 years ago, after the plant had been brought there by Neolithic nomadic tribes of Northeast Asia and China (Li 1975), it was established eventually throughout the Indian subcontinent. Universals of the ganja complex were:

cultivation of and experimentation with the *cannabis indica* variety of the plant; a religious justification of use; religious art, poesy, and rituals which celebrated use; an emphasis on the plant's psychoactive properties; and a strong folk-medical ideology which recommended marijuana as a panacea for physical, psychological, and spiritual ills. Undergirding these superstructural elements of the ganja complex was an informal economy and its socio-political organization through which marijuana was cultivated, distributed, exchanged, and consumed. The earliest descriptions of the ganja complex are given in northern Indian religious and literary texts and art. Yogic devotees of the Hindu god Shiva were among its most ardent carriers. Daubed with funereal ashes and sporting dreadlocks like the Great Yogi himself,[1] they diffused the ganja complex in many parts of the subcontinent.

The report of the Indian Hemp Drugs Commission (1894), an early paradigmatic work in drug studies, identifies elements of this use-complex:

> 435. It is chiefly in connection with the worship of Siva, the Mahadeo or great god of the Hindu trinity, that the hemp plant, and more especially perhaps ganja, is associated. The hemp plant is popularly believed to have been a great favourite of Siva, and there is a great deal of evidence before the Commission to show that the drug in some form or other is now extensively used in the exercise of the religious practices connected with this form of worship. Reference to the almost universal use of hemp drugs by fakirs, yogis, sanyasis, and ascetics of all classes, and more particularly of those devoted to the worship of Siva, will be found in the paragraphs of this text dealing with the classes of people who consume the drugs. These religious ascetics, who are regarded with great veneration by the people at large, believe that the hemp plant is a special attribute of the god Siva, and this belief is largely shared by the people. Hence the origin of many fond epithets ascribing to ganja significance of a divine property, and the common practice of invoking the deity in terms of adoration before placing the *chillum* or pipe to the lips. There is evidence to show that on almost all occasions of the worship of this god, the hemp drugs in some form or other is used by certain classes of the people. It is established by the evidence of Mahamahopadhya Mahesa Chandra Nyayaratna and other witnesses that *siddhi* is offered to the image of Siva at Benares, Baidyanath, Tarakeswa and elsewhere. At the Shivratni festival, and on almost all occasions on which this worship is practiced, there is abundant evidence before the Commission which shows not only that ganja is offered to the god and consumed by these classes of the worshippers, but that these customs are so intimately connected with their worship that they may be considered to form in some sense an integral part of it.
>
> 436. The special form of worship by the followers of Siva, called the Trinath or Tinnath Mela, in which the use of ganja is considered to be essential, is mentioned by many witnesses, and deserves more than a passing notice. A full account of this religious practice given by Babu Abhilas Chandra Mukharji will be found in Volume III Appendices of this Report. The origin of the rite, which it is said sprang up first in East Bengal, appears to be of recent date, about the year 1867. It appears to be observed at all times and all seasons by Hindus and Muhammedans alike, the latter

> calling it Tinlakh Pir. When an object of special desire is fulfilled, or when a person recovers from illness, or a son is born, or a marriage or other ceremony is performed, the god Trinath, representing in one the Hindu trinity, is worshipped. Originally one pice worth of ganja, one pice worth of oil, and one pice worth of betel-nut was offered to the god. But now ganja—it may be in large quantities—is proffered, and during incantations and the performance of the ritual, it is incumbent on all present to smoke. This form of worship is shown to have spread extensively throughout East Bengal and the Surma Valley of Assam, and according to one witness, it has penetrated even to Orissa (Indian Hemp Drugs Commission 1894, chapter 3).

The Indian Hemp Drugs Commission gives detailed portraits of the institutionalization of the ganja complex in the different social classes of various regions of India in the nineteenth century. The commission, comprising British civil servants, judges, and physicians, heard testimony from Indians of every background concerning the use of a wide variety of products derived from the two species of the plant, *cannabis indica* and *sativa*, such as hashish, charas, bhang, and other food or beverage preparations. They spoke approvingly of how deeply integrated and adaptive the items of the ganja complex had become in these diverse social strata (Indian Hemp Drugs Commission 1894).

In the nineteenth century, the ganja complex was transplanted to shores far away from India, and among an entirely new population. In the Caribbean, in the period following Emancipation, sugarcane plantations suffered acute shortages of labor as Africans sought to establish themselves as an independent peasantry or fled the countryside altogether. To replace them, the British government designed an indentureship program for importing laborers from the Far East and India. Although it was opposed by several indigenous interests both in Asia and the Caribbean, the program was implemented, and the first ship of Chinese indentured laborers arrived in 1837. As the Chinese proved unsuitable for plantation labor, however, Indians were indentured instead. The *Fateh Rahman*, the ship bringing the first contingent of them from Calcutta, docked in Port-of-Spain in 1843 (Williams 1970, 1982; Sherlock 1966; Parry 1968; Weller 1968).

Indians who enrolled in the indentureship program were recruited mainly in Calcutta and Madras, but these cities were lodestones for rural migrants from several surrounding Indian states and principalities. In the main, they were desperately poor farmers who were sufficiently venturesome to tear themselves from centuries-old parochial and religious loyalties in order to seek better lives in taboo lands across the seas. They differed, however, in caste and religious backgrounds, and thus brought with them a variety of skills or occupational specializations. They were joined presently by poorly capitalized but enterprising merchants or entrepreneurs, who paid their own passages as free agents and sought to earn a living by supplying the immigrants with familiar goods and services imported from home (Weller 1972; Klass 1961).

These Indians had embarked from Calcutta at the very time when the practices described by the Royal Commission, and particularly the Tinnath Mela (see above), were most widespread and popular. Moreover, Bengal had also been a traditional center of experimentation and cultivation of *cannabis indica*. Indeed, sinsemilla production was prefigured in this area, where "ganja doctors" could distinguish male from female plants as seedlings, thus enabling them to be separated and allowing the unfertilized females to realize their full potential of resin and flower production and cannabinoid potency. Transferred by them to the Caribbean, however, the ganja complex had divergent outcomes in the different islands and territories, such as Trinidad, Guyana, Suriname, and Jamaica.

Thus, in Jamaica, with the barest excitement, the ganja complex transcended the boundaries around the Asian population which had originally nourished it and had taken vigorous root among local Jamaican Africans. A majority of the rural Jamaican African population rapidly grew to believe that it was a beneficial substance, imbued with spiritual and religious properties, and they used it liberally from birth until death. Moreover, adapting the ganja complex to the harsh realities of the rural Jamaican laboring life, they thought that prolonged use built up workers' strength and made them more vigorous, so that they could work harder, faster, and longer. As a consequence, even employers who abstained from using the drug personally preferred marijuana smokers as laborers, and often provided ganja at the workplace to increase loyalty and productivity (Comitas 1973). According to Comitas:

> The roots of the Jamaican ganja complex can be linked to the Indian subcontinent. During the latter part of the nineteenth century, its prototypical forms were carried to the island by East Indian indentured laborers, recruited to replace the emancipated slaves in the cane fields. Present-day techniques and types of ganja use, critical parts of the ganja lexicon and much of the justificatory ideology surrounding ganja lend strong support to a claim of a direct India-to-Jamaica diffusion. The great majority of ganja users in Jamaica, however, are not East Indians, who form only a small minority of the population, but Black laboring people, both rural and urban, who are descendants of the African slaves who were forcibly brought to the New World in the seventeenth and eighteenth centuries.
>
> It is clear from prima facie evidence that ganja use in Jamaica is extraordinarily widespread. Although national statistics on these illegal practices are non-existent, various estimates of the number of users, ranging from one-third to two-thirds of the lower class, have been given by different sources. A somewhat more precise estimation can be based on the work of the Jamaican project team. For example, a survey of ganja smoking in one of the seven communities studied indicated that fully 50% of all males over 15 were smokers (half of these being classified as heavy smokers);

> 7.3% were former smokers; only 20% were non-smokers; and 22.3% were unclassifiable due either to conflicting information or reluctance by informants to provide information. If only half the unclassifiables were added to the smoker group, a very conservative procedure, a figure would be generated for adult male smokers of over 60%. If the 7.3% former smokers were included then over 68% of the adult males in the community were currently smoking or had smoked ganja in the past. After comparing these data with those derived from other study localities, it can be safely stated that the estimates given, from one-third to two-thirds of the lower class, do not misrepresent the extent of male smoking in the rural areas, In fact they tend to lend credence to the higher ranges of these more impressionistic estimates.
>
> Male ganja smokers make up only a part of the ganja using population, however, since women, in lesser numbers, also smoke. A larger pool of individuals including children, adult smokers and adamant non-smokers drink ganja teas and tonics for medicinal or prophylactic purposes. Many use the plant as an external tonic, and some make occasional use of ganja in food. Given the extent of non-smoking uses, one could estimate with considerable confidence that some 60 to 70% of the lower section of the rural population, men, women and children inhale, ingest or use ganja in some form—undoubtedly one of the highest rates of marijuana use for any population in the Western world." (Rubin and Comitas 1969, 37–38)

The ganja complex, by rooting itself deeply in the key institutions of rural African Jamaican life, ensured its survival and continuous elaboration for a prolonged future. Only a decade after its introduction, marijuana assumed important folk-pharmacological, economic, social, and cultural functions in the mostly African rural Jamaica, as it had done for centuries in India,

The cultivation of marijuana adapted well to work patterns common among Jamaican peasants, which were shaped by the wisdom "never to put all one's eggs in one basket" or, in other words, to avoid reliance on a single source of sustenance. Thus a rural householder typically combined different types of agricultural enterprise (raising a variety of livestock or crops) with nonagricultural supplements to his income or value (fishing, hunting, construction, arts and crafts, lay teaching, or preaching). Where "occupational multiplicity" (Comitas 1973) was necessary for survival, the addition of 200 roots of marijuana under cultivation, for personal use, barter, or sale, was a substantial bulwark of the household's prosperity. Many such householders therefore cultivated marijuana. Cultivating marijuana never consumed the whole energies of the household, nor was it the basis of syndicalization among cultivators. Indeed, it differed from other agricultural work in that one respect only. Whereas work parties (gayals) were mobilized, with traditional feasting, drinking, and ganja smoking, among the able-bodied in a community to assist the individual farmer to perform the heavy agricultural tasks, such as felling trees, digging roots, or posting fences, the cultivation of marijuana was always undertaken by the single individual—although it too entailed the onerous labor of forest clearing and daily surveillance.

The distribution of marijuana also entered unobstrusively into the preexisting marketing networks operated by higglers, or market women, and strengthened them. During slavery, when Africans had been allowed to cultivate self-subsistence kitchen gardens (to free owners of the responsibility of feeding them), trading in the produce was a rare dimension of freedom and had been dominated by women (Katzin 1959). Individual higglers had mapped over time their personal marketing routes and had achieved a degree of specialization, and each had consolidated a network of suppliers or peasant producers on the one side and networks of urban consumers on the other. These formed part of the legacy they bequeathed to the younger kinswomen who succeeded them after retirement or death. As they moved around the countryside, and between town and country, they served as power brokers and were important sources of credit, innovation, information, and gossip. The modest trade in marijuana increased their substance and effectiveness.

Likewise, the use of marijuana by various routes of administration was responsive to peasant status and grassroots political concerns. Just as in India, where the different social strata could be distinguished by how they participated in the ganja complex (either by drinking *bhang* or smoking *charas*), so too different styles of use, dosage, and administration distinguished age, gender, and class stratum in rural Jamaica. In childhood, mothers offered it as a medicine and tonic, often in infusions made by steeping marijuana leaves in illegally distilled rum ("bushrum" or "mountain dew"). In adolescence, infrequent or sporadic episodes of ganja smoking were among several bonds uniting peer groups. As young adults, the smokers began to lead more independent lives, centered around marrying, building a home, raising a family, becoming economically self-sufficient or even reasonably well-off, sports (football and cricket), and climbing the local civil and religious status hierarchies. Ganja smoking then fell in place with the rhythms of a busy life, and took place in smaller, more carefully selected company than in adolescence. Finally, in old age, as resources, cash, and mobility are restricted even as some senior citizens reap status and honors, marijuana is publicly forsworn and, as in babyhood, is again supplied discreetly and medicinally in teas and tonics (Comitas 1975).

While marijuana was differently valued by these different categories of users—babies found relief from teething troubles, their mothers gained prestige as "bush doctors," adolescents fed their sexual fantasies, young adults improved their soccer and cricket games, mature workers increased their productivity, and older persons grew in wisdom and respect—all agreed on the fundamentals of the ganja complex, such as the spiritual, "divine" provenance of the plant, its stimulant effects on artistic and religious expression, and its mission to heal.

Although the ganja complex exerted considerable influence on the world views and behaviors of rural Jamaicans and the cultivation, use, and distribution of marijuana were widespread among them, it was resisted by some local elites, as they were in the Indian motherland. In the Jamaican case, however, they opposed it not only because it carried the stigma of illegality, or because it smacked so much of the "superstitions" of the countryside, but also in deference to United States' policy and initiatives against drugs. Thus in Jamaican cities, it was acceptable only in the laboring classes, in criminal circles, or in the many minor dissident groups or religious cults which thrived in the ghettos of the unemployed and poor. It was in these ghettos that others of the ancient features of the "ganja complex," such as cannabis-inspired religious art, music, poetry, and ritual, were most strongly revived.[2]

In Trinidad, as well as in Suriname and Guyana, the ganja complex received a very different welcome than in Jamaica. Just as in the latter island, the Indians who settled in these colonies smoked plenty of marijuana at the time of their arrival and for some fifty years afterward. For example, Reverend John Morton, the Canadian Presbyterian missionary who proselytized many Indians in Trinidad, observed in 1859:

> It was a necessary feature in the training of helpers that they should be led to acquire right views as to the evils of strong drinks and narcotics. The pledge used at this time included a promise not to use or encourage the use of opium or ganja in any form . . . Ganja grows here freely, and is more commonly used by Hindoos of caste than either rum or opium. It is said to carry a man above his sorrows, to transport him into a paradise where the sweetest strains of music and the warbling of birds ravish his ears, where scenes of splendour and objects of beauty meet his enraptured gaze, and his soul is filled with indescribable ecstasy. The reaction of ganja does not seem so bad as alcohol or opium: yet, if followed up, are very injurious (Morton 1916).

Describing another Indian milieu in Trinidad, Morton wrote of his pastoral work in Woodbrook, Port-of-Spain, the capital city:

> One feature of that work is the holding of services in Indian hotels. Some of these are chiefly used by people from the country when they come to town on business. In others, local porters and jobbers are most prominent. In almost all, there is gambling and opium and ganja smoking. They sleep on the floor with or without a blanket to soften it. During a service in one, I saw a lad asleep on his chest as he stood leaning on a doorpost, from the effects of ganja (Morton 1916).

While in the 1900s the cultivation of marijuana in Trinidad was outlawed, its import from India, regulated by the customs officer and for distribution by licensed agents throughout the island, was permitted. In this arrangement, Parliament determined the maximum amount of the substance which could be imported, the customs officer imposed a tax and maintained a roster of the licensed agents and the amount each received, while the latter wrote down the names of their customers in a log kept at their local shops. The Indians, however, not only consumed the licensed imports but cultivated their own crops illegally. Some enterprising individuals had also sailed to nearby Venezuela to cultivate marijuana clandestinely for reimport into Trinidad.

But by 1915, the majority of Indians in Trinidad, Guyana, and Suriname had abandoned the centuries-old practice. An Indian informant, a much-traveled Presbyterian, said that long before his shop in Princes Town was raided in 1934, her father had wished to terminate his subagency to a large importer of legal marijuana in Port-of-Spain. She said that he made much more on cheap Spanish wine mixed with water than on marijuana; and that the latter attracted only the most backward, the most countrified of customers—people who rode into town in their bullock carts, who swore and were disorderly, and whom her father loathed. Eventually the ganja complex was sustained by a handful of elderly men (and maybe a few younger male acolytes) near the forested parts of the island. Apart from them, the only other users were small circles in the cities made up of sailors, criminals, entertainers, and prostitutes who depended on imported supplies to support fledgling, American-influenced local marijuana-using subcultures. The two groups of users were mostly oblivious of each other.

From the early 1900s to 1960, then, there was virtually no use of marijuana in Trinidad. The centuries-old cultural complex had evaporated. It had not been diffused to other Trinidadians, such as Africans, Chinese, Europeans, and Middle Easterners. In 1978, among the original bearers of the cultural complex, only a few Indians in their late seventies could recognize marijuana and could admit to actually purchasing it (as adolescents for their elders' use); but most younger Indians could not recognize the plant when it was shown to them. Advised that they were holding parts of a marijuana plant, they recoiled in horror, fearfully wondering whether they had been contaminated by the "dangerous drug" against which local and American media had warned them.

Why did the import of the ganja complex into Jamaica and Trinidad (or Guyana or Suriname) have such divergent results? The legal restrictions instituted in the 1930s against the drug and the subsequent police raids are not enough to explain the virtual extinction of use among Indians in Trinidad and the other territories. After all, similar laws had applied in Jamaica. And moreover, the decline had started much earlier; the laws remained very leniently enforced and were debated in a climate of public opinion more accommodating of use than in the 1980s.

One possible reason is the size of the Indian indenture and immigration to the various colonies. The number of immigrants to Jamaica was very small, and they quickly became indistinguishable from other rural Jamaicans (mostly of African descent). Too small numerically and too lacking in resources to form effective ethnic communities or associations, they posed no threat to abiding Jamaican institutions and social arrangements. According to this reasoning, Indian cultural items such as food, clothing, and ganja use became in short order common rural Jamaican property. By the late 1800s, therefore, the ganja complex was endemic in the Jamaican countryside and remained so until the 1960s when the fresh developments to be described in this book popularized it even further (Rubin and Comitas 1975).

Another explanation, also related to the size of the immigration, relates the disappearance of the ganja complex to the processes of assimilation which any large immigrant population undergoes in a host society. Thus, wide-scale changes occurring among East Indians in Trinidad, Guyana, and Suriname in the 1900s formed the context in which the 5,000-year-old ganja complex disappeared. The further proletarianization of the sugar laborers, the establishment of a class of proprietors producing canes on lands sold or leased by the sugarcane companies, the continuing flight from the countryside altogether to residence and employment in the urban-industrial areas, the appetite for education as a major road of upward mobility, the increasing conversions to Christianity (which involved, as Morton noted, the pledge against "strong drinks and narcotics"), and the drive for material prosperity were some of these typical processes. Seeking to assimilate, some Indians lurched into alcohol misuse (Klass 1961; Angrosino 1972; Yawney 1969).

Yet another explanation contrasts the relatively homogeneous African rural population in Jamaica with the more multiethnic and multicultural local populations of Suriname, Guyana, and especially Trinidad. In the latter, marijuana use has multiple significations in the more complicated social terrain, and prevails or not depending on an intense political struggle waged with cultural weapons.

Finally, this book argues that social-organizational, political, cultural, and economic conditions have to be accommodating, all at the same time, for the cultural package (the ganja complex) to take root deeply, grow, and perpetuate itself. When these conditions were ripe in the late 1960s and in the 1970s, the ganja complex was reintroduced, as this book describes.

THE GANJA COMPLEX TODAY

This book describes the continuing epic of the ganja complex in the post-1960s period. The Asian cultural package is first diffused to young Africans in Trinidad, Guyana and Suriname (and to young urban African populations it had not yet affected in Jamaica), who then rediffuse to it young Indians in those territories (whose parents and grandparents had tried to expunge it from group experience); next, cooperating as growers, exporters, and distributors, these young people introduce it to the African Americans, Latinos, and European American who are their neighbors in the Caribbean immigrant communities of North America. Their cousins in immigrant communities in European capitals, such as London, Paris, and Amsterdam, simultaneously introduce it to other local populations. Finally, 100 years after the immigration of Indians to the Caribbean, the religious and artistic components of the ganja complex have taken a distinctive form and have flourished as Rastafari and in reggae music (which are today widely accepted, commonplace cultural expressions in the global community).

This book gives the details of these events. In chapter 1, the general societal conditions in which the ganja complex was diffused or revived in Trinidad are suggested. These include modernization, the destruction of indigenous economies, high unemployment, inflation, a national government inadequately responsive to increasing poverty and despair, and the cultural bankruptcy of a community dominated by a comprador bourgeoisie. Chapter 2 traces the introduction of marijuana and the ganja complex. Chapter 3 outlines the development of the social-organizational pillars on which the ganja complex rested. In chapter 4, the religious aspects are portrayed in the influential Rastafari movement. Chapter 5 gives details of an important exogenous factor, changing public attitudes toward marijuana use and cultivation. In chapter 6, all the various elements reach full bloom, especially in Brooklyn and other immigrant communities abroad. Chapter 7 discusses variants of other contemporary marijuana use-complexes and showed how they were vanquished by the ganja complex. A theoretical consideration of these developments is offered in chapter 8. In chapter 9, the impact of the ganja complex and the marijuana economy upon the preexisting societal conditions is discussed, and the understanding of Caribbean society which their success has encouraged is explored. Chapter 10 offers insights on U.S.–Caribbean relations gained from the perspective of drug studies.

NOTES

1. Seated on a tiger-skin rug, armed with his trident, and befriended by a king cobra, Shiva, the Great Yogi, performed strenous *puja* at Mount Kailash in the Himalayas. So vigorous were his spiritual exertions that sweat poured from his matted locks, forming the River Ganges, the major source of water and life in the Indo-Gangetic Plain.

2. Of course, these early experimenters would later blossom into the universal Rastafari movement, in Rastafari liurgy, ritual, art, and theater and in reggae music. See chapter 4.

Chapter 1

Reviving the Ganja Complex: The Crisis of Caribbean African Youth in San Fernando, Trinidad, during the 1960s

If, in the human–drug interaction, the human part is to prevail, it must first be readied. It took a time of crisis for the ganja complex to be diffused to the African population of Trinidad and to be rediffused to young Indians whose great-grandparents had disavowed it.

Trinidad and Tobago, two islands forming one nation, lie about five miles northwest of Peninsula de Paria in Venezuela, South America. They are the southernmost islands of the Caribbean archipelago, and as Venezuelan nationalists have periodically claimed, actually belong to the South American land mass, with which they share a continuity in earth formations, crude oil deposits, soil types, rain forests, flora, and fauna. The islanders, however, share in the history and culture of the English-speaking Caribbean, a culture area which includes several other Caribbean islands, Guyana, Belize, and parts of Panama, of the Dominican Republic, and of Costa Rica. Many contend that Brooklyn in New York City, where over two million immigrants from these English-speaking Caribbean territories have settled, should now be added to it.

Trinidad is the larger of the two islands and its capital city, Port-of-Spain, is the nation's administrative, financial, and business center. Although it is only twenty miles across the Caribbean Sea from Trinidad, Tobago is an idyllic tourist attraction which still offers the oft-lauded charms of the colonial era. It boasts an untouched rain forest in the hinterland and is surrounded by sparkling beaches. Tobagonians, who are closely united by kinship and neighborliness, are renowned for their friendliness and hospitality. Crime and drugs are rare. By contrast, the shantytowns of Port-of-Spain can match Flatbush or Crown Heights in Brooklyn in any of the indices of inner-city desperation.

San Fernando is Trinidad's second-largest city and was the site of the ethnographic research reported in this book. Dubbed the "capital of the south," the title is meaningful because of the city's proximity to Pointe-à-Pierre, where one of the world's largest oil refineries, operated by Texaco, Inc. (USA) is located. Closer to San Fernando than to Port-of-Spain are also the local oil fields themselves, a self-renewing "pitch lake" from which asphalt and bitumen are exported worldwide, the refineries and estates of sugar producers, the gardens of many of the island's small-scale agriculturalists, and its remaining reserves of tropical rain forest. San Fernandians have a better chance of being employed than other Trinidadians or, indeed, than other West Indians.

More than 100,000 persons live in this bustling city. Originally a fishing settlement and trading post nestled around a wharf on the Gulf of Paria and extending a few miles inland upon the gently rolling Naparima hills and plains, it is now a greater metropolitan area which has absorbed residential enclaves and small townships in every landward direction. Crowds in the city center are swollen every day by the influx of people from these suburbs and the agricultural villages which outlie them.

San Fernando is a typical seaside Caribbean city. Built without the benefit of a plan, its streets crisscross one another unexpectedly. The original city is surrounded by the Long Circular Road and the Lady Hailes Highway. Businesses, schools, a sports stadium, a home for senior citizens, the unused rear of the grounds of the San Fernando General Hospital, the bus terminal, an abattoir, and wharves are strung along this rim. High Street climbs up out of a gaggle of fishermen's bars and rum shops at the wharves and ascends from west to east. It is lined by banks, big department stores, shopping galleries, and malls. Smaller businesses are wedged tightly between them, while the sidewalks offer an unbroken display of the goods of itinerant vendors. Several streets roughly parallel High Street from other west–east axes, along which more schools, businesses, residences, churches, and other public buildings are located. North–south streets and roads such as Coffee Street and Cipero Street also teem with homes and businesses, and Mucurapo Street is the site of the San Fernando Market, the main exchange for agricultural produce from the southern half of the island. Enclaves of inner-city housing, where deteriorating examples of prewar colonial architectural styles are exhibited, lie tucked in among these main streets. Other sections of low-income housing and shantytowns, as well as exclusive colonies of affluent homes, radiate out from the center toward and beyond the Long Circular Road and the Lady Hailes Highway. Some of them are described in greater detail below.

During the 1960s, youths (ages fourteen to twenty-three) in these low-income neighborhoods were facing a protracted period of crisis. Their plight was identical to the one which their age-mates on the other English-speaking Caribbean islands—Jamaica, Barbados, Dominica, St. Kitts and Nevis, Antigua, Grenada—were experiencing. Winnowed out by examinations in the fiercely competitive educational system, they had become high school dropouts without hope of further training. Few jobs were available for them. And since their parents had migrated abroad (mainly to America, Canada, and England) in search of work and were as yet unable to send remittances home, senile grandparents and the young persons were left to fend for themselves in deteriorating neighborhoods.

Thus the young people were pitted against an establishment which controlled and denied access to property, education, jobs, finance, and opportunity. In the transcript below, a bitter feeling of dispossession from their rightful estate still surfaced when two workers discussed their life circumstances in 1978. Although these young men had eventually found low-paid jobs in the oil industry at the end of the long period of unemployment which they describe, their good fortune gave them little comfort. They had suffered and seen too much deprivation. Both men had become Rastafari (see chapter 6), and the conversion is reflected especially in Turner's choice of a nascent Rastafari dialect to express himself:

Constable: *As you know I used to live in San Fernando. I used to be limin' on de block. We know San Fernando. I and you. Right? Dah is a long time, you know. Since we were small, you know. Bertrand Street. Scenes pass: Youth Training Center, Boys Industrial [youth detention centers], right? All kinda terrible scenes, you know . . .*

Turner: *You see dat? I does tell myself dat dah was my part for I to play den, eh. To see how I come from a good family, right? And then I just left my family and went in an institution [detention center]. From one institution to de nex' institution to de nex' institution . . . and it just keep on goin'. I tink about all ah dat. And then I get work.*

Constable: *Dis man here, de family he was from. . . . People had plenty respect for his brothers and for his mother. But de times dis man pass through! De times all ah we pass through! Onliest difference is that he spend more time in prison at a time dan me, and de both of us spend time in prison. 126 days. Flat! Ah go never forget dat. Other institutions too—we make Boys Industrial a coupla times. When I was a little youthman [14 years of age].*

But you see me and you. We ain't see trouble for nothing, you know boy. We ain't lime on dat block dong dey for nutting at all. No way! Dah was school, brother. Like school have a teacher, we does teach too. Because you meet a man on de street and call out: hey, hey come here. And you ain't go tell him nutting bad, you go rap with him. Now when I studying all dese times and I dig myself now . . . how far I reach, right? It was something else, brother. Something else. I could write it down . . . I feel I could make a book of it, you know.

Turner: *A book! Look, I look, I watchin' outside de window, is like if I seeing myself seein' everything that use to play [happen] with I, since I was a little boy coming up. . . . It was like growin' up in a wilderness . . .*

Constable: *Boy, dat life was really, really something. God! Look, his parents . . . use to be kinda ah big family. Dey wasn't rich. But dey was nice, very respected. If those parents had gone through life, if my father did go through life longer, you find my brother woulda been a big man in government, through my father. No, serious. . . . Look at Mr. Durity [deputy mayor of San Fernando]. He and my father were colleagues. Dey was pardners. Look at dis woman dey make mayor. Mrs. Kirton. I know she as my father's friend. So we have a part to play, boy. You understand? We have a part to play. Look . . . like our family really mash up. Listen, my family was no kinda down family, or hand-to-mouth family when my mother and father was alive. Ting was nice with dem. My father was doing kinda alright, had a house, shop, a shoemaker shop . . .*

Turner: *In dose times, shoemaker and carpenter use to have dey own workshop, you know. Dey was important people, you know. People use to sit dong in dey shop and talk. Dey was big in de church, dey use to hold good cash. Den dey was big in de PNM [political party which has formed the government since 1956] . . .*

Constable: *My sister and dem use to sing in de Anglican Church choir. Dey use to play piano. Dis man aunt use to run a private school . . .*

Turner: *Dey say frustration. Frustration is really something else, you know. Well den, dey had a time in my life when I gone to put dong my name to wuk with the Government Crash Program [stints of ten days' work for needy unemployed workers]. I went so far, man . . .*

Constable: *No Turner, I sweep de road.*

Turner: *No, no, listen. Den I tell my little brother, he use to wuk in some white people store: I tell he to go and put dong he name. And he gone and put dong he name too. As soon as I done do my work, I gone and I do he own. And when I do he own, I gone and put dong my name. You understand. Because he was the onliest fella use to give I—how much money you go get as a porter in a store? He use to give I something still. My father ain't alive, my mother in de States, she never use to send I nuttin' [remittances].*

Constable: *Before I start to push ganja [sell marijuana] in Short Street, l wuk in the Borough [the borough councils administer water, sewerage, road repairs, and other maintenance work]. Sexy was de man—when I say wuk, dis ain't no crash program. Dat time it was only dem old Indian people, you know, drunkards who use to sweep de road. First my big brother come and say he takin' de work, he can't make [survive]. De man was cryin'. But he didn't have nuttin'. Nuttin', sah! Den I come, and had was to take dat same work. I pay to fuckin' learn, boy. I pay. I pay, I pay, I pay dearly. I pay for mih mother, mih father dem too. So I pay to learn. Nobody not fuckin' me up. No way, no way. Anytime I talk about dat, my eyes does full, you know.*

Turner: *Dah is what I tell you just now: don't let we talk about dat. Because it have tings I does remember back too and it does hurt I. So dat I don't really like to tink about it. Well den, dem times was nice times, eh?*

Constable:	*Wha'?! You making joke?! Dah was my times self! Dem was de times self! Now ain't no times! Me ain't have no times now!*
Turner:	*Imagine. Fete [dance party] in Naparima Bowl [a ball room]. We startin' de fete. Because we is de first set ah people to reach in dey and draw two, three long tables so and it full with stocks [food and drink] . . .*
Constable:	*Men want to wear de best clothes, de sharpest tings. Dat time man fightin' clothes, endless clothes. Everyday is someting new! Sharp clothes! When man ketchin' dey arse gettin' clothes and ting—we had clothes like chupidness . . .*
Turner:	*I was tellin' Skinner so today. I use to wear hats!*

Over 17,000 young persons in the greater San Fernando area were still unemployed in 1978, the year in which many were interviewed for this study, and they felt keenly the same frustrations which Constable and Turner had articulated. Their fates had been in the making for over four centuries. The doomed history had begun with the importation of African slaves in the 1500s and had continued under the Spanish, French, British, and nationalist regimes which followed (Sherlock 1966; Curtin 1991; Parry 1968).

In the period of British colonial rule, which began in Trinidad in 1806 and ended in 1960, British government officers, British sugar producers and their agents, French planters, and Portuguese, Spanish, and African shopkeepers and artisans had commanded a labor force of former African slaves. The latter had fled the sugar plantations and headed for the towns after Emancipation in 1863, and had been replaced by British sugar interests with Indian indentured laborers imported from the Indian subcontinent. A few Chinese, who had proved useless earlier as indentured laborers in sugar cultivation, had opened small retail shops. Some East Indians had already followed their example and quit estate work or had come directly from India, independent of indenture, to do so.

These ethnic populations and strategic interests had realigned themselves but slightly since the 1860s, and then only to make more manifest the basic division between haves and have-nots. In the towns, Africans overcame tremendous odds to secure a place in petty commerce and manufacturing. Legitimate employment benefited only a small proportion of the labor force, while the remainder, like the parents and relatives of Constable and Turner, produced and exchanged goods and services, ranging from shoes to piano lessons, in a thriving informal economy (see preface and chapter 8). Indeed, until the early 1960s, the informal economy worldwide probably equaled or surpassed the formal sector in value and was responsible for the labor shortages of which colonial administrators complained (Myrdal 1944). Supported indigenously by the informal sector, a literate class of African publishers, authors, scholars, civil servants, schoolteachers, clergymen, skilled workers, and clerks was eventually formed whose sons would provide civic and political leadership in coming decades.

A boost to both sectors of the economy was given by the discovery of oil in 1910 and the subsequent establishment of oil fields and a refinery. While persons of European ancestry or expatriates monopolized the top executive and managerial positions, African and Indian workers secured well-paid, unionized jobs in the industry. The trade union leadership became a force in the 1920s and 1930s for the advancement of non-Europeans in the Caribbean through self-representation in government and the education of the young.

The colonial era was brought to an effective end in 1944, at the close of the Second World War, although independent nationhood would be achieved later, in 1960. Another economic boom had occurred during the war years, when local contractors and workers were in demand to build military bases and to provision American troops. But processes of modernization and development brought the economy and society of the islands more closely under American hegemony. The old British banks and companies were replaced by American ones, and many lines of local production, or the mainstays of the informal economy, were commodified and brought into the formal sector. Local production withered in favor of imports, and instead of the labor shortages of yesteryear, high rates of unemployment were now reported.

Following closely upon the shrinking job markets were waves of sustained migration, both legal and illegal, to the United States, Canada, and Europe. More than any other single cause, the removal of older adults or persons over twenty-five years of age through migration in the postwar period precipitated the breakup of families, or their reordering into transnational entities (Sutton 1990), and the rapid decline of housing stock and local neighborhoods in several Caribbean territories.

The achievement of national sovereignty and independence from British rule brought few material improvements. A particular bitterness which young people like Constable and Turner felt was directed toward the People's National Movement (PNM), the political party which had been forming the national government since 1956 and which had led the country to independence in 1960. Many of them had been in middle childhood or adolescence when the party had led public campaigns to bolster national identity, to encourage pride in islanders' non-European ancestry, and to commit the country to programs to alleviate unemployment and to remove the vestiges of four centuries of racism and white supremacy.

But the dismantling of colonialism and the campaign for national sovereignty and independent government had actually been the prerequisites for the Americanization of the economy and society, with its consequences of unemployment and migration. C. L. R. James, one of the founders of the PNM with Dr. Eric Williams, who became the prime minister of the independent nation in 1960 and remained in power until his death in 1982, had seen the challenge of self-government as follows:

> The governments of these territories have got to sit down and plan and decide, in view of the general level of social life and economic life, in view of the special situation in the countryside, in view of the dangerous political pressures which the unemployment and other problems are bringing to bear on the government, they will have to decide what industries will be necessary to establish . . . irrespective of the traditional profit motive. If we had 150 years . . . there would be no need for the telescoping of economic developments. But I see no possibility of individual entrepreneurs, either inside the West Indies or from outside the West Indies, developing the economy to a pitch at which it will be possible to feel that the economy is a going concern and sure to move forward, taking up the increases in population as time goes on. I cannot see it being done by private enterprise in the old sense of the term. There has to be a set plan, in which the State, taking all needs into consideration, not merely the ordinary economic demands but the social necessities of the population, will decide on a programme . . . to satisfy the urgent needs of the people and, this is very important because this is the political issue, to make an impatient people understand that some serious, tremendous, new and sustained effort is being made to satisfy the demands which are increasing everyday (James 1961).

Instead, under the pressure to Americanize and to become subordinate to American global political and economic imperatives, the independent government gave up dependence upon one metropolis to become subservient to the other:

> Little by little they were worn down until they are busy building schools, building roads, West Indianizing, and begging for grants, loans, investments . . . Dr. Williams . . . was going to show the oil companies where to get off. He was the mortal enemy of the American State Department and the Colonial Office. But now he is finished with all that. (James 1962, 162).

A more recent comment summarized the PNM achievement since independence as follows:

> In the final analysis, the PNM did not know how to use the political control which it had won in 1956 and we must see that this failure falls strictly in the logic of Afro-Saxon strategy which we adapted in the nineteenth century. Accustomed to advancing by denying our own worth, we have found it easier to rely on outside help in our quest for change. We have found it easier to rely on a Doctor [Williams] than to take up our own beds and walk.
>
> Instead of dealing with sugar, petroleum and the banks, instead of breaking the metropolitan stranglehold on the economy which had kept the West Indian people in chains from the start, Williams and the PNM adopted the Lewis [Sir W. Arthur Lewis, a Nobel prize–winning economist] prescription of industrialization by invitation. We

> hoped for economic transformation by borrowing capital, by borrowing management, by kowtowing before every manner of alien expert we could find.
>
> We failed to see that this kind of dependence in our territorial context amounted to nothing but obsequiousness, servility, and in the last resort, to a shattering vote of no-confidence in the population of Trinidad and Tobago (Best 1970, 4).

Thus, in the area of the economy, the most recalcitrant feature had been primary production for export under foreign control dominating both agriculture and industry. The arrangement remained firmly in place after independence. For example, the oil industry, which produces 81 percent of the value of total gross exports and contributes 20 percent of GNP "is in many respects a classic case of the effects of foreign direct investment through the multinational corporation controlling the important natural resources of a small underdeveloped country" (Farrell 1974). It is unresponsive to local economic needs, can employ only 15,000 (or 5 percent of total employment), and cannot be expanded. Government, having no control over decisions affecting employment, type of output, and the organization of production, finds itself in one stroke deprived of potential revenues and of control over important sectors of the national economy.

The dominance of a foreign-controlled oil industry also encourages the surrender of other economic controls, through monetary policy, devaluation options, and the like, which governments usually strive to retain for themselves. Since the industry serves as a model for all other manufacturing ventures, only the package of high capital costs, foreign finance, modern imported technology and technicians, and high wages but restricted employment has succeeded in producing value. Expansions of the oil industry, such as the fertilizer plant and paint factories, are examples of such successes; but in this area also, the oil companies have been indifferent to stimulating growth and creating jobs and have neglected opportunities to produce petrochemicals, plastics, and synthetic fibers, materials with which further industry could be built. Other successes are those industries—car assembly, breweries—which are jointly operated with foreign investors.

By contrast, industry and manufacturing which is controlled and financed by local investors are cautious and impermanent, tending to collapse when tax holidays, accelerated depreciation, tax-free imports of raw materials and equipment, and other such inducements are removed. Forays into quarrying and producing construction materials, or into food processing and the manufacture of garments and shoes, are made with the expectation of rapid turnovers, timed to periods of boom generated elsewhere, and subject to rapid transfers of capital. In the past twenty-five years, or in five five-year budget periods, in which generous inducements were offered, no more than 500 new industries have been created, yielding about 15,000 jobs: many of them became defunct a few years later.

Discoveries of fresh marine oil deposits and the increase in petroleum prices won by the OPEC in 1973 quadrupled the value of the oil industry and the share of government revenues. The increase, which has made Trinidad and Tobago the richest Caribbean nation, has not altered the traditional pattern. It has enabled the government to build, with Japanese technical assistance, an iron and steel plant costing over $4 billion. The plant will employ fewer than 400 persons permanently, will require continued foreign assistance to operate, is dependent upon imported raw materials, and will compete for an American market at a time when American companies are demanding tariff protection. No other sorts of enterprise have been encouraged by the newfound prosperity.

In agriculture, Trinidad still devotes 211,300 of its 270,000 acres of arable land to primary production for export: 121,000 in cocoa and 90,000 in sugar. Agriculture accounts for only 8 percent of total gross exports but employs 20 percent of the labor force.

Primary production for export, especially of sugar, has had serious adverse effects not only upon the economy, but also upon social relations on the island. On the one hand, the economy is particularly vulnerable to pricing decisions faced abroad and to the securing of preferential markets. The history of sugar production on the island has included depressions, layoffs, and low wages. At the same time, the plantations have been historically the scene of the oppression of persons, first of slaves and then of Indian indentured laborers. Because of the plantations, the growth of a class of peasant farmers, and of manufacturers and processors of agricultural produce, had been curbed. Today, estates, which are only 1 percent of all farms, still control 40 percent of farmlands.

The result of these conditions is that Trinidad and Tobago is unable to feed itself. Since imported food is sold at inflated prices, many of its citizens who are without jobs or who are underemployed go without food staples. The ready solution—to create new jobs by growing more food—is not easily achieved. The historic association of agriculture with plantations, and plantations with slavery or quasi-slavery, works against it, as do the higher wages and better working conditions offered by foreign-financed industry. Government has been unable to find candidates to take its offers of crown lands and agricultural loans; local investors favor only meat production reliant on imported stock feeds, imported tastes, and foreign techniques of production and distribution.

The principal areas in which growth has been experienced in the economy, particularly with respect to the employment problem, have been the public services and the commercial sectors. The PNM government, unable to expand either industry or agriculture, has itself provided over 50 percent of the jobs created while it has been in power. It maintains embassies abroad and a swollen civil service at home, and has added to the ranks of its army and police. It has employed over 45,000 young persons in a Special Works Program, the disguised dole which Constable and Turner had discussed.

Commercial businessmen have been the only class to profit from the government's policy of foreign-aided development. With the recently swollen oil revenues driving the price of foreign manufactures still higher, the importers and retailers of clothes, electronics, furniture, home accessories, motorcars, office equipment, tools, toys, books, and food have grown in number. Since 1973, their businesses are being constantly renovated and modernized, employing management, advertising, and accounting techniques developed in American enterprises. They have brightened town centers, as well as the shopping malls created especially to aggregate them, throughout the island. Foreign banks, serving these businesses, have also multiplied: in addition to the British banks of the colonial era, such as Barclays and the Royal Bank of Canada, there are the new facilities built by Citibank, Chase Manhattan, the Bank of Nova Scotia, Chemical Bank, and other American financial institutions. Through franchises to local operators, Kentucky Fried Chicken, McDonald's, and Pizza Hut add to the postmodern glass-and-steel glamour.

In the area of the economy, therefore, an antiquated, malintegrated, and inefficient structure had been preserved. The industrial parks and shopping malls have advanced along the northeast corridor and the north–south axis, homogenizing former agricultural communities into continuous urbanized swaths of bright lights and modern conveniences. Small towns like Chaguanas and Princes Town have been transformed into cities where commerce has been concentrated and an expanded class of middle-income workers is housed. But the structure nevertheless does not satisfy local needs for employment and reasonable prices for essential goods and services.

The same is true of social relations. In the modernization ideology of the Trinidadian moneyed classes, the pluralist conception of Caribbean social structure, bequeathed by metropolitan social science and accepted as conventional wisdom, has rendered invaluable service. In this view, the populations of the island are distinct from one another, not by their division into classes or according to their usefulness to the metropole, but by the differential shape of key cultural institutions. This belief precludes the hope of achieving a society, in the sense of an organic whole of cooperating participants, and has justified a politics of accommodation, compromise, and reformism rather than one of radical change.

Thus, Sir W. Arthur Lewis, the West Indian economist whose views had shaped the PNM's economic policy, had written: "A community which is mixed racially needs, more than other communities, to create for itself social and economic institutions which are broadly accepted." (Lewis 1950)

The egregious warning, with its casual assumptions concerning the nature and reality of racial difference, evidently had a manifold impact upon the PNM way of thinking. The maintenance of the colonial social structure was an immediate result. Indians would remain unknowable in the countryside, and in their rapid encroachment upon land ownership and the retail trades; the Chinese were to be inscrutable behind their flourishing businesses; Europeans would maintain their dominant economic and cultural positions and remain unapproachable behind the color barrier; while Africans, by virtue of their majority number, would constitute the nation (in which other groups were therefore minorities) and decide which government it should have. "The last apology or excuse for colonization will have been removed when Caribbean democracy can prove that minority rights are quite safe in its hands." (Williams 1957)

Dr. Williams had shown the same conservatism with respect to the issue of minority rights in his constitutional proposals in 1958 for a self-governing Trinidad and Tobago. While pressing for a popularly elected lower chamber, from which the government would be selected, he conceded to the second chamber of nominated members, among whom vested interests would be represented, powers far in excess of those enjoyed by the British House of Lords on which it was modeled. The second chamber in Trinidad, for example, was able to delay legislation in nonfinancial matters for as long as twenty-four months. It appeared as though he was personally afraid of the support his nationalist rhetoric had elicitied: "the delaying power of twelve months enjoyed by the House of Lords in Britain should be extended to twenty-four months in Trinidad, as the system is new and as we have only a limited experience of democratic process. That experience dates back only thirty-two years, a short time in the life of a man and an insignificant period in the life of a country." (Williams 1955)

In reality, the facts of everyday Trinidadian life belied these elaborate precautions. For example, over 17 percent of the Trinidadian population is of mixed origin. Africans and Indians had struggled in unity against the British for many decades and had cooperated in a general strike in 1937. There were Indian and African socialists who were committed to a common working-class ideology. Among native-born Trinidadian Europeans also, there had been a small but highly effective populist element. Primary and secondary schooling, sports, and religion were also arenas in which the different races and ethnicities commingled, sometimes competitively, often harmoniously.

Race in Trinidadian politics, in the 1955–1963 period in which it was most virulent, has proven to be an effect of the narrowness of political ambitions. On the one hand, there was Dr. Williams and his party of African professionals determined to show little more than that the black man could do the same things as well as white men. In the speech which gave birth to the People's National Movement (PNM), he had used the example of discriminatory practices against himself as a black academician seeking employment in Trinidad, to declare:

> The issues are not personal, but political; they involve not a single individual, but the West Indian people . . . mine was not an individual case. . . . I stand before you tonight . . . the representative of a principle, a cause and a defeat. The principle is the principle of intellectual freedom. The cause is the cause of the West Indian people. The defeat is the defeat of the policy of not appointing local men to high office (Williams 1955).

On the other hand, there was Dr. Capildeo and his party of Indian professionals, eager not to lose the opportunity to win the same recognition for Asians. When it appeared that the electorate had denied it to him by resoundingly defeating him at the polls, the good doctor resorted to hysterical calls to arms.

Behind the racist rhetoric, however, a more sharply and transparently divided version of the colonial society was forming. Economic forces have by themselves clarified its structure and reinforced it. Since 1970, when the growing numbers of the urban unemployed had attempted revolution (see below), the possession of wealth or secure employment had become a single interest to defend, uniting persons of every race, persons having different beliefs and enjoying in fact variable degrees of privilege. Thus a polyethnic, multiclass cause was forged, which supported the present government chiefly because its police had been successful in containing rebellion. Today, well-to-do or upwardly mobile Trinidadians no longer call their less fortunate neighbors "coolie" or "nigger," the derogatory names for Indians and Africans: they use a racially neutral term which is more abrasive because it is packed with the stuff of raw experience—"scrunter" (one who has nothing, one who is rooting about for something, like a pig does). "Scrunters" in turn have no use for making racial distinctions among themselves.

The changed shape of social relations has been registered in the composition of PNM representatives over time; and especially of the Cabinet ministers who seemed to exert most influence on the prime minister.[1] Beginning as a predominantly African group possessing few assets beyond education and newly won political power, today its prominent members include wealthy Indians with close, publicly acknowledged ties to business fortunes. Indians prominent in the opposition have also been bought over by ambassadorial appointments and lucrative government contracts. As a result there has been no effective opposition in the country.

Under PNM tutelage, therefore, none of the divisions among Trinidadians had been exorcised; but rather all had been submerged beneath a single, more insidious one.

Men's horizons are conditioned by the historical circumstances in which they find themselves. Dr. Williams had described his ruefully:

> Four and a half centuries of metropolitan control would weigh like an Alp, in the political sense, on the head of any country. They weighed equally, however, on Ireland, so that the time factor must not be exaggerated. But it must not be minimized. The other colonial areas of the world have been somewhat more fortunate than the West Indies. One hundred years . . . of British hegemony in the Gold Coast, sixty years of British control of Nigeria, a century and a quarter of French rule in Algeria, made it impossible for imperialist attitudes to harden and crystallize to a similar extent as in the West Indies. From another angle, the vast size of India or Indonesia reduced metropolitan overlordship to a control at the top hardly touching directly or visible to the millions of peasants at the bottom; the West Indies, by contrast, are so small that colonialism was something you touched, saw, heard, and felt everyday everywhere. All these other victims of imperialism have had decisive advantages over the West Indies. They had a language of their own, a culture of their own, a religion of their own as in India, a family structure of their own as in Ghana, a sense of values of their own which they could oppose to Western Imperialism. We in the West Indies have nothing of our own—a few artifacts and place names are all that remain of the aboriginal civilization. We are a people transplanted into slavery to a transplanted crop, and we have remained political satellites of the metropolitan economy whose economic interests we were intended to serve. We have become in the Martiniquan saying "peau noir, masque blanc," a black skin, a white mask, a European culture in an Afro-Asian environment. That is our history. This is our heritage. That is our dilemma (Williams 1960).

This lament—that a Caribbean culture does not exist and cannot exist—is gainsaid by the events to be described in this book, but it is the wisdom presiding over the PNM regard for culture. Having failed to recognize real social movements among the population (or having grown hostile to them) and having neglected to participate in developing economic institutions which actually serve everyone, the government was unable to recognize a national life which required institutions and resources through which it might be strengthened.

Two cultures had formed in Trinidad in 1978, one dominant, the other still emergent. The dominant one was that of the social classes which supported the government and its policy of Americanization. Competitiveness, corruptibility, materialism, consumerism, and adoration of the metropolitan life are all expressed in its mythic vocabulary. This culture does not need new educational approaches, national archives, historical or social research, theater, or the arts. A television set and a passport are sufficient. Its symbols are those of the glossy advertisements, showing happy, polyethnic (but fair-skinned) gatherings in fashionable settings, with people drinking rum under blue skies and a clear sun. A study of the aspirations of youth in the mid-1960s had noted the degree to which consumerism and social apathy have been formative in the f moneyed Trinidadians (Rubin and Zavalloni 1969). An analysis of the essays of the Trinidadian European secondary school students from professional or business backgrounds revealed their utter indifference to school. Instead their repeated concerns were about security and the maintenance of a sun-soaked, privileged lifestyle. The African and Indian students, who became the important persons or government ministers in the 1990s, had expressed a "messianic" interest in social conditions; but they reported an equally intense drive to acquire the material possessions which conferred status.

The attitude of the Trinidadian European students had become the norm for the whole graduating class by 1978, and the messianic urge of their African and Indian schoolmates had been quite submerged under the successful accumulation of wealth. On the part of the emergent elites, therefore, their culture also betrayed bad conscience.

The culture of the dominant class was widely expressed in the everyday lives of the underprivileged and disenfranchised, but it often malfunctioned there. The fashionable gatherings of rum drinkers too often degenerated into the drunken brawl. Among the poor and unemployed, competitiveness and corruptibility translate into woundings and homicides; materialism and consumerism equals theft, the police, the courts, and prison; while adoration of the metropolitan life without an airplane ticket can only be expressed through self-hatred and frustration. Low-income Trinidadians, therefore, were obliged to identify themselves through other symbols than those offered by the glossy photographs. In the first place, their culture must be therapy and repair.

That work of therapy and repair, aided by the use of marijuana, is described in subsequent chapters.

THE LIMES

The modification of social relations in Trinidadian and Caribbean communities can be chronicled by the changes of structure and function which the neighborhood "limes" had endured. Constable and Turner had discussed them in their conversation. These street corner associations of mature adult males (Liebow 1962; Whyte 1959), to which boys were occasionally admitted, were assembled for many recreational purposes (sports, rum drinking, gambling), but also served as networks through which labor and capital could be mobilized for production in the thriving and extensive informal economy (see preface and chapter 8). Indigenous artistic production, including the world-famous steel band, calypso, and carnival, also issued from them. But as the informal economy was emptied subsequently in the period of modernization, they degenerated into the play group of adolescents. Then, as modernizing elites barricaded themselves in luxurious suburbs and consolidated their wealth and power, they functioned as gangs of young adult property offenders. Finally, after a brief political and cultural revival, they vanished as a sociocultural form.

San Fernandian limes descended these rungs of the ladder to extinction. When World War II ended, areas of low-income housing comprised nearly all of the city. Only the predominantly white suburbs of St. Joseph's Village and Vistabella, and two residential enclaves where wealthy Indians had built homes, were set apart. The rest of the city was subdivided into several neighborhoods where the majority of African and Indian San Fernandians lived. The boundaries of each neighborhood were defined by the common use of a Chinese-owned shop for daily provisions, or of facilities such as standpipes or electricity or telephone junctions; by the postman's or itinerant vendor's stakeout of the city; and chiefly, by settlement patterns based on kinship, affinal, and other social ties. Prominent neighborhoods where many events reported in this book took place are long-established, lower-class, nonwhite communities: Prince Alfred Street, Roy Joseph's Scheme, Rushworth Street, Bertrand Street, Coffee Street, Cipero Street, Mon Repos, Vistabella, and Navet.

These neighborhoods housed nonwhite San Fernandians indiscriminately. They lived in uniformly modest structures, many unpainted and unadorned and constructed by homegrown architects with very individual approaches to style and design. Most properties were unfenced and permitted an uninterrupted flow of traffic and social intercourse between homes from street to street.

Despite their outward appearance, however, neighborhoods were by no means homogeneous: between neighbors, there were critical differences in occupational status, prestige, and prospects which were not clearly recognized or appreciated in the 1950s. The Prince Alfred Street neighborhood was typical of their composition during that decade. It contained thirty-four households in twenty-four houses, with fifty-nine adults, an unnumbered category of older siblings, and seventy-one children under the age of sixteen. Among the latter were some of the young unemployed persons who are the major actors in this book.

Among the adults, the parents of these youngsters, were: two families of foreigners, both jewelers from Bombay, India; an Indian upholsterer; a Chinese shopkeeper; an Indian printer; an African lay preacher; an Indian law clerk; two teachers, one African, one Indian; an African trade-union president, an Indian assistant town clerk; and an Indian junior staff officer at the Texaco oil refinery.

There were also: the African proprietress of a "parlor" (a small shop located in one of the rooms of her home), an Indian taxi driver, four Borough Council laborers (two Indian and two African), an Indian car salesman, an

Indian mechanic, two African seamen, an African butcher, and an African night watchman.

Then there were: an African washerwoman; two African sweepers, husband and wife; two African bottle-retrievers-and-washers; the African mistress of a wealthy Creole contractor; an Indian nut seller; an Indian sweetmeats seller; an Indian who was an itinerant hardware peddler in the countryside; and an African freelance joiner/carpenter.

Limes were the street corner associations of adult males through which multiple interactions were mediated among the different strata of neighbors. Just as uniformly modest housing concealed them, the variety of interpersonal relationships which were developed in the lime, under an ideology of equality and local loyalty, also masked the hierarchization and variance among adults. Representatives of both the formal and informal economic sectors cooperated through the lime for mutual advantage. Thus, in addition to the ties of kinship and affinity, which united nine African and five Indian households, patron–client ties forged in the lime coupled other households. Neighbors with respectable jobs in the formal economy organized esusus (credit associations) and kept money in trust for the others. They advanced it, with literate and informed assistance, to launch small businesses, such as a tire repair service, a market stall, or a taxicab. They also contributed professional services—accounting or legal assistance—to these businesses. Although only two motorcars distinguished their owners' compounds, in an emergency they were placed, with the few telephones and refrigerators, at the service of the needy. The joiner/carpenter, the washers and sweepers, and the food sellers earned the major portion of their incomes in the neighborhood itself, but at discounted prices which benefited the neighbors. The Chinese shopkeeper guaranteed the credit without which cash-poor neighbors could not survive, but in return monopolized the market for day-to-day grocery and household needs. Finally, small neighborhood churches and political ties further integrated the neighborhood. During the 1955 electoral campaign, the entire Prince Alfred Street neighborhood, both African and Indian, supported the People's National Movement (the so-called African party) and was a base for party organizers.

At the same time, other forces were already at work to enlarge the differences between neighbors. New opportunities which self-government had opened up had excited the ambitions and competitiveness of all non-European Trinidadians. Positions as civil servants or political party functionaries, in the police, in the army, and in development projects were now accessible to qualified nationals. The postwar economic boom in America was also absorbing migrant labor. On Prince Alfred Street, for example, almost the entire category of older siblings was migrating out of the neighborhood during the 1950s.

Among those leaving for the United States were: seven teachers, five Indian and two African; three Indians with clerical skills; an African music teacher; two African nurses; an African policeman; an African carpenter; an African calypsonian; and an African musician. The migration of several others of this age category could not be traced during fieldwork.

The removal of young adult workers from the community, as well as the commodification of lines of local production (for example, food prepared on the sidewalk had been replaced by foreign fast-food franchises) destroyed many of the earlier functions of the lime and particularly its role as the cornerstone of the informal economy.

A new phase in the structure and function of the limes thus occurred when they were inherited by the succeeding generation during the late 1960s and early 1970s. With the introduction of free universal education in 1955 and the demise of the informal economy in the 1960s, the competition for upward mobility was focused powerfully upon the educational performances of younger children. The educational system in Trinidad requires entrants to survive hurdles at ages eleven, sixteen, and eighteen and at each stage ruthlessly eliminates failures, or the majority. Thus parents and older siblings were compelled to finance private tuition and enlisted church and neighborhood support to ensure academic success for younger children. The popular belief following self-government was that there were unlimited opportunities for the suitably educated: the competition to secure school places or redeem lost ones caused families considerable anxiety.

The optimistic beliefs, as well as the competitive and contrary emotions released by actual dramas of acquiring and securing status, were exuberantly expressed by youngsters when left to themselves. Deprived of designated or equipped play areas and other recreational facilities, but enjoying freedom of movement throughout the neighborhood, they converted the lime into a play group.

In this form, juveniles, mostly male, lacking leaders and often suffering parental disapproval, convened on every possible occasion for sports—football, cricket, volleyball, marbles, draughts, kite flying, wrestling, and many others—or to engage in learning, discussion, and joking sessions. Intense competitiveness animated all these activities. When, however, a lime confronted limes of other neighborhoods, it found itself unified by exclusive recruitment from a neighborhood and by remaining kinship ties. Clashes between limes were frequent; and the territorial assets of a neighborhood, such as fruit trees, sports gear, or unoccupied spaces (empty lots and abandoned buildings), had to be vigorously defended.

Important areas of the childhood experience of all non-European San Fernandians were filtered thus through the lime. Persons separated today by wealth and social distance had shared through it critical developmental stages of childhood. When a magistrate convicts a marijuana user, for example, the two may well have shared a common backyard and the youthful adventures it had sponsored.

The polarization of class attitudes, especially when it occurs in as brief a process as it has been in Trinidad, is painfully felt in a small city like San Fernando. Everyone is distressed and pushed into extreme attitudes. A prominent San Fernandian businessman, enriched by the modernization of his enterprise, was asked to recall the history of the city and his boyhood. He speaks of the lime as a lost childhood paradise and for this very reason flirts with the idea of a police state as a solution to the problems of his former liming partners:

> *You ever read James' cricket commentaries and 'Beyond a Boundary'? You should look at them, you know. Den you get a good picture of the richness of de lime. De language, boy. And de skills. Dah is why you see I really happy we still livin' in the heart of town. And then, you see, the business is an old one too. So my children still growing up around.*
>
> *But dem limin' days was the best of my life. Out of school, home to leave my books and to change, and is dong the hill. Sometimes I didn't even go home from school. James does describe where he really learn to appreciate good batting and good sportsmanship. From the limers. From de people on de street.*
>
> *Well you know my family is half-Indian, half-black. My mother's people are real Creoles, old-time Trinidadians. Dey used to own estates and a lumber business. And den my father's people from de plantation: hard-working Indian people. But he was into all kinds of things: a really unusual man, I have to say. You know, he used to be very active in sports: he was one of the pioneers in boxing in Trinidad. He didn't box himself but he promoted boxers. That's what I'm tryin' to say, you see. When I was growin' up, we used to know all sorts of people: not only Creoles and Indians on a standin' with my parents, you understand: but with the boxers, cricketeers, athletes, people who used to work for us, carpenters and so on from the neighborhood. Dose were the people I used to lime with: their children and families. A sort of respect and mutual understandin' used to exist.*
>
> *Well, of course, I have no social contact with dese people anymore. Trinidad change over the years. And a lot of them just waste their lives, to be blunt. Your father don't have to start off in business or anything like that for you to succeed. Dey have opportunities but people don't take them. Look, the government push jobs, Special Works, scholarship, housin'—but the young fellas in town feel dey too high to do low work, or some foolishness. How it is the Indian succeedin'? Dey have endless Indian millionaires around. And as for this Rasta business, well if dat is not chupidness, tell me what is. Is very foolish to be a Rasta, is as simple as dat: you goin' to get put in jail. So why dey wearin' dese locks?*
>
> *I'll tell you somethin': the other day Boots came in here and start beratin' me in front of de whole place. Dat jackass Daniel was here stirrin' it up: dat is the work of all you intellectuals, it look like. I use to feel dat way too. Dat I above it all, dat de mind is de important thing and havin' ideals and havin' concern and all dat. Well,*

now I realize dat dat wasn't really me. And all of you will come around to dat understandin' too, you know. Well, Boots accuse me of bein' a racist and an exploiter. As I was sayin,' I pass through all de stages of limin' with dese fellas and when nobody had money, it was my father's pocket change what keep it goin', you dig. We play sports together, we hang out together. All around 1970 so, I had my sympathies: I use to have a little place up on the Coffee where dey use to come and put on dancin' shows, drummin', skits and plenty talk. All around den de ganja ting come up: I use to buy it, I use to use my contacts in de country to show some of dem same brothers where to get it. But now as you see dese accusations comin' strong, and when you see men burnin' dong people store in Port-of-Spain—and dey threatening somethin' for Carnival dong here too—well I have to choose my side, you see. Long ago, people here use to laugh about a military takeover and so on. But now people talkin' differently. Chief Inspector Burroughs handlin' this situation by shootin' on sight, and I for one have nothin' to say about it.

Dey had somethin' about Trinidad long ago. You see me? I would never leave this country to go and settle anywhere. A man wants a place over his head, some security, somethin' for his children. Dat is all there is to it. And if you could have it with sunshine thrown in, and de sea . . . and well, life more leisurely here. I was in London for a while, you know. Every time I remember one of dose rushes at de subway station, dat same moment my mind blank out you know; and it openin' up . . . on Tobago. Yeah, I have a piece of land there: de place is like a balm. Any time you see tings goin' hard, my mind does just turn on Tobago.

No, long ago in Trinidad people use to live together. Not everybody was rich, but you didn't find people starvin' here. People use to do their business, but they still use to find time to sit dong and lime together, play sports together, cooperate, you know. Everybody know their place, you see. But dey spoil it up. Dey really spoil it up.

By the early 1960s, the optimism which had characterized the previous decade had been dissipated in the minds of many who had supported the anti-colonialist campaign and the nationalist government. Citizens found out that the opportunities were limited. In the Prince Alfred Street neighborhood, for example, twelve out of the forty-three young males who had limed together were singled out by their educational attainment or parental favor. Henceforth, the two groups would be distinguished by dress, speech patterns, range of extra neighborhood contacts, and interests generally. Eventually, the twelve would produce a management consultant, three university lecturers (PhDs), a magistrate, a university lecturer (PhD)/librarian, a doctoral student (as of 1978), and five qualified (BA or MA) secondary school teachers. Five of them reside permanently abroad, four in the United States and one in Jamaica.

The physical appearance of neighborhoods also began to change. Throughout the 1960s, the houses of the more prosperous, when they had not migrated to suburbs or abroad, were being extended, renovated, or completely rebuilt, and strong fences were built to protect them. The remaining housing, however, had torn roofs, unreliable flooring, broken windows, and muddy, unkempt compounds, and were under constant threat of demolition by landlords eager to build commercial space or more luxurious, high-rent housing. By the end of the decade, only fourteen of the thirty-four households on Prince Alfred Street remained. Several houses had been torn down, and only thirty-three adults continued to live there. Three landlords had acquired all the property on the street; one had fenced in the entire area that had once been occupied by nine houses and had made a sort of playground and pleasure garden for himself and his children.

Throughout the 1960s, therefore, another shift in the function of the lime had been occurring. Gradually it had become the exclusive property of the young adolescents not selected for advancement. Kinship and neighborhood ties of sociality had been eroded. Plagued also by daily domestic squabbles over upkeep and other expenses, these limers were nearly always on the street. Denied access to further education or employment, they had no money just as the ethic of consumerism had gained ground in Trinidad.

Thus making money again became a major preoccupation of the remaining limers, but in the absence of the informal economy which had thrived earlier. Most individuals combined legal and illegal means to earn a living. Among the legal means were the costumed carnival bands and steel bands (steel pans are high-quality musical instruments created from discarded oil drums), which offered seasonal employment to musicians, instrument makers, designers, wire benders, mask makers, tailors, and vendors. Producing artistic or recreational items such as toys, Christmas trees, kites, and handicrafts was another lucrative occupation for the nimble-fingered. Such incomes were supplemented by odd jobs—carting, laboring, cutting hedges and lawns, working as mechanics, carpenter's and mason's assistants, mattress makers, and the like. Illegal means were the ones indicated by Constable and Turner, such as petty larceny, burglary, pickpocketing, pimping, and gambling.

Competition and violence marked all these pursuits. Steel bands and carnival bands, struggling for the limited funds and small public recognition with which the nationalist government rewarded "folk arts," and manned by competing limes with a history of animosity between them, clashed often, with stabbings, woundings, bottle-throwing, and sometimes murder. In illegal operations, pickpockets and shoplifters who "worked" the department stores during rush hours cooperated with fellow limers against those of other neighborhoods to claim turf and informed on one another to the police. An endemic illegal activity was gambling in its many forms (cards, dice, lotteries, cockfighting, races, stickfighting), which attracted crowds of limers and workers of a neighborhood. They redistributed money in violent, noisy confrontational transactions.

Conflictive relations between unemployed young people with frustrated educational ambitions produced a social type much celebrated by newspapers of the day: the "bad john." Typically, the bad john would be prominent in his lime on account of his courage and daring in street fights, or because of superior skill in playing the steel pans, in criminal activities, and in physical combat. Against other limes, he was an aggressive war chief. By the 1960s, bad johns had impressive records of arrests, convictions, and imprisonments. Often the bad john acted on behalf of landlords, businessmen, and politicians against competitors, bad debtors, and troublesome tenants. He spent what money he had on the upkeep of mistresses, and on clothes, jewelry, partying and liquor, restaurants, movies, and gambling. The bad john cut a style which many young Trinidadians desired to emulate. Constable was claiming to have been one when he boasted about the way women supported and served him.

In the mid-1960s, the viability of this sort of life lessened: the bad johns in particular were hemmed in by the de rigueur duels and clashes and by police arrests and imprisonments. A few became converts to evangelical Christian sects or Islam (Black Muslims) and "testified" (preached) their faith at busy street corners, where huge crowds were drawn to the spectacle of a famous criminal speaking sacred words. But a greater number were among the speaker/organizers who were now differentiating themselves among limers, urging "peace and love" among the "brothers" and abstinence from liquor, gambling, and violence. Their discourse focused on their common social problems. In the end, therefore, the limes assumed an overtly grass roots political function.

At the time, the tastes of unemployed Trinidadians were being altered in response to new stimuli from abroad. The civil rights struggle in America, and later the struggle against the Vietnam War, preoccupied islanders. New fashions in African American music, radical literature, and also "pot" or marijuana use were diffused. Individuals on the lime acted as middlemen in the cross-fertilization. For example, with a sound system and the latest hit records from America, a limer could earn money by hosting parties where he charged for food and drinks. The parties, subsequently called "blockoramas," were enormously popular as venues for exhibiting the new styles and attitudes. The same organizers were also spokesmen for radical ideas, and made available for reading and discussion in their limes the works of Fanon and Césaire, or of Cleaver, Carmichael, Malcolm X, and other metropolitan militants. In this manner, the parochialism of limes was further broken down: limers preferred to leave their own neighborhood and to join another lime, where there were better conversation, more music and books, cultural activities, and maybe an experiment in communal living. As individuals matured as effective speaker/organizers, loyalties to them superseded narrower ones; and loyalties to clear thought, good speech, and good organizing challenged loyalties of kinship, restricted neighborliness, and shared personal biographies commemorating hard times.

By the late 1960s, speaker/organizers had grown sophisticated in their calling and could make articulate, erudite assessments of themselves, the limes, their transformations, and their future. The resulting ideology was Black Power, or a call for jobs, Afrocentric education, and strategies to alleviate poverty and to rid the country of continuing racism and European control of key resources.

Particular limes, having good speakers and organizers who were by now recruiting islandwide for revolutionary groups such as the National Joint Action Committee and the National Union of Freedom Fighters, were the scenes of extraordinary excitement from 1968 to 1970. On Prince Alfred Street, for example, the lime included two nationally known leaders flanked by very able and articulate local neighborhood luminaries, including two exceptionally gifted high school students, a calypsonian (then at the start of an illustrious career), and a painter and sculptor. They had turned an abandoned two-storied house into a meeting place which remained open twenty-four hours a day. Limers and visitors frequented the place to circulate books, discuss them, or write personal journals. The latter often contained, in addition to the details of daily stresses, stories of police harassment, models of utopias, elaborate plans for the reform of colonial society, and coded accounts of experimentation with marijuana. A few individuals from limes in the cities of Port-of-Spain, San Fernando, and Point Fortin eventually formed bands of marijuana cultivators in the hills which remained active until the last were murdered, as "guerrillas," in 1973.

Marijuana, or pot, which had been recently introduced as an item of the American counterculture, acquired a key symbolic importance in this context. Limers said that its use quieted a gathering, inducing conversation and reflection. Because its use defied the law, it legitimated other forms or symbols of rebellion.

Finally, in 1970, the limes made their last effort as limes. Learning that the Trinidadian government had remained inactive while five Trinidadian students had been detained in Canada on the charge of destroying a computer center at Sir George William University while opposing the war in Vietnam, limers broke out in spontaneous demonstrations in the streets of Port-of-Spain and San Fernando. In Port-of-Spain, they marched into a Roman Catholic cathedral to hold a meeting and had to be evicted by the police. In San Fernando, the windows of businesses on High Street were smashed. The following day, 100,000 persons demonstrated in Port-of-Spain, the largest gathering of its kind ever to take place in the Caribbean. The police arrested many.

University students and members of the country's political opposition promptly joined the limers in the demonstrations and, bypassing the speaker/organizers by virtue of their superior education and "political experience," quickly usurped leadership and policy-making roles. Without a concrete revolutionary program, however, they reiterated the limers' demands for an end to unemployment and racism. Their most significant move was to organize a march into the predominantly East Indian countryside to demonstrate solidarity with East Indian workers and unemployed persons, who received them warmly.

In April, after two months of unrest and marches, 6,000 daily paid workers at Brechin Castle sugar factory protested against the Industrial Court, Prime Minister Williams's earliest weapon against labor.[2] When plans for a general strike were announced, the government declared a state of emergency and ordered the arrest of Black Power leaders. Fires, alarms, and skirmishes with the police followed in downtown Port-of-Spain, and a curfew from dusk until dawn was imposed.

On April 21, a faction of the 750-man Trinidad Defense Force mutinied and declared support for and solidarity with the limers. The mutineers also questioned the displacement of the original speaker/organizers from leadership. Several days passed before they were forced to surrender by the loyal army and the police. It is possible that the rebels were disheartened by the simultaneous appearance of a U.S. naval task force offshore, as well as of two determined Venezuelan destroyers. Finally by May, the island had returned to normalcy.

"Normalcy" in San Fernando has prevailed from 1970 to the present day (2000). It has meant the uninterrupted growth of business and the consolidation of the wealthy or lucky in their privileged positions. San Fernandians have the highest per capita income in the Caribbean, and recent Central Statistical Office surveys indicate that they are the largest consumers of credit, who buy more cars, stereos, and household appliances than other West Indians. Three new suburbs have been added to the city in the last decade to accommodate the continuing settlement of younger African, Chinese, East Indian, and European professionals, businessmen, or management-level staff. Their expensive houses and neighborhoods are often designed and landscaped by foreign consultants and boast all the modern conveniences one expects to find in a prosperous town in Florida, for example, where many do eventually migrate in retirement.

Business places in the city have undergone constant renovation and modernization and, in the inner-city areas, continue to press upon low-income neighborhoods. The poor and unemployed, numbers swollen by internal rural–urban migration and driven from the inner city by high rents or abusive and neglectful landlords, have also contributed to the expansion of the city. Their suburbs include the teeming working-class settlements of Pleasantville, Cocoyea, and Marabella. In the midst of the modernization of the city, between ghways linking it to Port-of-Spain, these neighborhoods have to ntain decent living standards against steeply rising prices, irregu- of water and electricity, housing shortages, and the lack of effective welfare and health provisions.

The Black Power revolt was the last effort of the limes. From their earliest functions in the thriving informal economy to their attempted revolution, they had served as an effective curriculum of learning in business and competitive skills and eventually, in the philosophies of togetherness, cooperation, and reconstruction. At the same time, the realization of these goals after 1970 seemed to lie beyond the immediate political interests, competitive individualism, and parochial outlooks which remained inherent in the form.

In the early 1970s, therefore, ex-limers, caught in a paradox of social organization, lighted on marijuana, the drug they had recently discovered. Unconscious, perhaps, like so many other human actors at critical points in history, of the magnitude of their deed, they resurrected the long-buried local Indian tradition of the ganja complex, penetrating to its deeply ingrained, 5,000-year-old social, economic, religious, cultural, and political behavioral patterns. Adapting it by "Africanizing" it, they created a powerful tool for extending their revolutionary sentiments while providing at the same time for their material survival.

NOTES

1. Prime Minister Dr. Eric Williams died in 1981 and was succeeded in the office by members of his own party, the PNM. George Chambers served from 1981 to 1986, A. N. R. Robinson from 1986 to 1991 and Dr. Patrick Manning from 1991 to 1996. In that year, a coalition of opposition parties defeated the PNM and formed a government headed by the first Indian prime minister, Mr. Basdeo Panday.

2. The Industrial Court was appointed in 1979. Its major decisions undermined the many gains labor had made in previous decades, especially the right to strike.

Chapter 2

How the Ganja Complex Was Diffused

In this book, drugs are viewed primarily as a cultural good (for example, "the ganja complex" rather than "ganja" or "marijuana") which, in order to have perceptible effects on humans, must be integrated into a broader cultural pattern incorporating much more than only the use of the pharmacological substance. Marijuana was a kind of coin which picked up the energies, positive or negative, of the informal economy (see preface and chapter 8), or of the reorganization taking place in such groupings as the lime, and it circulated these energies so as to strengthen and augment them and extend their sphere by mobilizing new adherents.[1]

Thus marijuana, the "herb" or "kaya," the valuable substance which was in such demand in Trinidad in the 1970s and continues to be a staple among contemporary drug users, was certainly not the same as the marijuana which had grown unnoticed for at least fifty years; and the ancient ganja complex itself, which had been brought to Trinidadian shores by Indians fifty years before that, was reinterpreted to respond to more topical, present-day concerns. It represented both cultural survival and cultural innovation. Thus what Trinidadians paid for in the period of this research was a cultural good, a kind of contemporary entertainment, a real-life drama, which allegedly conferred educative and therapeutic benefits upon those who enjoyed it. This chapter shows how this unique cultural product was fabricated.

In the early 1960s, the young, unemployed, urban Trinidadian African male limers, influenced by pot (marijuana) use abroad among metropolitan militants and countercultural artistes, were curious to experiment with it themselves. At first, unaware that the plant was tropical and could be grown copiously on islands like Trinidad (where in fact a few elderly Indians were cultivating it), and thus before local cultivation and marketing could be organized, they relied on imported supplies. Use was contained very exactly within this particular population for the greater part of the decade, first in Port-of-Spain and then in San Fernando, before spreading to young, unemployed African males elsewhere on the island. The practice was diffused to other populations, such as employed or wealthier Africans, Europeans, Indians, and Chinese only after all the "eligible" African youths had been initiated. Only when that stage was completed was the practice exported to Tobago and other nearby Caribbean islands.

At least two features of the contemporary ganja complex put a definitive stamp upon it: first, the arrival from abroad, or the "foreign" origin, of marijuana, the raw pharmacological stuff, and second, its primary adoption by the particular population of young, urban, unemployed African males. These twin features determined the early organization of the traffic and the pace at which marijuana became endemic in the low-income population as a whole, and its subsequent spread to other populations. They also dictated the pace of local cultivation.

With respect to the first feature, more than 8,000 Trinidadians emigrate legally every year. Since the 1960s, the destination of the larger number had been the United States. Poorer migrants headed for Brooklyn in New York City or the U.S. Virgin Islands, while wealthy businessmen searched for homes in Florida. Many settled abroad permanently and established cross-generational links between a household in the metropolitan center and several households in a local island community. Some traveled seasonally, such as agricultural laborers and nonskilled workers, or wealthy Trinidadians who vacation abroad frequently to steep themselves in metropolitan life. Many Trinidadian businessmen and professionals also need to visit abroad periodically for work-related reasons. Finally, students attend a variety of educational institutions in foreign countries.

In Trinidad, there are few areas completely isolated from the flow of persons and communication. Migrants leave from all parts of the island, while within the island there is a sizable internal migration. One is often surprised to find visitors—tourists and students of many nationalities and ethnicities—in the smallest or remotest village.

Abroad, West Indians find themselves in circumstances unlike those in the Caribbean. Persons from different islands are brought together to share separate, non-European neighborhoods and an impoverished metropolitan life. The exclusivity between islanders, fostered for centuries by the separate political ties which each island maintained with the colonial power, is removed. West Indians also fraternize with non-Europeans from elsewhere, such as Africans and Asians in Europe, and African Americans and Latinos in America. They assume a politically conscious non-European identity where it may not have been formerly a matter of concern on the islands. Marijuana in metropolitan centers served as another conduit for the exchange of contacts among non-Europeans, and between non-Europeans and marijuana-using Europeans involved in liberal causes, or the civil rights and antiwar movements.

An informant on Prince Alfred Street, the neighborhood described in chapter 1, was a student in England in the mid-1960s and reports that he had been radicalized there by racial and class issues and by the contacts he had formed with other militants, European and non-European, through using marijuana. He used his brokerage between these groups to supply marijuana—or hashish—from Jamaican distributors to the others. When he returned to Trinidad, he smuggled in a few ounces of hashish for his own use, and to "turn on" some of his boyhood friends.

Radical political beliefs figured largely in this case. However, while there were many Trinidadians like the informant, the diffusion was not accomplished through their agencies only. A climate of unrest existing throughout the world system in the 1960s—from students, antiwar activists, Black Panthers, and civil rights marchers in metropolitan centers to nationalist struggles abroad, the expansion of U.S. business, and the disintegrating limes in peripheral Trinidad—was the structural condition which many populations adopting marijuana use faced in common. Other diffusions from abroad which also proved acceptable included African hair designs, the ideology and rhetoric of Black Power, and radical or countercultural lifestyles.

In addition, music was itself a very important borrowing, and a conduit for communicating positive attitudes about marijuana. The Beatles, other European American rock music groups of the early 1960s, and African American musicians endorsed drug use and countercultural ideas and sang about them. Their music was influential among young Caribbean Africans, and Jamaican musicians started blending it with local traditions in a continuing syncretism which would result in the 1970s in reggae, a music explicitly inspired by and centered around marijuana. Reggae then advertised marijuana use around the world and remains a potent musical form and source of countercultural ideology in the new millennium.

Brought from abroad in these circumstances, marijuana was prepared for use and consumed in quite specific ways. Since cigarette papers were as yet unavailable, it was chopped up very finely and stuffed into an emptied-out cigarette, to make a "cigarette joint." Another detail was that the "cigarette joints" were then smoked communally among the limers described in chapter 1.

The second, more definitive feature of the contemporary ganja complex was the identity of marijuana users with young Caribbean Africans, who soon proclaimed that marijuana originated in Africa. The ganja complex, packed with 5,000 years of promoting material and spiritual self-sufficiency and peace, adapted itself well to the conditions of young Trinidadian Africans which were set forth in chapter 1. They needed urgently to discontinue the petty criminality and violent feuding!

THE LONG INCUBATION PERIOD

In each locale where it eventually became commonplace, marijuana use had a typical incubation period. This conclusion was drawn by combining direct observations (1976, 1977, 1978, 1979) of several different stages of it in cities, towns, and villages in Trinidad and in a number of Brooklyn and New York City neighborhoods, and from reconstructions of the period from accounts of Caribbean persons from every part of the Caribbean diaspora.

There were several constant characteristics of the incubation process:

The first was the length of its duration. The period of incubation was at least five years long and it worked more or less to segregate initiates totally from the general population. Typical settings for use on the islands were family homes which had been deserted by adult family members migrating abroad, while New York offered the abandoned apartment buildings of Harlem and the Bronx and, in Brooklyn, the commercial lofts of East New York, Brownsville, Crown Heights, and Flatbush. In Trinidad, for example, use was initiated in some neighborhoods of the two large cities, San Fernando and Port-of-Spain, around 1963 to 1965. It remained the secret of the earliest experimenters in their rundown redoubts and did not establish itself in similar neighborhoods of the same two cities until 1968 to 1970. Meanwhile, in rural Trinidad, in hamlets at the center of villages which bore a resemblance to the affected neighborhoods in the cities (i.e., unemployed African youths imitating urban lifestyles lived there), no one would have heard of marijuana until 1970, when a few venturesome individuals would have tried it for the first time. Use would remain their secret, shared only with their closest companions, until 1975. In more remote areas, where planters and their sons actually grew marijuana and cared for marijuana plants from seed to maturity, no one actually used the drug until as late as 1976 to 1978.

Thus, all told, more than ten years from onset elapsed before marijuana use was introduced to the larger Trinidadian population.

Second, during the incubation period, initiates were always young (eighteen to twenty-four), urban African males just awakening to the suspicion that they would be unemployed, underemployed, or unemployable for the better part of their lives. Attention had been drawn to this feature above.

The responsiveness or even aptness of marijuana for young, urban, unemployed African males was remarkable. In the early 1960s, use seemed to have been contained within the communal gatherings of the limes with an exacting exclusivity: use outside of these social parameters was punished, sometimes by mental disturbance.

For example, the informant from Prince Alfred Street reported that he had introduced hashish to two middle-class initiates and to an unemployed limer in the summer of 1967. Only one middle-class recipient felt that he had been affected at all by the substance but was unimpressed, while the other stopped his experimentation after the first couple of profitless attempts. The unemployed limer, however, has continued smoking heavily every day since then to today (2000). During a later return trip, the informant discovered that the practice had become entrenched among all the other limers on Prince Alfred Street. All of them were young African males, with the exception of young Indians[2] or persons of mixed ancestry who identified themselves as African.

Newspaper accounts and police statistics left the same impression. In the early 1970s, when marijuana offenses were published in the island's newspapers for the first time since the early 1900s, the reports came from Port-of-Spain and the urbanized northeast corridor, and from San Fernando and its suburbs. The occupations of offenders included: unemployed, laborer, sailor, fisherman, gardener. A large category was labeled bandits, who had been caught allegedly in possession of both marijuana and arms. Where names can be trusted to give a clue to racial identification, mostly Africans were involved. Offenders fell in the age category of thirteen to thirty-five. Schools in which a "drug" problem had been uncovered were not the island's elite schools, but those where rejected pupils—often the children of poor but ambitious parents who had not passed the qualifying examinations at the end of primary school—were being coached for examinations at the intermediate and senior levels.

Fieldwork conducted in 1975 in Raw Deal, a village of 100 households and 535 persons about eight miles from San Fernando, confirmed marijuana's partiality for young African males. This example of a village in which marijuana use was only one year old also indicated how long marijuana had remained confined to the cities before being diffused elsewhere. Observations in the village recalled reconstructions of the situation in the mid-1960s in San Fernando.

An exhaustive household survey was completed in Raw Deal, which was selected because it was 50 percent Indian and 50 percent African. In 1975, Africans were the only users and dealers, despite the equal ethnic distribution of the village population. At first, only two African males older than thirty years of age were users, and only one African woman, aged twenty-three, had tried the substance. Ownership of property and achievement of educational or occupational advantage in a family were found to be factors which sharply divided nonusers from users.

Marijuana use was adopted in Raw Deal's population of young, unemployed African males thoroughly. Everyone who was young, male, unemployed,

African, nonpropertied, and lacking educational/occupational opportunities was a user—all except one person, who was discouraged by the others because he grew clumsy, noisy, and agitated when he smoked marijuana. Moreover, he had a history of epileptic fits.

Marijuana smoking in 1975 in this village was still a communal, rather than an individual, activity. It was confined in the affected population with a kind of ritual restriction. For example, when the boundary of "young, African, unemployed male" was violated, the sole offender became mentally ill. The prohibition might explain why use had been confined for so many years to only a few neighborhoods in San Fernando and Port-of-Spain before venturing beyond.

The African villagers in Raw Deal are the descendants of a company of American Baptists who were rewarded with land in Trinidad for service to the British Crown in West Africa. They arrived in the 1900s. Intermarriage between the family lines continuing down to the present day, when first-cousin marriages are still common, has produced a village composed of hamlets. Each hamlet contains a cluster of homes belonging to a kindred, and the hamlets are further connected to one another by a consanguineous or affinal tie.

Because all the original American settlers were landowners, every parcel of village lands carried a family name. Over the years, however, these properties had been alienated. Chinese and Indian landowners had purchased some, while a few villagers had prospered at the expense of the rest and had bought them out. Thus, African Raw Dealers were relatives divided by land ownership.

The consequences of a father's drunkenness, or lack of business acumen, were being keenly felt by dispossessed Raw Dealers in 1975. Property values had risen, and land ownership correlated strongly with advanced educational and occupational standing. Most propertied persons in Raw Deal could afford their own homes and usually had jobs in industry or public service in San Fernando or elsewhere. Some had extensive agricultural holdings, and had contracts or grants from the sugar companies and the government to produce sugarcane, fresh pork and poultry, vegetables, and fruit. Their sons and daughters were reared to function productively on the land, in the home, and in jobs, and doing well in school was an important filial obligation. For Raw Dealers, therefore, land ownership had moral and symbolic dimensions.

The Worthy family once had extensive agricultural holdings. What had remained of them—a five-acre parcel of agricultural land and two lots in the residential part of the village, where the family lived in an attractive house—had fallen into the hands of one particular branch of the family. The inheritor, a Mrs. Worthy, was thought by villagers to have used obeah (witchcraft) to acquire the property. Her daily displays of acquisitiveness, and those of her immediate family, added to the unsavory reputation. The older of her two sons was especially derided by young, unemployed African

Raw Dealers, on account of his strong disapproval of liming, gambling, marijuana, and their other pastimes. His three sisters and himself were young pillars of the Baptist Church, and they were the life of all its sports and social activities. He had divided the house into two apartments by his own labor and expense, reserving the ground-floor apartment for himself, and worked at home ("in the yard") to consolidate a thriving business as an independent welding contractor.

The younger son was raised to follow and exceed his brother's example. To avoid any contact with other young Africans in the village, he was made to play cricket, football, and table tennis with a club in another village dominated by Indians. He attended social gatherings at an Anglican Church in yet another neighboring village. He had been apprenticed to a welder in San Fernando and then secured a maintenance job at the San Fernando General Hospital, through an uncle's influence. He took night classes in drafting at the San Fernando Technical School, and also correspondence courses from a technical college in the United States.

But the young man had an Achilles' heel. He was passionately fond of the latest style of African American popular music, funk music, which Trinidadian marijuana users had made their own. From time to time, therefore, he lingered near the juke box in the major store at the main village junction, which was also the favorite haunt of Raw Deal's marijuana users. One night, two of them, boyhood companions and consanguines, drew him into conversation and gave him a cigarette, which he later supposed to have been a marijuana "cigarette joint." He believed that it was the first time he had tried smoking the drug, but he could not be sure. But there was another first in store for him the following night: he slept with a woman—a sex worker—for the first time. He had found her in San Fernando.

A week later, he supposed he smoked again, as before in the course of a conversation with village limers while listening to music at the jukebox. Three days later, after having behaved oddly, and feeling high (he said) either on account of the marijuana or the "runnings" in his penis (for he also said that he had contracted a venereal disease from the sexual encounter), he destroyed all his college notebooks and correspondence course texts, and slammed his new transistor radio into the wall of his bedroom. Then he broke through a window into the Baptist Church, where he stationed himself at the altar, shouting profanities. Later, kicking and screaming, he had to be taken by his mother and older brother to the San Fernando General Hospital, where, on admitting that he had used marijuana, he was treated for mental disturbances resulting from what the doctors called a "cannabis syndrome."[3] In a few days, he was transferred to the mental hospital in Port-of-Spain and was kept for six months on a regime of tranquilizers and other psychotropic drugs.

He was released in 1976. A vacant-eyed young man, he used to wander through the village in dread that his current "normalcy"—jobless, dependent on his medications, docilely obedient to his older brother—would be eroded by a single further (putative) puff of marijuana.

The story of young Worthy showed to what susceptibilities a middle-class male may have been prone if he had used—or even imagined he had used—marijuana outside of the strict social parameters in the incubation period of its introduction to Trinidadian communities. In 1980, when there was a more varied and more numerous using population which did accept persons like Worthy, "being African" and "being dispossessed" still ensured that such a user would be welcomed and embraced warmly and supportively in marijuana smoking. An affinity or resonance between the drug and that identity persisted.

Marijuana's partiality for young, unemployed Africans was all the more remarkable in the remote Indian villages close to the rain forests of South Trinidad, where villagers and their young sons actually grew marijuana in 1975. As marijuana use increased nationally, middle-aged Indian subsistence farmers in these villages had been drawn into brief but lucrative stints of cultivating marijuana. But the only experimental marijuana smokers were the younger sons of the very few African families resident in such "Indian" villages. The middle-aged Indian growers, non-users who preferred alcohol, were very apprehensive that their sons' association with their African agemates would seduce them into experimenting with marijuana. The fear was realized rather quickly afterward at this late date in the Caribbean marijuana phenomenon.

The diacritic "unemployed, underemployed, or unemployable" was also strikingly maintained in the incubation period, as in the case of Raw Deal. Not a single young African wage-earner smoked marijuana. The diacritic "young" was also exacting. Initiates were typically dependent upon their families or were persons being sponsored as dependents eligible for immigration by their relatives abroad. Indeed, the same young males often showed up at different incubation settings on the islands and in immigrant communities abroad as they followed a unique migratory itinerary up the Caribbean archipelago and across North America or Europe. For their sojourns in Brooklyn, for example, these young males retreated from such haunts of petty criminality as Fulton Street to set up "communes" in abandoned apartment buildings where they experimented with marijuana use. In seclusion they also found respite from their immigrant kinsfolk's disapproval of unemployment, drugs, and liming.

Although it may at first appear contradictory, the signifier "urban" applied very well to initiates in rural areas. In the countryside, African families al-

ways lived on the main trunk road and were likely to hav
employment, such as in the civil service or in technical craft
nopolized the modern, public areas such as the grocery store
and cinemas, and dressed more fashionably than other "coun
dreamed of the city and visited as often as they could afford t

The boundary drawn around "males" was also hard and fast, and only a few females had experimented with the drug in 1976.

And finally, initiates always emerged from the protracted (more than five years) incubation period as dramatically changed persons and (many) as fledgling marijuana distributors. This outcome reflected the passions and associational rearrangements described in chapter 1, which clandestinely occupied the lime during those several years in seclusion. At the beginning of the incubation period, initiates may have been drawn from a single neighborhood; but because the informal economy and the lime had been destroyed, they would have been fiercely individualistic and violently competitive over the few hustles which provided income. As they became more experienced in both marijuana use and seclusion, however, these groups of experimenters in abandoned buildings accepted members who were not from the neighborhood. New ideologies of "brotherhood" and "togetherness" were formulated as these expanded groups of experimental marijuana smokers acquired political and cultural functions. In 1970, they surprised Trinidad when they surfaced as a political force. The details of these events were provided in chapter 1.

EARLY ORGANIZATION OF THE TRAFFIC

Throughout the period in which use was restricted to young, urban, unemployed African males in San Fernando, the marijuana traffic reflected the peculiar social characteristics of that population. Limers, preoccupied with the legal and illegal pursuits with which they maintained themselves, were all equally responsible for procuring supplies of the drug. A supply was more or less equally divided among the limers. The supplier gained a quantity for personal consumption and perhaps a few dollars in profit.

This arrangement was mentioned by persons interviewed in every San Fernando neighborhood, when they were describing the period up to 1970. Later in the research, informants from such far-flung English-speaking Caribbean communities as Belize and Panama confirmed that it had obtained in their home communities too. Marijuana was around. It was smoked communally for the most part, obviating the necessity of individual purchases for private, individual consumption. The trade depended on imported substances, smuggled in irregularly by seamen or travelers. Their prices were idiosyncratic. Relationships between city demand and the growing country supply were marked by distrust, robbery, and violence whenever the urban and rural principals in the exchange came into direct contact. A yeoman service was accordingly performed by the "country" African or Indian schoolboy, the traveling salesman, and taxi drivers, who acted intermittently as couriers or entrepreneurs in the traffic.

Two large drugstores in the city, run by prosperous middle-class owners, supplied MX and LSD, which were also used in this early period of experimentation. Later, when demand for those psychoactives was completely eclipsed by marijuana, these drugstores remained connected to the traffic through sales of cigarette papers (to make joints) and other paraphernalia for smoking marijuana.

In Raw Deal, the same arrangement could be directly observed in 1976. Here, a year after its introduction, all smoking remained communal in the group of young, unemployed African male smokers, in an abandoned building not far from the village center. Although $1 was charged for each joint, the dealer one day became the consumer the next. A young man would assume the role of dealer as cash became available to him, or sometimes as a result of sheer good luck, and the small profits earned were used to buy a pair of sneakers, or clothes, or to make some contribution to the household, or for gambling, rather than being reinvested in the traffic.

In Raw Deal, however, indications of the changes which had already occurred in San Fernando were also apparent. Demand was rising, and by the end of the summer of 1977, four young men had differentiated themselves as suppliers of regular, daily quantities of marijuana of fairly uniform good quality. When a return visit was paid to the village in 1978, there were even more users, wholesale prices had climbed upward, and only two of the four young men had specialized as the village's regular dealers. Remaining members of the earlier smoking group, or lime, were not involved in dealing and only consumed marijuana. Communal smoking by the lime had disappeared and was replaced by individual consumption by the purchaser (and his selected personal friends).

When regular dealers had emerged a few years earlier in San Fernando, the consequences for the traffic were dramatic. The development stimulated demand for marijuana further and encouraged the growth of use throughout the low-income population generally and in the middle classes. And second, it spurred local cultivation.

These two consequences are discussed below.

GROWTH IN DEMAND

Marijuana use spread beyond the social parameters which had contained it throughout the late 1960s and early 1970s, and especially after 1974 to

1976, when former limers had succeeded in establishing permanent marijuana-selling operations (see chapter 3). By 1977, an estimated 17,000 San Fernandians were users of marijuana. The estimate of 17,000 users in San Fernando is derived from the attendance at a Peter Tosh concert in Skinners Park, organized by a leading San Fernandian Rastafari block leader. At least 17,000 concertgoers had turned out to hear Peter Tosh, a leading Jamaican reggae musician and Rastafari, sing "Legalize It" and to see him blow smoke from a huge spliff (a Jamaican-style cigar-sized marijuana joint, wrapped in "fronto," or raw tobacco leaf) in the faces of policemen. The audience would have included unemployed users and dealers, as well as their younger working-class clientele, from San Fernando and surrounding villages. If some non–San Fernandians are included in this count, most middle-class users would have been excluded. Older persons than would have attended the concert had also become users. Most employed persons in low-income neighborhoods—manual or poorly paid but skilled laborers, lower-echelon white collar workers, and civil servants—had become regular users. In addition to the total penetration of the low-income milieu, marijuana use also appeared among the middle classes, both African and East Indian. In San Fernando, the number of users also included a quite distinct quantity of Europeans, either from Trinidadian families or abroad, some of whom had derived the custom from living in North America or Europe rather than in Trinidad.

Several reasons may be advanced for the growth of use. The chief of these, the establishment of regular selling operations, has already been noted and will be discussed at length in chapter 3. As limers became regular dealers, especially after 1974, marijuana was readily available in the city. Their simultaneous conversion to Rastafari, outlined in chapter 4, requiring them to wear the highly visible dreadlocks and furnishing a religious justification for the cultivation, distribution, and use of marijuana, satisfied many segments of the population about the beneficial effects of the substance. Opposing the consumption of alcohol, meat, and other "nonnatural" foods as Rastafari, they forced Trinidadians to be aware about health, diet, and religion, and introduced skepticism toward the accepted wisdoms in these fields.

Moreover, the continued use of marijuana by limers, and its self-righteous use by the Rastafari among them, lessened the threat of illegality. Fear of the "fantasy lands" to which marijuana was said to transport its victims was also decreased as users reported the tonic effects they had felt, and as the drug acquired a folk-medicinal reputation in the relief of stress, asthma, fever, and bowel difficulties. The Rastafari enthusiasm for the substance and its adoption by increasing numbers in the low-income milieu became mutually self-supporting, each allowing the other to thrive.

At the same time, protest, which had been the original medium for the diffusion of the practice, had been generalized. In Raw Deal, for example, young informants had been more heavily circumscribed by the institutions of land and family, both controlled by conservative elders, than they were in San Fernando, where these institutions had already been weakened for many over the past few generations. The adoption of marijuana use had coincided very nicely with the collapse of these institutions in Raw Deal in 1976. The young men began to smoke marijuana at a time when court disputes over land were being waged by the several branches of families, thus highlighting the importance of land simultaneously with the dispossession of those without it; and when the burden of unemployed sons was creating daily, evening-time quarreling in the village. Similarly, in middle-class groups, other sorts of dissatisfactions with life sanctioned illegal, nonconventional behaviors.

In San Fernando, early middle-class use closely resembled the ganja complex which had been established among unemployed African youths. The case of the informant from Prince Alfred Street may be recalled. The young man was pleased, on his return from abroad, to discover that his radical philosophical and political views were shared by age-mates from whom he had grown apart in following his educational career. His use of marijuana was supported by theirs and did not cease on his return, as in the case of other middle-class persons who had experimented with the substance abroad.

A young middle-class Indian in another neighborhood made it his late-afternoon ritual to share a couple of joints with the local distributor before going in to dinner. The son of a deceased magistrate and landowner, the young man began liming with the young African dealer in early childhood, and the relationship warmed through a series of transactions of mutual benefit to both. The young landlord has found the services of the dealer, an expert burglar, invaluable in maintaining control over his properties and his tenants. Reciprocally, the dealer has received help from his friend to escape an early conviction for armed robbery and to set up a mechanic's shop. When he was arrested for marijuana distribution while fieldwork for this research was proceeding, his friend paid the bail.

In the case of three brothers, proprietors of a large business, marijuana helped solidify a link with Black Power during 1969 and 1970, when they had brief, youthful political ambitions. They smoked marijuana on the various limes with which they were acquainted and opened a reading room, club, and bar to provide a meeting place for Black Power discussions—participants would often bring marijuana with them. The brothers also used the Black Power chic to capture a market for the line of "black" cosmetics and aphrodisiacs they were manufacturing. Today, while continuing to use they have nullified these former alliances.

The case of David F. caused a scandal which was exhaustively r[illegible] in the nation's newspapers and weekly news magazines. In December 1976, the seventeen-year-old Trinidadian European youth, son of the managing director of Trinidad's oldest extant company, burned down the house of a wealthy contractor in their affluent neighborhood. The young man and his friends had been using the house for smoking marijuana while its owner was on an extended visit in Europe. The fire was deliberately started. The young man and two companions, also Trinidadian European youths, were arrested, released on bail, then recalled into custody when the police learned that a British passport had been obtained for him, and that a flight to England was planned. Botts, a dealer in Port-of-Spain who claimed that David F. had bought marijuana from him, remarked:

> *Some of dese white boys does hear de talk on de block, and den dey does go home and feel dey dreader dan dread [more Rastafari than the Rastafari themselves]. And dey didn't use to believe it, but now dey go learn dat the police is for real.*

The growth of the marijuana phenomenon by 1978 had completely transcended all the boundaries in which it had been contained earlier. This unbounded growth accounted for the appearance of quite distinct complexes of use, to each of which attached a unique body of effects. These distinctions figured even in the operation of the trade (see chapter 7).

Thus, in San Fernando at the time of writing in 1978, marijuana smoking remained imitative of metropolitan fashions among categories of users other than the initial using population. It featured in polydrug use, which included alcohol, cocaine, and LSD. Marijuana, in these circles, enhanced a party: it heightened an appreciation of leisure-time activities, stimulated the various appetites, and sometimes produced drowsiness (see chapters 7 and 8).

For unemployed Africans, firmly anchored in the ganja complex, marijuana was reported to "bring togetherness" and to "keep us cool." Then, after 1970, and especially while regular selling operations were being established, "it made us think constructive." Finally, as use crossed class and other boundaries, the distinctiveness of the unemployed Africans' complex of use deepened into Rastafari, which ritualized use and prohibited the consumption of all other intoxicants. The assumption of dreadlocks, Rastafari speech conventions, and a meatless, saltless diet distinguished persons whom marijuana now caused "to see the light." The arrival at these distinctive religious rituals would then complete the successful diffusion of the 5,000-year-old Asian ganja complex to an African population in the Americas near the start of the twenty-first century.

Chapter 2

GROWING MARIJUANA FOR DEMAND SINCE 1960 TO THE PRESENT DAY

When the city-generated demand for marijuana had affected local cultivation by stimulating Indian peasants to plant it, all the conditions for the flowering of the marijuana economic system, for the firm foundation of its institutions, and for the unbounded expansion of demand were finally met. The ganja complex had thus acquired the wherewithal for survival and continuous self-perpetuation.

Indian marijuana cultivators were a very distinct sort of people. In joining them with unemployed city limers, the marijuana economic system had brought into association the two most marginalized populations in Trinidad. It had integrated the extreme ends of rural and urban segments of the informal economic sector (see preface and chapter 8).

These marijuana growers were Indians who had fled the sugar plantations in the central Naparimas to settle close to the rain forests in the southeast of the island. They had supported themselves in the informal economic sector by subsistence farming and animal husbandry and by hunting and gathering in the rain forests. Some families gathered wood and road-building materials and had found occasional employment in former times in the now-derelict cocoa and coffee estates which French Creole[4] emigres had owned. Nowadays the only employment to be had in these districts is irregularly offered by the Special Works Program or by the County Council.

Thus Indians who grew marijuana were clearly distinguished from the majority of East Indians who remained behind on the plantations, eventually to become large landowners or landless laborers. The organization of their villages, the way families distribute themselves spatially, their religious observances, their relationships, and their uses of one another and of their resources and time—all uniquely identified them. The villagers in this part of Trinidad are less involved with the outside world than elsewhere: there is no running water supply, no electricity, and no employment. One eats what one grows or catches and uses what one makes.

Firsthand data on marijuana cultivation were collected in a growing village of ninety-eight households near the town of Rio Claro in the rain forests of southeastern Trinidad. Apart from activities related to marijuana, a day is spent hearing about disputes over domestic animals and their errant grazing habits, trespassing, learning how to trap birds, eating wild bananas and pineapples, watching Hindu priests at their devotions, and hearing their conch shells being blown to summon worshippers to prayer. Night falls rapidly, and then there is nothing to do, except indoors. Marijuana revenues had recently brought two generators which keep a bar/poolroom and a poolroom open until 10:00 P.M. In the village were several young men in their twenties, the sons of affluent Indian marijuana growers, who complained mildly about the lack of excitement in such a small village, but who had no desire to visit out: a group of them claimed that they had not visited San Fernando, the nearest large city, for nearly eight months.

There were a number of versions of how the idea of marijuana growing was introduced to the villagers. One major grower said that a relative, on a home visit from Canada, had suggested to him that business opportunities in marijuana were coming. In 1960, with seeds which an uncle had obtained in Port-of-Spain, he and another villager went into joint production. Another grower claimed that it was the district medical officer, fresh from his medical studies abroad in the early 1960s, who had first put the idea of cultivating marijuana to him. By 1970, nearly everyone in the village was a marijuana cultivator: it had been one of the earliest villages to begin. In 1976, only two households were not or had not been so engaged. One belonged to the village contractor, who had his hands full with the constant renovation and modernizing of houses in the village. The other was headed by a very nervous newcomer (the remote affinal relative of a villager) who devoted his whole interview to proving how highly he regarded the virtue of minding one's own business and how scrupulously he practiced it.

Myths of origin notwithstanding, cultivation and use may have been sustained clandestinely in this area since the 1900s. A renegade Hindu priest, one of only two older Indian men discovered to be marijuana users in this research, lived in a community nearby; and very old men, while disclaiming use, now or ever, cupped their hands to smoke tobacco cigarettes as though they were holding a *chilum,* a clay pipe used for marijuana smoking in India. At the same time, the curious fact that only recently had use become widespread among the young sons of Indian growers has already been noted.

These growers had quite limited ambitions in the trade. They showed little incentive to remain long in business, being wary of both the police and their city clients. Their intention was to make enough money to finance a legal enterprise, such as a farm, a bar, or a poolhall, and then to retire from all association with marijuana. Thus, there was a rapid turnover of villages going in and out of cultivation. For example, the village where this researcher had lived in 1976 had been a major supplier since 1970. A roll call of San Fernando distributors could be made as they drove into the village to make purchases. In 1977, however, a brief visit had been enough to ascertain that there was no more cultivation and trafficking here. Families had settled down to their newfound prosperity and concerned themselves anxiously with good schools for their younger children and the provision of public services generally. Their erstwhile clients bypassed this village and sought out others.

This kind of grower demonstrated little interest in innovative techniques for producing marijuana. There were no well-tried procedures of cultivation and processing aimed at delivering greater potency, weight, color, and appearance or superior taste. Marijuana was planted at least twice a year, on plots the cultivators had cleared in the rain forest. It was tended by camps of growers and their sons, who spent weeks in the forest attending to the daily chores of weeding, irrigating, and protecting the plants. The best crop was planted in June and July and was harvested in December. Another crop was sometimes planted in December and harvested in July, but the marijuana was said to be unhappy with the rains which begin falling in July. Often the marijuana was harvested prematurely, for fear of theft or police detection; but sometimes, when it was brought to maturity, it rivaled the best available anywhere.

The size of plantations rarely exceeded 2,000 roots: this production level was achieved in the early 1970s and had not been exceeded. Although the police and media had popularized the idea of El Dorados[5] of marijuana in the forests, if these claims—"police raid destroys $50M worth of marijuana"; "raid destroys 120,000 trees"—were true, the clearings would have been as conspicuous as sugarcane plantations. Both geographical limitations and the motives of growers suggested a more modest size.

Finally, these growers have been indifferent to the challenges of marketing. In the early days of cultivation, they often sold quantities as little as an ounce. Since the 1970s, however, planters refused to sell less than a pound at a time. Buyers were expected to do all the traveling, the (sometimes perilous) transfer of the purchase from the countryside to town, and all further marketing. For example, all exports of marijuana from the island in 1978 (to the United Kingdom, North America, and other Caribbean islands) were organized in the city by the city distributors, and growers took no part in them.

An exceptional character in this context was a young Indian named Darius. Born in a country district, he grew up in limes in Port-of-Spain, where he had been sent to live with a relative. While attending a technical college there, he learned to use and distribute marijuana. In 1974, he returned to his birthplace to cultivate marijuana himself, but then discovered that it was more lucrative to purchase marijuana from other planters and to function as a middleman between them and the city purchasers. Until the advent of Rastafari, however, he was the only planter to have read books on marijuana and to have had ideas about improving cultivation. Using the skills he had learned in draftsmanship at technical college, he built proper ventilated racks for planters to use when drying marijuana, in order to preserve its quality. Moreover, he was the only planter to have made overtures to the distributors at their selling locations in San Fernando, and helped to set up some of the new ones. More details of this aspect of his role will be described in chapter 3.

About cultivation, Darius confided these opinions:

> *Let me tell you more about de plantin'. Around about 1968 den, as I was tellin' you, ganja cultivation sprang up in those three areas: Jeffers, Guaya, and Biche. The*

population of cultivators was about 50 people or so, right? After de years pass and people grew more conscious of ganja, you find de planters increased. Around 1970 in de same area, de numbers must have been anywhere between 300 and 500 people, until the police cracked it up around 1972. Man, long ago when you went down to Biche and you asked about ganja, often people would ask back for seeds: man, we always hear about dis ting: Get seeds. You know. Seeds would be something strange to the planter. So dat means dat in dose days, the population of ganja cultivators was small, very small. But by 1973, everybody was aware.

I would say dey had over 2,000 planters in all. Say in 1972 in Biche, out of a total population of close to 5,000 people. Dey would have adults and young people. De adults may be gardeners or woodcutters or doing some wuk [had temporary employment]. But de young people who comin' up from school, dey come up in a poor area, after school dey cutting cocoa for people and dat sort of shit, you find dey started plantin' marijuana. So I would say dat from 1972 when only adults were plantin' to 1974 when de youths started to plant too, the population of the whole place was involved.

I thought that as a young man I was ambitious, I was very fortunate. But I didn't know dat there were more fortunate brothers dan me livin' in Biche area. So when I went dong dere and saw a lot of big houses and a lot of cars and fancy tings, I wanted to know who owned all these tings. And then I found out it was youths like myself who owned all dese tings. Same guys who cutlassin' and pickin' cocoa for people, gettin' a dollar here and dere: some of dem reach close to half a million dollars.

Of course, de size of a marijuana plantation varies. For example, it varies with de environment de planter is in. I was de first planter in Diablo. I planted one task of land. Dat is about 4 lots of land. And every lot has about 1,000 trees. So I planted about 4,000 trees. But I would not be so precise in sayin' 4,000 trees, because you have to make allowances for losses. So for de 2 acre of land I gettin' less dan 4,000 trees. Again like in life, in marijuana dey have a male and female; and de male is impotent, it does not contribute anything to a man's head ["high"]. So out of your 4,000 trees, you have to weed out males. So I got about 3,000 trees really, yieldin' about 450 pounds of marijuana.

You know there is a way of calculatin' dis ting. One marijuana tree could give you a poun' of ganja; likewise, one tree could give you two poun's too. Dis is my personal experience. But I like to break it dong to de minimum—one tree givin' a quarter-poun'. So 100 trees give you 25 poun's approximately. But den trees are so different in my experience. Raisin' a field of marijuana trees is like raisin' 12 children in a family. All de children doesn't come out de same way. All doesn't be bright or whatever. Same way with marijuana.

But let me stray from Diablo a bit. In other places is more fertile. A fella might go to Guaya forest or Mayaro or Biche or Charoma or Nariva forest and you find dat is virgin forest. You find he has an opportunity to plant more, threefold, fourfold, dan in an area like where I am livin'. So you find up dere you have proportionally more marijuana growin.' And a proportional quantity of products comin' out too.

When a man starts to plant marijuana, he thinks about money. And when he starts to cut de land, he thinks dat de more land I can cut, de more money I can make. So when a man is in primitive forest, he cuts de most amount of land he can cut and plant de most amount he can plant. A man does plant up to an acre. Fellas go out on deir own, calculate how much dey could plant in a year and act completely alone. Dat is de usual ting. When he come out with dat, he make a few thousand and decide whether to go back in again dat year or not.

Most planters does plant only once for de year. De time dey choose is de rainy season, June going back to September. You find dat dose guys, de most dey will come out with is a 300 pounds of marijuana. Less dan two acre, because de land fertile dong here.

Until recent times even if a man come out with 1,000 pounds of marijuana, he wouldn't make much money. Because de police wasn't as heavy on de planters as dey are now. So you find dere was a lot of marijuana aroun' and de price was cheaper. So for de year a man use to make $20,000 or $30,000 and he cool wit' dat. And den he will go back a next year because he feel, like me, dat dey have a future in marijuana.

I am not dimmin' myself of dat view, I am still holdin' dat view seriously. What make me stray from it a little bit is how de police operatin' at de present time. A few years ago I use to see myself pushin' marijuana for 20–30 years to come and makin' someting out of nothing, someting that had no value before.

But you see planters have children and people don't stay long in de business because of dat responsibility. And as de law becomes more drastic, even more people will stay out of it as soon as dey can. A fella might stay in it for two-three years. I know men who plant ganja for one year or two years and say: I had enough, I'm not planting anymore. Dey just can't take de jammin': dey not hardcore men. So for most people de amount dey plant and de amount of time dey plant is inconsiderable. But den I know men who plantin' longer dan I am in business, or since I in business.

But now dey have good business all over de Caribbean too. Like St.Vincent, Grenada, St. Lucia, and all dese small Caribbean countries. Dey so small, dey cyant grow, but de ting spreadin'. Look at Barbados, it can't cultivate marijuana period. Dat is one flat islan'! So a lot of our money makin' here dependin' on de foreign market. Dey had some men sendin' 200 pounds of marijuana to Canada every two weeks. Dis makin' money man. Dey should let de ganja run and let de foreign money run. Look in Jamaica, I hear de ganja does earn more dan de bauxite, banana, and all dat chupidness all put together.

The most recent development in local cultivation has been the settlement of villages by young urban Africans, all of them Rastafari and former city dealers, who have commenced cultivating marijuana themselves. One such settlement comprising twenty-five Rastafari brothers had become well known in 1977 for the quality of their ganja, and for the fact that they dealt strictly by Rastafari principles. They sold marijuana only to other Rastafari, in an arrangement of trust in which scales ("an instrument of Babylon": see chapter 4) were not used. One brother in San Fernando purchased two and a half pounds in this manner; and on returning home discovered that the package was short by at least half a pound. The next morning he returned to the settlement and received a good three-quarters of a pound without argument to make up the loss.

After two years of operation, the elder brother in this group had been able to construct a $50,000 house, where all the brethren have access. A motorcar was purchased next for the journeys they made to San Fernando.

The Rastafari and other growers (such as the sons of the former Indian growers) opened up other areas to cultivation than the original southeastern rain forests. Other growing villages have been: San Pedro, Mayaro, Guayaguayarere, Manzanilla, Piparo, Tabaquite, Biche, and Penal. The Rastafari were the pioneers in moving into the more inaccessible rain forests, such as those northward along the eastern coast, near towns like Matelot, Toco, and Cumana. They had also started cultivating in Fyzabad, Gran Couva, and the Northern Range.

In 1978, Rastafari brethren were planning innovations in cultivation to surmount the threat posed to large plantations by surveillance by police helicopter. Sinsemilla production techniques, developed in the United States (northern California and Oregon initially) and Jamaica, which requires fewer intensively cultivated female trees to produce a higher potency and greater yield per plant, were being implemented.

NOTES

1. Marijuana has been called by many names in Trinidad and the Caribbean. In Jamaica, Hindi names like "ganja" have been retained. In Trinidad, the metropolitan terminology—"pot," "grass," "weed," "tea," "herb," "reefer"—was followed at first; later, an attempt to appropriate the plant and its uses as indigenous to Trinidad resulted in "tampee." Gradually, however, "ganja" and Rastafari words like "i-tions" or "i-cient herbs" became commonplace. "Kaya" was a name coined by Bob Marley, the famous Jamaican reggae musician, in his song "Kaya."

2. Many Indians and persons of mixed ancestry claimed they were "black" or "African" during the contentious Black Power years. See below

3. In 1976, "cannabis psychosis" was held responsible for many cases of mental disturbance brought to Trinidadian hospitals, when doctors discovered that the patient had smoked marijuana. Patients were treated with hourly mixed dosages of pheniamazines (Melleril, Artrane, Chlorpromazine, Haldol). Side effects of these pharmaceuticals included euphoria, Parkinson's-like effects, and excitability, followed by acute depression. A reader is surprised to discover these effects recorded in the clinical reports of patients, after a few days under medication, and to find them attributed to the continuing agency of marijuana. In young Worthy's case, he had smoked no more than two puffs of marijuana over an interval of two weeks—and he could not even be certain of that!

4. Chacon, the last Spanish governor of Trinidad, had invited French planters, fleeing slave revolts fomented by English agents provocateurs on the smaller islands, to settle the interior of the island. By so doing, he hoped to stave off being invaded by the English himself.

5. El Dorado is the name given to the (mythical) cities of gold which lured European explorers and adventurers to the Americas.

Chapter 3

Economic and Social-Organizational Underpinnings of the Ganja Complex

In the initial stages of experimention or well into the incubation period, there had been few profits to be gained through the distribution of marijuana. Initiates were dependent upon such sources of irregular supply as returning migrants, students, and sailors. A user, happening upon a source, would share the marijuana among his fellow initiates without the intention of even recouping whatever money he might have invested in it. The marijuana was consumed communally, in a secluded place. Since no wrappers (cigarette papers) were as yet available, tobacco was emptied out of filter cigarettes and replaced with finely crushed marijuana. The filter packing was then removed, and the cigarette was lit and passed from hand to hand. Later, the fine paper backing was removed from the foil paper enclosing Du Maurier cigarettes and used as wrappers to make joints. Corn (maize) sheaves, raw tobacco leaves, and brown paper torn from paper bags (the latter with some concern for the lungs!) were also used for want of wrapping papers.

DIFFERENTIATION OF "PUSHERS"

The increase in the marijuana-using population of San Fernando from about 5,000 limers around 1970 to over 17,000 in 1977, as well as the proliferation of local cultivators, are the work of the original users, the unemployed African limers who advertised marijuana use and made it available in the city throughout the period. In accomplishing these results, the young unemployed persons found themselves organized in a novel form of social relationships, the *block*, or *gate*; and they converted to Rastafari. The first of these simultaneous developments is described in this chapter, the second in chapter 4.

As demand rose in San Fernando after 1970, the early organization of the traffic proved inadequate for supplying consumers with reliable or regular quantities of marijuana. To ensure that the city was supplied regularly, certain conditions had to be met. In the city, for example, a technical division of labor in the traffic was required. Selling operations had to be run by more than one person. One had to buy from growers in the countryside and to bring the marijuana back to the city—a day's work, often—while others had to remain at the selling location in the city. Otherwise a location could not acquire a reputation for permanence and regularity. At busy selling locations, several persons might be needed to parcel out the marijuana and to sell it.

Many San Fernandians interviewed during this research were sure that the entrepreneurial urge—to find a way of keeping a selling operation open twenty-four hours a day (a task requiring manpower and organization) and supplying it with adequate amounts of marijuana (a task requiring further organizational and business skills)—first emerged in one of five limes, around 1967 to 1969. These five limes were all centrally located.

In Short Street, just off High Street, the main shopping center, where taxis going to and from all corners of the island may be found, was a very depressed neighborhood comprising the dwellings of manual laborers, sex workers, and petty thieves. One building was supported by remittances from abroad. Two active tailors, a shoemaker, and a bar paid the rents in another. Hogarth, a seaman and former bad john, used it for selling regular supplies of both local and imported marijuana. In time he attracted Stevens, Constable, Simpson, Carl, Stanley, and Blueberry, all from other San Fernando limes, to operate the block with him.

Close to this block, but further removed from High Street, in a more variegated, more thriving lower-class neighborhood, were Borneo, Arctic, Ruhr, and Sadowa. Just off Mucurapo Street in the Roy Joseph Scheme, close to where the San Fernando Central Market is located, along with many drugstores, wholesalers, and other businesses attracting large crowds, were Louis XIV and Machiavelli and about six other neighborhood limers.

Further along Mucurapo Street, into a portion of it which used to be called Prince Alfred Street, was an extremely large lime, for a long time an attraction to limers outside its immediate neighborhood. Stevens dominated sales on the street after moving from Short Street, among Sabinus, Buen Retiro, Sachs, the Jaguar, Ras Chari, Saida, Tug, Argyll, Bunuel, and others.

A fifth lime, along the busy Cipero Street, was somewhat cut off from the chain stretching along Mucurapo Street, from High Street (with Hogarth) at the north to Prince Alfred Street, at the southern end. Kuper, Singham, Mao, Cancian, Dyson, Pitts, and Barnes started and operated the selling location.

In these five limes, the persons mentioned generated considerable excitement as they entered into variously principled, variously durable alliances among themselves while striving for efficiency in the traffic.

In the interview below, the Jaguar from Prince Alfred Street recalls his career as a distributor, beginning in 1974. He gives a detailed picture of the series of minute transformations which culminated in the block. Neighborhood limer and neighborhood limer, husband and wife, coworker and coworker, fellow gamblers: these are some of the relationships which were tried out in the five limes for their efficiencies in the traffic, before the block emerged as the most efficient. Some of them have survived in the block.

Corresponding to the evolution of socioeconomic relationships was the increasing sophistication of the trade. In the Jaguar's career, the technical aspects of the marketing of marijuana themselves passed through several transformations. Thus, in the beginning, when marijuana was of secondary importance economically, and in the first stages of transformation after 1970, marijuana was packaged in $1 joints only: first, "cigarette joints" made from emptied-out cigarettes and then, after wrapping papers became available, hand-rolled. At this time, purchases from growers rarely exceeded a couple of ounces.

Later, as transformations approached more closely to the block, there was greater variety in packaging. Catering to different sizes of income and consumer tastes, distributors not only sold joints but 3-bags, 5-bags, 10-pieces, 20-pieces, half-ounces, and ounces.

Finally, after 1976 to 1978, when blocks or gates had been recognized as distinct socioeconomic entities and after the conversion of their members to Rastafari, the minimum purchases from growers were pounds, and export was organized to the smaller Caribbean islands, in quantities of several pounds at a time. The Jaguar says:

> *De first man bring ganja on de block was a man name Pascal, a half-Chinese brother. He and Riad: a tall Indian boy who use to live by de corner. Pascal and Riad use to get de marijuana from Cobra in Port of-Spain. But I wasn't aroun' when it come really: I only come to smoke when ganja did build up on the street. You remember Tinker? Tinker give me my first smoke. All dat was aroun' 1967.*
>
> *When I get de first smoke . . . I-man didn't know nuttin' about ganja . . . I and I start to roll under the house dey. Laughin' and carryin' on eh! I wasn't with Jasmine yet, I was under Miss Vio dongstairs dey. After dat day, I get to like it.*
>
> *I really start pushin' aroun' about 1973–74. At dat time dey, de pusher on de block was Stevens. Dey use to have [plenty ganja] here: dah was one ah de mos outstandin' places, right? But dey had Short Street: Short Street had it time. When Stevens come he takeover, because he had everyting. He use to have X [Mandrax, or Quaaludes], ganja. And you find fellas use to go off on X too. Dat cool dong now. Yeah, so Stevens was de man.*

Well, my time come in. Well, you ha' to say it come in late, late dong. It had others like Ras Chari, but den, dey use to carry on for Stevens, right? Stevens had Ras Chari, Bunuel . . . a lot of young fellas on de block use to push for him. How he really get out a here . . . something happen, and he get a better place in Roy Joseph Scheme and he become famous dey now. Den I start up. I start up about a year after he done leave here already. A year after.

My first visit to get ganja . . . you know a fella name the Priest. From Poona? You know Brahma? You must know dem. Dem days he use to push a motorbike. A thin dark Indian fella. Short. You must know the Priest. Well, I use to go up in de country . . . nah, dat time I never use to go. But he come on de block. Somebody say: dah is the Priest. Well, he talkin'. And when he done talk and ready to go, I call him. I say I would like to buy a piece of ganja. He say: you really want dat? He say: you'll go for it now? It was a Saturday, never forget it. I say yeah and we jump on he bike and we gone Poona. Dem days the Priest was de man: he only selling pound and half-pound, not 10-piece [$10]; 2 ounce and ting. An ounce dem days was about $15.

Well, dah is what I start off with. An ounce. I pay $15. I use to work at Carvalho [a Portuguese-owned furniture store] dem days, eh? Makin' mattress and ting. When I work, if I get a week work and I have more to go, always use to borrow money —I didn't have to gie mih mother no money eh—I always use to borrow a little piece . . . And I had intention to buy a piece a ganja, to start to push . . . So I make sure I had mih money. But I didn't expectin' de man dat day, eh. But I had dat money put away to get dat ganja anytime. So I did take $30 so from de store.

So from dat $15, I make about $80. Dem days I was new on de block. So I ain't diggin' for police, because police ain't diggin' for me. Dem days dey wasn't so heavy, you know. Nowadays, like dey more . . . itch-y.

Well, I use to live with Jasmine, den, you know. So I come home. I couldn't roll ganja. Pack dem in cigarettes. Man had to roll out [empty] de cigarettes, cut up de ganja fine, fine, and pack dem in de cigarette. Cigarette joints . . . So I roll out about 80, pack dem away in a Flexpan tin, hide it under mih mother house, bathe, change mih clothes and went out on de block.

Dem days I hardly eatin': only drinkin' fruit juice. Well you know de fellas on de block: well, look . . . Didn't have no big pushers den, right. De fellas who buyin' . . . like Argyll maybe would like to buy . . . ah telling you fellas who wasn't in de limelight ah pushin' yet, like Argyll, Peaches, King. All those who pushin' now? None was pushin' when I start off. So I tell them and I start to get sale. Word pass: look, the Jaguar have someting nice dey.

Dem days I use to push heavy. I was de onliest fella den you could come any day or night and I have ganja. Because I stayin here all de time while de rest ah fellas gone limin'. Is dey I start to come famous.

All den I couldn't roll [make joints], de first man roll for me was the same half-Chinee fella, Pascal. Me and he was always friends because we grow up together, you know. So now he start to pull good with me because he know Poona too. So he use to wrap for me now. He use to go in de Scheme and get wrappers. So now me and the Chinee going, buying, coming back dong, wrapping out. And both ah we on de block. Second time we must be buy about $130 in ganja: half lb. When Pascal come in de ting—because he always smokin'—we use to take out a piece one side for we to smoke. Nothing big. So from dat half-pound ah ganja, after I take out de piece, *you know how much I get? More than 250 joints. Pascal rollin' now: so dis is not cigarette joints. And now me and he pushin' on de block.*

So now de block get heavier, you see. Anthony come on de block. A little dougla boy who use to go Benedicts [St. Benedict's College, La Romaine]. He startin' to have paper: wrappers. He come with wrappers. Somebody else come with ganja. Dennis. You know a fella name Dennis use to come here and lime with we? All ah dem have someting small. But de real heavy man is Pascal and me.

Well, Pascal and me didn't stay together too long. In de few weeks we were together, we really lick up a lot of cash though. Den well, he start to push independent and me too. But we really lick up money. I get so develop in de ganja, I even start goin' for my own paper now.

Dey had a fella . . . Rommel. He had a brother in Carenage [Carenage docks, near Port-of-Spain]: use to work on a boat. So when I get develop in dis way, I use to get my paper too. Rommel use to push too: he was from Erin and we use to work together on de same shift at the Public Transport Depot [The Panther had recently landed a new job cleaning buses]. As cleaners, right? He use to go for ganja: we use to hire a car; I really get big, man. I use to know all de drivers: I use to get one from de Poona stan' to come and meet we at work 2 o'clock in de mornin' when de foreman and dem sleeping. And we use to go Poona, Poole, San Pedro, up in Kildare Trace, all over, lookin' for ganja.

Meanwhile, Jasmine carryin' on de ting at home: she get famous too. Dem days now I sellin' 10-piece, ounce and all kinda ting. I pushin' off . . . leh me see . . . if I start off with one and a half pounds on Friday, by Sunday evenin' I done dat. And back in de country. Dat first buy I make in Kildare Trace, by an old one-foot fella: da was $30 for de car, and Rommel take half-pound and I take one and one-half pound. We use to go regular dey, early in de mornin'. Because we did know de people good. We use to get good ganja. At dat time now, is dollar piece I use to deal in, rather dan joints. De onliest way I would keep a joint is for if a fella ask me for dat: den I wrap it out and gie him. But dollar piece in a piece a brown paper. Some people use to give wrappers too, but not I.

Rommel use to do the same thing dat time: cigarette joints. But den I say: hear nuh, if we get wrappers, I could wrap out joints for you. So dah is how we sight up wrappers from he brother in Carenage, Port-of-Spain. Because he was on a boat so we put it to him. We was really brave in dem days, you know. We jus use to lef de work and go Carenage. Dem days up dey, dey use to sell double pack [of cigarette papers, or wrappers]: 4 for $2. In Carenage, Rommel brother set us up with a whole box for $25. So now we hustlin' papers. Wrappers at $1 a packet.

I really get big. I had about 3 arrests. First one was past Brother's Road. In a bus with two poun's ah ganja. I waitin', waitin' for a taxi and I see a bus comin' so—me ain't ha' to pay, ah workin' in de bus company—I get on. I did see dis man scopin' me from head to toe and I did say: is police. But I say: is my money, I ain't throwin' away no ganja. So dey hold me. A white boy from up on de Coffee who use to come here by Boots: well, he bail me out. Ah get a $75 fine and I had to pay a lawyer $35 to talk for mih. And I lose de two poun's. But dat didn't stop me, I had money —I had to buy TV, fridge, fix up de house; we use to eat. Plenty time fetein' [partying]. Dah is how de money come and run . . . so I start off with two poun's again.

Is de las lock-up dat break me. A Saturday Randy Pierre [San Fernando's inspector of police] come by me. I was wrappin' out a five joint for a fella. And Jasmine say: look a stranger comin' up de yard. But he already come up on me. I did only have time to run and drop de ganja outside de back. About two poun's again. Well, he come inside and search and ting. He find de five joints. He take dat. Den he call me and send me for de ganja.

Dey lock me up. Dah was the early part ah 1977. Ned mother stand mih bail. I had $250 in my pocket. In de house, dey say: turn out your pockets. So I take out de money. Dey say dey feel dey should charge me for traffickin'. You know, sellin' ganja. Dah is a different charge from possession. Ah man in de back say: take care all you count de money and gie he back correct. Dey tell he: Eh, you want to get lock up too?!

You know, when dey take me in de car, Pierre call Jasmine and hand she de money roll up. She thought all de money was dey, just roll up: and he drive off fast after dat. You know how much he give she: $9. Den dey charge me for possession. Dey charge me in court . . . Is de prosecutor who save me. When dey ask whether I had other convictions, de Crown Prosecutor open a book and he say: no. Although I did have two. You see, Jasmine brother wife—Charlie wife—did know dis policeman, because Jasmine talk to he. So dey charge me $700. I had to pay half one time. Everybody was frighten: de Indian woman who take mih bail, Jasmine. But den de Indian woman say: don't dig nuttin'. And she and Jasmine gone. Dey did already put me in de cell; but when dey didn't take me out to go Port-of-Spain, I get a little glad. And in de evenin' Jasmine and de Indian woman come up with de money. Since den I really ain't pick up.

The period from 1969 to 1976 is filled with failures and successes of the sort described by the Jaguar. While the search for an appropriate socioeconomic form continued on the five limes, migration from them was taking place to other parts of the city, where the newly arrived brother would lend himself to transformations in neighborhoods there.

Thus, from Prince Alfred Street: Stanley went to Short Street, where he "had" the block for two years. Then he helped Jeru and Joseph set up neighboring blocks. Next he went to Vistabella, his grandmother's neighborhood, where, in addition to setting up his own block, he helped establish Simba's and Baraka's.

Vim joined his family in Cocoyea, building a prosperous block there continuously from about 1974 to 1978.

Matos went to the adjoining street. Naz also moved to a street nearby. Both built prosperous blocks in these locations.

From Short Street: Gentleman Slim went to New York and established a block in Brooklyn which he still operated in 1978. Mistry went to his own neighborhood on Coffee Street, starting off Xenophon, Takis, and others in turn. Stevens went to Prince Alfred Street and later to Roy Joseph Scheme. In neighboring areas like Carlton Lane and Leotaud Street, Ras Blaka and others were supplied by him; then opened their own blocks.

From Cipero Street: Botts, Kuper's younger brother, went to the housing scheme on Rushworth Street and developed what is perhaps the most prosperous block in the city in 1978. His associates include Ras Iron, Boyee, Prince, and a number of others. Singham settled in Duncan Village. Cancian built up a block with nine other very religious Rastafari in La Romaine. Pitts and Barnes went further up Cipero Street, developed a block there, and were the first, after 1976, to become heavily involved with export to the other Caribbean islands. They were personally responsible for the introduction and spread of marijuana use, Rastafarianism, and block organization in Barbados.

The climate of trial and error, of striving to succeed in the marijuana traffic, left a palpable feeling of exhilaration in San Fernando. Loquacious and expressive young men (and even by now a few young women) were being exercised very vigorously to show their aptitude in business. Learned abilities as bad johns, gamblers, or as the spokesmen/organizers of 1969 to 1970 could be assets. Often age was a decisive factor: the first marijuana smokers were men in their thirties in 1974, who were among the "many to be called" towards, experimenting towards the block; but frequently younger men, more experienced in use, trafficking, and Rastafari, and furthest removed from former manifestations of the lime, were "the few chosen" to realize it. Among the latter, associations and eventually blocks emerged which were more stable, their members more committed, contented, and creative than among the former. Other assets included: supportive parents, inherited patron–client ties in the neighborhood, a grandfather committed to African reclamation of the land (Botts), and other such formative influences upon character and resolve.

Words were found to express the motivational exertions experienced in the passage from disintegrated lime to block. Such social, cultural/motivational, economic exertions expressed themselves in the symbolism of marijuana, which now made men "think constructive" and led them "to see the light." They are also the central feature of Rastafari.

Matos, a leading Rastafari block leader in San Fernando in 1978, describes the passage as one from "the fleshical" to "the heartical":

> *First time, de way I-man a-see de block, you know . . . It come like . . . in dem times, it was just fleshical. Like most ah de time, most ah de brethren just a-come for most ah de day and just sit up and na do nuttin' and just gamble along de way . . . and waste time, you know.*
>
> *But den, in dis here time, de inspiration start to come on. It come like . . . brothers start to locks up [grow dreadlocks, as Rastafari believe the Bible enjoins] from dem times. But dey didn't know de way; dey didn't see de light. As man locks grow, man ha' wisdom open, right? Man start to see through different lines. Man start to sight de light. And when man see de light, is just . . . man's works to be seen. Dat is de heights: within de man a-see de light, his works . . . people ha' to see.*

So den it come like different brothers start to stray. Like who a-stay for Jah, trod de road a Zion. And who a-stay in de fleshical, although they might even have locks, dem just trod a nex' road. So den dat start to divide up even the brothers.

All in 1967 so, it was just de fleshical. It was just dat plenty brothers a-live around de place, dem gather in one place, dem lime and gossip whole day. And just a-gamble among dey self. It was like . . . nuttin' as far as I concerned. Even de las' few days here was more dan dem days, because dem days was really nuttin'.

Ganja start to come in, you know. And dah . . . as the herbs come in now, it come like dah was de light. Is dat is what start up everything heartical. Because within through de herbs, brothers like see de wrong . . . dem a-dealin'. And brothers like even see de way and begin to trod. Just time and time.

More times is de ganja dat come . . . You see, de Father does come like a tief in de night in dis here time: so like many ah He missions does come in and you doesn't know how it come and when it come. Like den even we don't know how Rasta come on de land. Because it was here from Creation. So den de herbs was always from Creation. So de man cyant pinpoint: is dey it start. All man know it was around. . . .

Dem time, it was anyone a-deal it still. You know. It come like one man might have a portion, dis man might buy some from he and bring it dong smaller and sell I when I come or a nex' man. You will never know who a-deal in it because you might come and ask anyone: give me someting, you know. When it start to come, is like everyone use to have someting. Or it might come and meet you in de town. Who have, have; or who ain't have still smoke, you know.

But dem time . . . you see, man didn't sight up de light in dem times still. So den it was just aroun', to open I on an I-ditation [meditation].

More times, I-man use to buy and sell and to dwell on de block dey, you know. All in de time ah Pascal and Ras Chari on dis block I-man na did sight any big pusher yet, you know. Because man might have someting and by Friday, he have nothing; while de smallest man might have a portion dat day. It come like . . . is just man seek for love and within dah man have de love, man ah deal with it, you know.

So through dem times, it come to . . . like, on every region you go, you go hear . . . well, dah brother dong dey real good [has a good marijuana business], and dah brother good, you know. A certain time, it just rise up so 'til every brother was just good. Dem block just superb you know.

De most highest place in San Fernando come to be Prince Alfred Street, you know. Dat come to be one of de established places. Dey come like how Observatory Street stay in Port-of-Spain. De gate by Doctor and dem—a kinda established place for Rasta.

From dey plenty brethren branch out. But den men rise up in all regions, because well den, de mystic [the Rastafari message of the Inner, or Rasta, Self] was in de air, you know. People just start to knat up, knat up, knat up [grow dreadlocks]. Den dah was just de callin', you know. Because well den many were called and few go be chosen. In dis time Jah go be choosin'; it dem times it was just de callin' you know.

Man wasn't knat up in de Black Power times, you know. But man a-thinkin'. But in dem times de block was jus' zes up: anytime you pass, people in de road, de road full up, de house full up, you know. It used to lively up de street in a form. But den it was still darkness de brothers a-deal in dem times, you know. So dat had to mash up anyway: it wasn't firm still.

What is de block? De block is where people a-come to do business.

CHARACTERISTICS OF THE BLOCK OR GATE

The block, or gate took shape in the various neighborhoods in San Fernando gradually between 1974 and 1978. In time, as the links with blocks in New York City and elsewhere multiplied and were strengthened, blocks acquired a multinational form. A block is a novel form of socioeconomic organization among former San Fernandian limers. It has certain distinguishing characteristics, which are derived from the technical requirements of the marijuana traffic and from the unique social inheritances of the San Fernandian limers. They are:

- *Loyalty*: There is a certain loyalty between a leader and from one to as many as nine young men and women whom he leads. The appearance of the latter—women—should be marked as another novel feature of block organization. Women had not figured largely in liming activities.

  This loyalty may occasionally astonish an observer. It rests upon appreciation of the leader's oratorial skill and the quality of his Rastafari message. People associate with a particular leader because he will make them "see de light," or encourage them to be more "upfull" (orthodox) Rastafari: he will clarify Rastafari thinking and help them seek out Rasta ways of doing and being.

  Thus, the division between leader and led is thought of in religious or caste terms. In deference to this belief and to Rastafari doctrine, terms of equality are used among brethren, the leader being distinguished sometimes by the term "elder brother." In the egalitarian ideology, there are neither "leaders" nor "led."
- *Division of Labor*: The division between leader and led, however, is also a definite division of labor in the conduct of the marijuana traffic. The leader usually has made the initial purchases of marijuana; makes frequent trips to the country to purchase it or decides upon some strategy to be supplied regularly; arranges personnel on the block; decides how and when to package the marijuana; and has formal control over the redistribution of surpluses.

  The led perform services required on the block, such as packaging and selling marijuana; and also shoulder domestic responsibilities, especially when block members have young children. Both leader and led perform all functions (other than the specific leadership ones) without distinction—even household ones. They smoke from his supplies of marijuana, eat from his store, and receive small advances of cash or marijuana to meet a few everyday needs. If someone is arrested, the leader is expected to arrange bail, and to pay a lawyer and the fine. Similarly, if someone is ill or has some urgent, unexpected expense, the leader will help.

The leader is always under pressure to redistribute his surpluses in a manner to ensure the survival of his block. Older leaders, men in their thirties, the first smokers and experimenters, and younger ones, men in their twenties, are distinguishable in this matter: the former have greater difficulty in resolving the problem and have a higher turnover of personnel; while the latter have succeeded in finding satisfactory ways to reinvest ganja revenues, creating more stable, more loyal, more innovative, more "I-ry" (good for I-man = more genuinely Rastafari) blocks.

- *Coresidence and Ritual*: At an accelerating pace, block members live together and share in communal rituals, religious celebrations, and feasts. A variety of intimate relations exists among many coresidents. Often, for a youngster whose parents have migrated abroad, the block is the chief source of support, instruction, and care.

DESCRIPTIONS OF SOME SAN FERNANDO BLOCKS

The following descriptions were selected from field notes describing San Fernando blocks. They were written in 1977 and 1978. They indicate the degree to which block performance depended upon the personality of the block leader, his relations with his associates, his involvement in the neighborhood, the richness of his Rastafari conceptions, and the symbols he generated. When customers purchased marijuana from a block, they recognized that these were qualities or attributes of the commodity they had bought and anticipated that they would profoundly shape their experience of it.

Despite the broad similarities which identified them as a novel socioeconomic form, blocks diverged in many particulars: in the manner in which the contact with growers or other suppliers was made, in the quality of marijuana which was purchased, in the process by which decisions were made as to quantity and as to who made purchases, whether marijuana was produced by the joint, ounce, or pound, in the utilization of labor power, in the number of persons supplying the labor, in the type of relationships which existed among the laborers, and with respect to the redistribution of whatever surpluses the traffic produced. The descriptions of a few selected blocks below were selected to illustrate them:

Vim's Block

Vim is a young man of twenty-four, who is extremely sensitive to movements of racial and class politics. Phenotypically Indian, as are the other members of his family, he grew up in a mixed neighborhood: one in which there were both Indians and Africans and in which there were both those who would make it and those who would not.

The family identified itself completely with those who would not make it, both Indian and Africans, but in this neighborhood, however, they were mostly African. The children, therefore, became very "black-heart" as they were incorporated into the lime, and in the case of Vim, lived through, in heart and mind, its transformation into a block.

This identification is a matter of importance to the family as a whole, and one learns to appreciate the fact best when it is questioned. When they lived in this neighborhood, Vim's father was a salesman in a hardware store and earned very little; his mother did equally poorly, selling Indian pickles and savories. Eventually, when Vim was about ten (1964), his father built a concrete house in a considerably superior suburban area with plenty of unoccupied land surrounding well-built houses, although it was by no means a luxury suburb. The father also launched his own business as an itinerant salesman, selling hardware goods from his recently acquired station wagon in the country districts. Vim did not move with the family, but stayed on a street close to the lime; he would later have a child by a young woman here, and his sister would also become the common-law wife of Ras Chari (who would establish the block here) and the mother of his two children.

The eldest daughter, however, "turned out different." She had been sent to commercial school, where she learned shorthand, typing, and bookkeeping, and in 1968, she married her first employer, a moderately prosperous Indian dry-goods merchant. This change in her fortunes caused her to adopt abruptly her husband's racism: she began to treat her brothers and sisters strictly as guests, disallowing them any familiarity with her possessions and her new home.

Vim's icy regard for this betrayal, not only of the family's "black" experience but of the hopes the family had placed in her, the one on whom dollars were invested for education, is central to his critique of money and Babylon, the bourgeois pagan world. When the family, as an ideology and an organization, is played out as a strategem to advance aspirations, a weak link is fatal to all its members. Vim recalls bitterly how no help was ever forthcoming from her; how she used her younger brothers and sisters as servants whenever she requested the labor, and forgot about them afterward. He quarrels with his brother-in-law, whose racism is in fact quite indigestible: a fight almost erupted between them once, when the brother-in-law tried to demonstrate the thickness of "Creole [African] people's skins" by fiercely pinching Ras Chari's infant son. Whenever this sister and her family visit, Vim is provoked into taunting his parents for tolerating their presence; they are clearly sympathetic toward him, especially his father, who takes the occasion to display his knowledge of current Rastafari speech, thereby making the brother-in-law uneasy; but they contain the quarreling as best they can.

Vim dropped out of school when he was eight (1962). He explained that he determined to master "many things so that I would have something to say about them afterwards." This career took him through pitching marbles, kite flying, slingshot hunting, and, finally, the Boy's Industrial Home, for stealing food from a shop. When he was twelve (1966), however, he managed to work out a position for himself, as a "son"/helper, with a "white lady" who lived in yet another part of town (though still not too far away from the old lime).

It was while he was living at this woman's home that Vim began to smoke marijuana. While maintaining daily contact with the old lime in his first neighborhood, Vim tried it, experimentally and with great fear for his mental health, as others were doing at that time. Like everyone else in these circles of experimenters, he began to develop his point of view on unemployment, Black Power, and politics.

Vim does not have a great deal of respect for books and did not read Frantz Fanon[1] and the radical literature as the others did. He contented himself with the digests by others of what they had read, and for the most part agreed with what he heard. On the other hand, he has an enormous confidence in his own analytical ability, while his combative conversational style ensures him an audience and heated exchanges of views. The first materials he uses in his thinking are the earliest relations he has experienced, those within his family: and as the drama of his eldest sister unfolded, it deepened his ironic understanding of the forces which shaped his "trials and tribulations." At the same time he profited from the real strengths of his family: a cheerful, adaptable father and a quiet, immensely dedicated mother, and their determination to cope and survive. For Vim, his relations with his associates and his conception of Rastafari were modeled on an ideology of the "family." This emphasis in his thinking distinguished him from many other Rastafari, who invoked "community," "nation," and "race" instead.

Thus, while he accepted the fact of discrimination, he refused to see that it justified violent protest: there were alternatives persons might explore, if they did not waste time protesting, gambling, and provoking "the man" (authorities). Gradually, as the marijuana traffic expanded and after Vim became a regular distributor, he retired entirely from gambling houses, cinemas, and dances, preferring to devote his free time to his vegetable garden, which he had prepared in the unoccupied land behind his father's house.

Vim took no active part in the Black Power uprisings in 1970; he talked with the brothers, he limed with them, exposing himself to the same risks of arrest, carried the Black Power sloganeering to the "white lady" who lodged him, but otherwise, he said, tried to stay out of trouble. After the uprising, he and his brother, the Champ, went about the growing blocks preaching his Rastafari gospel of non violence and self-help with great rhetorical flourish. His personal block took shape under a street lamp close to the white lady's house. By now, he was purchasing marijuana in half-pound batches, and could call on any one of a number of young men to assist him in wrapping out the marijuana in exchange for free supplies for personal use.

By 1973, Vim had been expelled by the white lady after his first marijuana arrest. The raid had been on his parents' house where he used to stash the bulk of his supply; but a certain coolness had alienated the white lady and himself, on his side because of the recent Black Power consciousness raising, and on her side, on account of the rumors she had heard of Vim from nonsmoking neighborhood youths who wanted Vim's downstairs apartment for a table tennis and weightlifting room.

Vim relocated the block near his parents' house, where Gregory, his permanent assistant, coped with sales which could now be measured in pounds. On Carnival Tuesday of 1974, Vim, who is about 5'6" and as slight as a ten-year-old, was arrested on the much more serious charge of attempted assault on a policeman who tried to arrest him for marijuana. The police confiscated several pieces of jewelry, cash, and marijuana. He was sentenced to six months' imprisonment and lost substantial savings to pay lawyers' fees and other legal expenses.

The costly setback did not shake Vim in his Rastafari beliefs nor his conviction that poor Africans' best hope was investment in alternatives, such as the ones marijuana and his garden promised. He revived his block around his parents' house in 1976, with Gregory, Brink, Moray, and Jeff, all Africans and Rastafari, to help him sell marijuana and tend the garden. Moving sales between different campsites in the late afternoons, when many customers sought marijuana smoking, he soon enjoyed the patronage and following of Indian youths from villages in the nearby sugar belt.

In addition to the ideology of self-reliance, which had removed them from petty thievery, gambling, and idleness, Vim offered his associates the garden, marijuana, marijuana revenues, and the very real benefaction of his family. Gregory especially benefits from it; for while the others have at least one parent, Gregory has only a very aged grandmother, who is more his responsibility than he hers. Vim's mother and sisters cook vegetarian meals for the young Rastafari in the evenings, using the produce from their garden; and whenever they feel to lounge around the veranda or beneath the house, where the Champ and Vim have their rooms, they are made to feel welcome. By the end of 1976, they had converted others in the neighborhood to the belief in Jah and Haile Selassi-I's divinity, to shun Babylon, to manifest the true "Ethiopian" I-man, the inner man, committed to "going forward."

The innocence of Vim's family's, so far as marijuana use and sales are concerned, has been established in spite of being subjected to considerable skepticism in the research. The only connection they have with the traffic, apart from the encouragements mentioned above, is that Vim's mother keeps his cash in her dressing table with her lingerie—quite a customary hiding place for money and other valuables in Trinidadian households. Vim also made innumerable marijuana contacts in the country while assisting his father in his business; but while his father tolerated his use of marijuana, Vim has never requested him to use his motorcar to carry his marijuana.

Vim sells a pound of marijuana in one or two days. Brink and Jeff sell on the streets around Cocoyea. Gregory remains near Vim's parents' house, while Vim sometimes sells in the mornings at the main offices of the Water and Sewerage Administration, and on some weekend nights, outside dance halls and parties. No more than four to six hours a day is given over to selling, although it may take two men a couple of hours extra to wrap out a pound every two days. On most evenings, from 5:00 P.M. to 8:00 P.M., the block—Vim, Brink, Jeff, Moray, and Gregory—is in session at its movable campsites, attracting scores of customers, some of whom remain behind to hear Vim and the Champ. While they remain, they smoke marijuana, sometimes free of charge. On one exceptional evening, when Vim was joined by brothers from another block, he shared smoke which would have been valued commercially at about $80.

Though generous, Vim is often angry when the recipients of his largesse do not immediately run out, cultivate gardens, and become Rastafari, as Vim has been instructing them. The marijuana which is consumed on evening sessions and which Gregory, Brink, Moray, Jeff, and the Champ consume makes serious inroads into his capital. Nor have things always worked smoothly with his associates. When he was restarting his block in 1975 after the big arrest, having lost savings and jewelry, he had to sell off his $500 stereo equipment for $150 to make his first purchase of marijuana. He entrusted the money to Gregory, who lost it while gambling. Gregory was not as yet the committed Rastafari he is now.

Today, Vim supplies food, clothing, and sometimes shelter for his associates, and has been fortunate so far in avoiding further arrests. A police corporal lives close to the block, but according to Vim, he became a policeman through passing exams and not from rising up through the ranks: he contents himself with little jokes at Vim's expense. His wife, however, exploits her position as a policeman's wife whenever she can: her latest usage of it was to seize fourteen of Vim's chickens, in the knowledge that he would grumble but do no more.

Vim's associates are content and hope that the block will soon specialize in 5-bags, 10-pieces, and ounces. Gregory, whose father is dead and whose mother is in England, has nothing besides marijuana, now that he has been expelled from school. Brink is slightly better placed, in that he may eventually get work through his father, himself an unskilled Texaco worker. Jeff's father is also in New York, and he is out of school, without qualifications, living on an aunt's kindness.

Apart from his associates and some others among his clientele, Vim has no close ties with anyone else in the trade. Frequently, however, he travels to buy marijuana together with one of the leaders on another large, prosperous block, where Vim's message is well respected and which has two gardens under cultivation, following Vim's advice. By traveling together, they save costs and are able to pool their knowledge of the countryside, and since their combined money is often more than $1,000, they are able to use the large sum to extract bargains from the growers.

Stanley's Block

Once, the occasion arose at Stanley's block for those present to go out and buy a meal. The Rastafari are very strict about diet and normally prefer to eat home-cooked, saltless, vegetarian food, but it is not always easy to prepare food on all blocks, all the time. Stanley led the way to a largish concrete house where a pair of sisters and two friends had set up a "parlor": they sold sandwiches of curried chickpeas or potatoes, homemade buns, sugar cakes, coconut pastries, fudge, and a variety of local drinks or tisanes, such as mauby and sorrel.

The sisters are bespectacled and in their fifties. The parlor business enterprise is clearly a hand-me-down from a more genteel past, when it was for social gatherings, church functions, high teas, bazaars, civil receptions, and women's associations that the delicacies had been prepared. The sisters are African, but they have fair complexions and "good," curly-straight hair. They kept up a lively conversation with Stanley, chiding him about not visiting them for so long and wondering whether he was as true to the Rastafari faith as he claimed. He answered with quotations from the Scriptures and his own jokes at their expense. Their witticisms and choice of expressions, or their English generally, were distinctive. Evidently, the sisters belonged to a latter-day emergent African leadership class, the same which had produced Trinidad's prime minister and the various luminaries of the court, the professions, and the civil service who ruled the country today.

If one looks past the kitchen into the living room, there is a faded picture on a table with artificial flowers in a vase, of a young man wearing baccalaureate cap and gown. The young man had fought for Britain in World War II and had died on a combat mission with the Royal Air Force. The picture adds to the story of this household. The sisters, deprived by fate of their main avenue to the local bourgeoisie, one which they had prepared with love and by their personal sacrifice of savings and luxuries, had persevered by teaching in primary school. In retirement, they gave cooking and sewing lessons, and with two friends, an Indian divorcee and an unmarried middle-aged African woman, had started the small neighborhood business as a shield against inflation and thc high cost of living. They are genuinely fond of Stanley because he insists upon his dignity as an African and approve of the Rastafari on account of him. It is a dignity which their lives had helped to build.

The sisters' house indicates the kind of neighborhood out of which Stanley operates. It started out as an enclave of poor but respectable and tremendously ambitious African and Indian residents: their houses, some of them falling into serious disrepair, with pianos and stuffed furniture, remain as monuments to that status. Then, as sons and daughters who did not die in the RAF moved their families out, the bereft and the nonachievers were left behind, and the area was settled by a fresh wave of families, this time laborers, the self-employed, and the unemployed.

Stanley enjoys the same relationship of loyalty and support with the neighborhood generally as with the sisters. Since it had been his neighborhood from childhood, he is known to the older residents as well as to the newcomers. One of the latter, a carpenter, and a group of them, all self-employed Rastafari leather workers, receive commissions from him. Stanley was incorporated from childhood in the local lime, which has all but vanished. Stanley learned to use and sell marijuana on the Prince Alfred Street lime where Cindy, his wife, used to live, and which was the lime of Vim, Ras Chari, and many others.

The local lime had been very exclusive. It had a large proportion of "redskinned" adolescents, like Stanley himself; exulting in their fair skin and "superior" status, they had little intercourse with the other limes in the city. Indeed, they had a reputation for being "very aggressive" on Saturday mornings, when members from various limes would jostle on High Street, to steal from stores and pick pockets, and at parties and dances. Most of them have left the neighborhood, some migrating abroad.

Stanley's mother and aunt, who raised him, had a tarnished respectability in the neighborhood. An upper-class status attached to them on account of their color (they are phenotypically white), because they were comfortably off, and because they traveled frequently to New York, but no one knew their exact circumstances. Stanley does not remember his father and during his childhood was half-indulged, half-neglected. He dropped out of school when he was eleven (1955) and had reached the exhibition class (when exams are taken for the government exhibitions, or scholarships to secondary schools).

By 1956, he was being supervised by a probation officer after he had been caught stealing and soon after, on account of a second offense, was sent to the Boys' Industrial Home, a correctional facility for youthful offenders, where he was taught tailoring. For a several years afterward, he practiced that trade at men's clothing shops in San Fernando.

Stanley is a skillful manipulator of persons, especially when they are young, impressionable, and insecure. He has the patience and the insight of a professional analyst, and manages to help a person articulate her or his problems while making himself indispensable to the solution of them. Apparently, he has scored his chief successes in counseling with young women, two of whom have borne him sons. But he had been Cindy's sweetheart since 1964, when he had joined the Prince Alfred Street lime, and he would later father her three sons. In 1965, Stanley was already a San Fernandian spokesman for the Youth Power Organization, which had formed principally around the issue of unemployment. From 1965 to 1969, he was one of the organizers of a commune in the Waller Field area of north-central Trinidad; and, because of his indefatigable aplomb, talked some government officials into donating the use of land-moving equipment, fertilizers, insecticides, seeds, and expert advice. The commune cultivated tomatoes and herded goats. On weekends, Stanley visited the Prince Alfred Street lime in San Fernando to court Cindy. Gradually, members went out on visits and did not return to the commune; Stanley, who always finds himself in charge of finance and who always finds difficulties with the job, left on account of a quarrel related to the sale of the goats, their last valuable asset. Subsequently, Stanley was very active during the Black Power rebellion in 1970: he participated at all the major demonstrations and ran the gauntlet of police batons at the famous rally on Frederick Street in Port-of-Spain. He was among the many arrested for distributing literature "subversive to the public order" and was detained at Nelson Island, an offshore penal institution. On his return, he moved in with Cindy and together they organized a block at Lord Street Corner. At the height of the rebellion, marijuana was smoked openly on this block, which is in the busiest part of San Fernando, in deliberate defiance of the police.

After 1970, Stanley inherited the block Hogarth had started in Short Street. It was to become the biggest, fastest block until it was finally broken down in 1978, after repeated police assaults. The spectacular success of this block was entirely Stanley's doing. By 1975, he had converted to Rastafari, and his tenure of the block coincided with his own personal process of "going dread." Being a man extremely talented in the field of person and situation manipulation, and being also shrewd, endowed with gifts for drama and effect, he displayed this process in public, provoking reactions in all those associated with him.

The block was located in a neighborhood which had traditionally sheltered retired workers, sex workers, and criminals. One woman maintained a functional home with remittances from her husband in America. Stanley won her trust so completely that she offered shelter to any transient recommended by the block. At length, when her husband discontinued his support, Stanley contributed the money for the upkeep of the household. When jewelry and "hot" items, like shipments of denim jeans, T-shirts, or electrical appliances were received as payment for marijuana or in exchange for marijuana earnings—again, a policy adopted by Stanley more than other block leaders—persons in the neighborhood received items free of charge. A bicycle was purchased for a disabled seaman's child. Stanley even gained help from a wealthy Chinese businessman who had made a parking lot on the street for his shops on nearby High Street. He showed Stanley places in the lot where he could hide marijuana, and promised to assure the police that his parking lot was unmolested by block members—a ploy to draw attention away from the block's marijuana sales.

Stanley also experimented with methods of presenting marijuana to the public. In 1975, he was selling huge joints wrapped in pink papers; distributors in nongrowing country areas (such as Raw Deal: see chapter 2) resold them as two joints at home. Stanley also smoked from a chalice (a local waterpipe, made with a coconut, hard wood, and rubber) to share marijuana and promote communal use on his block.

Stanley has "belly" (courage), a qualification which attracts many admirers. A very tiny man who bears in fact a remarkable resemblance to the Emperor, Haile Selassi-I, he wanders all over San Fernando, when there are no bench warrants for his arrest, detaining a preacher, a teacher, or a nurse—any "hypocrite"—in the midst of Saturday shopping, and lecturing the victim on Jah Rastafari, probing their beliefs, and holding them up to ridicule. When his dramatic gestures and outrageous sallies have attracted a sufficiently large crowd, he launches into a massive, many-sided attack on bourgeois institutions, or Babylon. Stanley is a marvelous speaker: his jokes, his quotations from the Scriptures, his cornering of an opponent for a barrage of abuse and instruction are rapidly and crisply orchestrated. His voice shifts from satirical tones of affected Jamaican (Rastafari) dialect to those of Trinidadian ribaldry as he weaves arguments together.

As he moved from Black Power, took stock of the debacle of 1970, and struggled toward conversion to Rastafari, he took along on the quest all the young people who came in close contact with him. By 1975, the block had become the meeting place for calypsonians, musicians, artists, and performers drawn from the many Caribbean islands, some returning from abroad, students of all ages, and workers. Stanley operated a branch block not too far away, where his closest friends from the old Prince Alfred Street lime could meet him more privately in the evenings. Coincidentally, it was located on the very spot where a licensed opium and marijuana dealer had sold drugs until 1914.

Stanley is a man of contrary moods and motives. Sometimes he used to sit on a stoop behind his branch block, talking to a few friends about Jah Rastafari, about what "dreadness" and "going forward" meant, dreaming about a future in which, comfortably off, he would devote all his time to worship. In the moonlight, he looked like the image of those ancient North African traders, Phoenicians and later Muslims, fired by religious zeal and business acumen, whose trading networks had spanned the world as it was known in those ages. On the other hand, he has proven himself on occasion to be more avaricious, more obsessed by the immediate dollar, than any other Rastafari marijuana distributor in San Fernando. The trait has won him many detractors, even among those who admire him for his obvious strengths.

All the personnel at the courthouse in San Fernando know Stanley—lawyers, magistrates, warrant clerks, court clerks, welfare officers—and many of them admire his spunk. He marches into business places to solicit financial assistance for his various schemes, acquiring notoriety if not capital. In one case, he seriously embarrassed a San Fernandian businessman, a self-styled mystic and devotee of Eastern religions, whom he had approached for help to fight a constitutional case over the right to wear dreadlocks: the businessman is long-haired. He makes it a point to pay regular visits to the elected parliamentary representative for this part of San Fernando, an old schoolmate of his.

The police do not like him at all. He has been arrested on five occasions since January 1976—for escaping custody, for assault, and for marijuana possession and sales. It is allegedly on account of his prior attachment to them that the Short Street block and its branch were finally destroyed in 1978. To raze the building thoroughly, the police pressured the mayor to authorize demolition of all buildings in the vicinity where block members might find shelter. On another occasion, he and seven other Rastafari were shackled and manhandled by six policemen and shorn of their dreadlocks. Stanley claimed that the sacrilege "disoriented" him and that he was brought "close to madness and schizophrenia" when he saw his dreadlocks, "the color and fullness of golden herb," lying on the ground. It is one of his best stories, and while it is embellished anew at each telling, there remains in it earnestness and sincerity, which carry over into his analyses of the brutal hypocrisies of neo-colonial society, for which the story had acted as a springboard.

Stanley retaliates against the police by making daring escapes from squad cars. He has friends among the warrant officers, who will pretend not to have seen him at large when there are outstanding bench warrants for his arrest. For the dreadlocks-shearing incident, he has filed a constitutional case to argue that his civil rights had been violated. Meanwhile he tries to convince more people that the Rastafari are not unkempt hooligans but serious practioners of their religious beliefs.

Cindy's three sons are a considerable asset to him in gaining public goodwill. These children are very beautiful, lively, alert, intelligent, well-groomed, and captivating. No sooner does a young woman smile in their direction than Stanley presents himself, shoving a sweet-smelling child into the delighted woman's arms, and beginning to lecture why it is essential to these children's future that he be Rastafari. The children's welfare nurse, a middle-aged, middle-class Jamaican woman who visits the children at home once a week, has declared that there is no other gentleman in San Fernando but Stanley! Graduating schoolgirls (eighteen to nineteen years of age) help Stanley to sell marijuana and take care of household duties while he attends to his business. Since Cindy is as independent as Stanley and lazy to boot, Stanley often finds himself responsible for all the cooking, washing, and baby-sitting in the household, so that these services rendered by the female public must figure as economically significant services.

It is rumored that Stanley has accumulated a lot of money during his ten years of selling marijuana. His own intense interest in money has always made for difficult relations between himself and those who work with him. As a result his block is unique in its high turnover of personnel. Stanley has mentored several young men—Jeru, Dense, Richie, David, Andy, Kenrick, Joseph—as they established themselves in the marijuana trade and as Rastafari; but all have discontinued the business association with him after only a short period of time. The complaint is universal: they will support Stanley in all his endeavors, and continue to look to him for advice and instruction, but they prefer not to work with him. Beyond the obligatory redemption of legal dues and supply of food, Stanley is impossibly reluctant to part with money, and he is quick to answer any query concerning redistribution by saying that children are the first priority and that his had consumed the money in question.

For example, it was a quarrel between Stanley and Jeru's father which caused Stanley to withdraw from the Short Street block. The father is a Water and Sewage Authority employee, and in 1970, when Stanley was selling marijuana at Lord Street, had operated his own block, together with Argyll and Sabinus, at the Library Corner. These blocks were closely allied, since all the members had originated from the same Prince Alfred Street lime and had branched out from Ras Chari's block there. The Library Corner block was abandoned within a few months. Its three owners had conceived it largely for political reasons: they wanted San Fernandians to smoke marijuana openly in the heart of the city. The location, however, proved to be too conspicuous and ill-protected to serve permanently as a block.

In 1977, Jeru was one of Stanley's associates on the block, together with Bunuel, Kenrick, Andy, Dense, and Richie. Stanley had worked out a system by which an amount of marijuana was given to each young man on request, at a price worked out to please both Stanley and the particular young man. The latter was also supplied with cigarette papers to make joints. In fixing the price, he would have estimated a surplus for his own use and for his cash needs. Stanley was thus able to accumulate a steady supply of cash daily, in sufficiently large quantities to take advantage of bargains when buying marijuana wholesale in the countryside. In this manner, savings of over $6,000 were accumulated by August 1977. Jeru's father, claiming that he was acting on his son's behalf, wanted the money to be either redistributed or banked in a joint account in a safe deposit box.

Stanley resented the interference. He complained that he had all sorts of plans: there was acreage outside San Fernando where he had persuaded Dense to build a hut near the one he had already constructed; he was hoping to bring this land under cultivation. He had already started a herd of goats with three ewes, a ram, and a few kids. Richie and Cindy were allotted funds to build coops (vending stalls), which were to be stationed at the Library Corner, to sell apples, grapes, and vegetarian Rastafari food for the coming Christmas season, when thousands of shoppers saturate that area. He needed money to buy more goats from the interisland boats arriving from Grenada and to buy fruit and vegetables from the wholesalers; he needed money on hand in case of arrest and to pay lawyers' fees for his upcoming constitutional case, which he was confident he would win. He was interested in traveling to Tobago to establish a branch or a trade connection, since cigarette papers and marijuana fetched much higher prices in all the smaller islands, where Trinidadian Rastafari were beginning to introduce marijuana and Rastafari. Cindy and the children were also planning another trip to New York: there, she would sell marijuana for greater profits in U.S. dollars and buy karate shoes, jumpsuits, T-shirts, and materials for making incense sticks, which she would ship to Trinidad for retail, again for substantial profits.

But Stanley was principally upset because, when it was a matter of money, he never liked to give accurate accounts: he does not say how much he paid in the country for marijuana; he does not like to dwell on the financial details of his various schemes. Then there are expenses such as the children's forthcoming trip or his eldest son's bicycle, imported from the United States, which he has to defend constantly. He likes quoting Malcolm X: "If it's not for the children, who the hell is it for?"

Provoked in this case, he retaliated by handing over the $6,000 to Jeru's father and signing as one of the owners of a joint bank account; but disbanded the block by leaving each associate to buy and sell on his own. The outcome was immediate: supplies of marijuana became irregular, and the block was unable to keep payments and favors flowing smoothly to the neighborhood. The old woman whose house they used and who cooked for them closed her doors. Stanley remained as one individual buyer and seller among the several who came and went until November 1977, then left altogether, to join Richie, Cindy, Dense, and David at the Library Corner coops. Jeru, Bunuel, and Kenrick were left with the task of reorganizing the block, but the police smashed the house which sheltered it in May 1978. Today, Richie and a few other youngsters still spend some of their time there, but they never have more than a few joints to sell.

Stanley withdrew to his grandmother's neighborhood to live. He started a block at his grandmother's house and continued to manage the coops at the Library Corner until they were pulled down by the police in February 1978. Finally, he was left only with the block near his grandmother's house. His associates—David, Richie, Dina, Betty, Jessica, and Assata—sell in the neighborhood. Cindy, of course, continued to sell marijuana herself at the house: she made her trip to New York late in 1978. The trip to Tobago was made, with David and Dina. Relationships are brittle with all of these associates on account of Stanley's worsening stinginess. The young women in particular received little benefit from the services they rendered, other than marijuana for personal use and the promise of protection in case of arrest.

Stanley is a transitional type in the consolidation of Rastafari in San Fernando. Others like Vim, Botts, or Matos are younger, more scrupulous, and more principled in all their transactions, especially financial ones. At the same time, they have profited from Stanley's struggles as a Rastafari. Stanley has not become the kind of inspired Rastafari prophet Port-of-Spain boasts, whose charisma is overwhelming: he is recognized to be pragmatic and levelheaded even in devotion. But these unresolved conflicts in the man show the lines along which resolutions to conflicts must be made in the movement as a whole.

Bott's Block

Bott's block is situated in a government housing project of some forty-two apartments on Rushworth Street which dates back to the 1950s and where low-income families have had a long tenure. Bott's father was a respected, if spendthrift, civil servant. His grandfather, who also lived with the family, had won even greater renown as a neighborhood scholar and expert in African history. He now lives on land he has acquired near Chaguanas, in central Trinidad, and advocates African reclamation of the land. Bott claims him as the most influential person in his life.

From an early age, Bott had been an innovator in his neighborhood lime. Big built and imposing in a slow, amiable way, he persuaded three others, while still in primary school, to join him in making kites for sale to more privileged classmates. In those days, kite flying was a cutthroat competition: a well-made kite would have ground glass glued into its bows and frills. Other weapons, like razor blades, were sewn into its long tail. Thus armed, a kite could attack other kites while in flight, either ripping them to shreds or cutting them loose. During the Christmas celebrations, Bott and his little company made imitation Christmas trees, using a discarded broomstick for the trunk, and for branches, wire models on which closely cropped green streamers were stuck. They also made toy trucks from scraps of wood, using discarded thread bobbins for wheels. The toys fetched a good income for the four boys.

As a teenager in the early 1970s, Bott worked as an associate with Mistry, a fellow limer who had formed a block on Coffee Street. It was a part-time association during which Bott held other menial jobs. Finally, in 1976, with help from Mistry, Bott invested his savings in a block. He had already joined Rastafari and was preaching his grandfather's message of an African exodus from the city to return to the land.

From the beginning, Bott tried to make sure that the associates on his block were as directly involved in the profit sharing as himself. Each of them—Ras Iron, Buen Retiro, Prince, Boyee, Haji—received marijuana at discounted rates from him to sell on the block. Each Rastafari followed his own initiative to do so. Profits were then recollected in the form of an esusu (an informal credit union), each member being obliged, on risk of forfeiture of former contributions, to pay weekly dues on the date specified. He even brought four middle-aged heads of households in the housing scheme into the esusu: being government employees, respectable, and elders, they added seriousness and discipline to the effort. They could also bank money legitimately. The move won further neighborhood support for these Rastafari.

The esusu has so far afforded cars for Bott, Prince, and Boyee, which are used as taxis to enhance their profitability. For the sum Bott raised toward their cars, Prince and Boyee have been obliged to make additional weekly repayments out of their taxi fares; but the money is needed for the capital they are currently accumulating to buy land and material for a house. So far, only Buen Retiro, the handsome womanizer of the group, has forfeited once and was forgiven the penalty!

Bott has used esusu funds to buy five acres in the countryside near Moruga in southern Trinidad where there are many derelict cocoa estates. In February 1979, he bought a Mazda pickup, which he painted green, gold, and red (Rastafari colors), to be used for transport in developing the land.

The block continued to operate prosperously in 1979. Bott has recently secured contacts to export marijuana to the United States in exchange for U.S. currency and goods.

Matos's Block

Matos's block also deserves special mention. The son of an Indian market vendor and nephew of another, the young man was early apprenticed to buying and selling vegetable produce. At the same time, as the son of an African handyman, he was incorporated in a wide network of African kin. He was yet another member of the Prince Alfred Street lime, and was introduced to marijuana smoking there while in his early youth.

By 1974 to 1975, he had established his own block, with some encouragement from Darius, with whom he still enjoys cordial relations. Kip, Busy, Doc, and Carey have remained his closest associates from the start. Buen Retiro has a close business relation with him too, although he has stronger ties with Botts.

Matos runs his marijuana operations quite separately from all others. He makes marijuana available to his associates at preferential rates and has urged both Kip and Busy to use their profits to set up coops and gardens, which they have done. His own profits he invests in his market stalls, where other Rastafari block members work.

Now that his mother and aunt are old and retired, Matos has plowed his profits into building their market stalls into a quite sensational phenomenon in the San Fernando General Market! First, he acquired two more stalls, so that with the two belonging to his brother—Jerry, a block leader in Cocoyea, at the southern outskirts of San Fernando—a section of the market, comprising six stalls, is militantly Rastafari. Matos and Jerry work long hours in Port-of-Spain and in the countryside, winning bargains from planters and shippers from the smaller islands, in bulk purchases of potatoes, onions, fresh vegetables and fruits, hill rice, pigeon peas, spices, beans, sea-moss, and homemade drinking chocolate or other agricultural produce. The stalls are piled high with provisions for the big market days on Saturdays and Sundays, and they are routinely offered at slightly lower prices than those prevailing elsewhere in the market. Consequently, huge crowds of shoppers of all ages mill around the stalls, under the Emperor's many portraits, in the sweet smell of devotional incense, with reggae music blasting from the high-quality speakers of a sound system. Matos, his brother, and six associates attend to them in a blur of many busy hands, sloganeering—"Food for the People"—quoting Rastafari aphorisms, and distributing handbills with Rastafari messages and advertisements.

The market stalls are run like block endeavors. Associates receive provisions daily, plus a weekly cash payment and marijuana for smoking. An esusu, much like Bott's, has been recently started among them; and the two youngest members, orphaned by their natural parents, live with Jerry in Cocoyea.

Matos regularly finds new opportunities to make money. For example, during the Carnival, he set up a booth with a bank of blenders to make banana punches, peanut punches, sea-moss and soursop drinks, and a variety of vegetarian savories and sweetmeats. He claims that the booth made over $10,000 during the season. He also has entered the import–export business. He commissioned Doc to make carvings, each capable of concealing two pounds of marijuana, which he has twice taken successfully to London. His Rastafari girlfriend there knits him unusually designed tam-o'-shanters and buys materials for making incense, pictures and clip-ons of the Emperor, clothes, and shoes which he carries to Trinidad to sell. His last expedition ended in a bust at Heathrow Airport in London, but, undeterred, he now has larger plans for a London–New York–Trinidad linkup.

Recently, Matos bought a van from the post office. In excellent condition, it is a big help in all his lines of business. He has set aside a sum of money to purchase land adjoining another Rastafari's in Toco, on Trinidad's north coast. He has $20,000 in hand to begin a Rastafari newspaper with Jerry. In 1978, he invested another $20,000 to sponsor a tour by the famous reggae singer Peter Tosh. The shows drew attendances of more than 17,000 in San Fernando and Port-of-Spain. Buoyed by this success, he is preparing to sponsor shows by other Rastafari star artistes.

Darius's Block

Darius's block also demands special treatment. Located several miles outside of San Fernando, it magnified some of the features of organization. Darius is the dealer–grower–block leader introduced in chapter 2. His financial investments, as well as his professed beliefs and personal trustworthiness, are the cement binding his six subsidiaries to him: in turn, they are a guaranteed outlet for his marijuana. Since he deals in bulk quantities, the preferential rates at which Darius sells to his subsidiaries are more noticeable than the smaller percentages on the average block or between cooperating blocks (for example in 1979, he charged $125 per pound instead of the usual $200 to $250). Also, Darius sells first to his subsidiaries—an inestimable advantage in times of scarcity.

Although Rastafari does not serve as an additional bond between Darius and his associates, they have been affected by it. The group does not live together—and they are each too prosperous to have to depend on one another for bail—but they do meet to arrive at common sentiments and ideas. The group approves of the Rastafari religiosity and its emphasis on "natural" living: like the Rastafari they explore disciplines and practices such as yoga, holistic health, diet, and the cultivation of marijuana. These interests have confirmed Darius in his traditional Hinduism, which he interprets with a new, Rastafari-influenced enthusiasm. Thus, he has performed regular pujas (devotional prayers and offerings to the various Hindu deities) since becoming a marijuana distributor.

Another bond is Darius's restless ambition to find a way to turn his wealth to socially significant ends. For example, he wants to make a feature film of the Pullul Brothers, a group of notorious Indian bad johns who were based in the countryside rather than the city and whose lives and exploits illuminate the harsh realities of Indian life in rural Trinidad. Another idea is the revival of folk theater and cultural activity, such as Indian dance and singing, in Piparo and in his associates' villages and neighborhoods. He knows himself to be a single link between many marijuana growers in the country and block leaders in the city: a powerful influential link between two sources of enormous value, manpower, and creative energies. But while he is tantalized by the fact, he does not quite know how to further it or to profit other than financially by it. The awareness, however, is enough to put a distinguishing mark upon his entire group.

In turn, Darius has hastened the process of block formation among the city blocks by ensuring regular supplies to beginners and by acting as stockpiler against times of scarcity. He was eager to tell his own story, from which the following extracts are taken:

> *Marijuana has uplifted the unemployment problem here in dis country. You know people could tink of sendin' their children to study medicine because of ganja. Business houses, car firms, construction industry—all of dem make a lot of money because of ganja. Dey had people who just five years ago had no money, were poor, didn't know TT$1,000. And now dese same people have accumulated anywhere near to TT$200,000 or $300,000. Dis has made them uplift deir standard of living: dey have built pretty houses, furnished dem, educated deir children.*
>
> *About six years ago, I was a dropout from high school and so forth. Dat was de Curepe Educational Institute; and afterwards I did draftin' for three years at the John Donaldson Technical Institute in Port-of-Spain. I got a diploma from dat course. But I was de type of person who didn't like to work for no one. I had dat kind of mentality, dat kind of consciousness in me dat make me believe that I could make my two ends meet. So I tell myself—well, I leave myself alone and I didn't want to work for nobody—I come up in de country by my relatives and stay here. I started doin' a little gardening and so on, for about three years.*
>
> *Meantime, I been hearin' about marijuana all over de place, dat people makin' a good raise, and I was interested in takin' part in it, not knowing that one day I would be one ah de top-rankin' ganja men in de country today. I didn't know dat. I didn't even use to smoke den.*
>
> *So I started plantin' marijuana and I would never forget . . . it was one Carnival season when I make de first TT$700 in ganja. Tings were so tough, the ting was so*

scarce, it was green marijuana I sell to make my first $700. It was a time like this, a week before Carnival. People just wanted it and dey tell deyself: well, once is marijuana, dat good, dey buyin' it. So I made my first $700. Dat was four years ago (1974–75). De same Jaguar. . . . The Jaguar contribute to dat $700 too. Yeah. So I tell myself, dese same fellas who buy dis $700, dey coming back for more again, and where I go get it from?

So I say leh me make an investment and even if I make a piece of bread on dat investment, I still making somethin' for myself. And I could always go back and plant.

So I started buyin'. In dose days, ganja was selling at TT$300 a pound. So I buy 22 poun's, and de man trust me another poun'. Eventually I made a profit of about $50 per poun'. And it gie me a sort of incentive to invest more money. And while I investin' dat money, I start to plant, so dat I even had more money to invest.

"I had planted only one task of marijuana (1/8-1/10 of an acre) really didn't know de real whereabouts of how to cultivate it, because, before I began, people use to say: dis is de hardest ting to grow, de hardest ting, man; you just cyant grow dis, you have to be a God-gifted man to grow dis ting. But I got seeds while buyin'. And I started to plant. You know, I believe marijuana is a prime necessity to man, I will always keep on plantin', plantin', plantin'.

Eventually, I realize dat while I plantin' fellas coming to me here to buy and dat it was more worth my while to sell rather dan plant. So I started buyin' and sellin'. And I started to see money. Money dat people in a lifetime cyant save. Sometimes the money I make for a month it takes a man a whole life to save. Owin' to de good reputation I have—when I say reputation, I mean my behavior, my dealin's, my principles, my policies and so forth—people tend to believe in me. I have plenty planters dealin' with me and since they could not meet my demands, for frequency and quality because I wanted someting for a boomin' block, to make it more faster—I encourage people to go into plantin' it, and bringin' it de way I wanted it.

I could tell you about anybody you want to know about in San Fernando. Anybody. Because all ah dem deal with me at some time or another. And some of dem I even start off on dey blocks. So anything you want to know, I could tell you. The Jaguar, Stanley, Matos, Kenrick, Peaches, Botts, Baraka, Simba . . . anybody!

But when I first start off on de city blocks, is good licks I get. Is not dat you advance a portion of ganja and den don't get anyting back for it. Is character I does look for in a man, you know. Hardcore men, dat is what I does look for. So what I really don't like is de run around and de talk. So in de end is with only a few a dem dat I stay good. Some ah dem does be shame to come to me now: so when times hard, like now, dey does send for de ganja. See Matos now: he is a sound fella. He and Botts . . .

One ting I appreciate in de Rastafari is de religious feeling you know. Dat is, from those who really have it. To be careful how you do things, what you eat . . . I sight up dat religious form too, you know. I is a very religious man: a Hindu, and nobody could take it away. I always do a puja, to give praises.

Finally, Darius's block looms large over the entire San Fernando network, without dominating the other blocks. While Darius can be relied upon to have marijuana to sell most of the time, the option of city block leaders to buy elsewhere, or to make their private arrangements with planters, has not been threatened.

INTERBLOCK RELATIONS

The distinctiveness of the various blocks was translated into the quality of the marijuana they sold. Customers got a flavor, so to speak, of the different block leaders and the ideologies they represented in the marijuana they consumed. In 1978, there were 110 blocks in San Fernando. On most blocks, one pound of marijuana could be sold in one and a half to two days: thus in the San Fernando area, some 20,000 pounds (excluding exports) were sold yearly. If the price paid to the planter per pound was that during fieldwork—TT$275—and if the yield in joints was estimated at 1,000, selling at $1 each, then each pound of marijuana generated about $1,275 in revenue. The traffic in San Fernando, therefore, amounted to a business worth about $25.5 million yearly.

This figure remained, of course, an estimate. The number of blocks fluctuated seasonally. Locations handled a greater or smaller volume of trade, in a shorter or longer period; the price per pound varied seasonally or according to quality, or according to a variety of supply conditions, such as police operations; and a pound of marijuana was very often resold in the city by the pound, half-pound, ounce, 20-piece, 10-piece, 5-bag, or 3-bag rather than by the joint, yielding in each case less than $1,000. Additionally, a portion of each pound was usually reserved by the block leader and his associates for their personal use.

Some 500 persons, mostly male, in the San Fernando area derived their yearly incomes from this $25 million. Dependent upon them—and involved in varying degrees with the traffic—were several women, children, or other relatives.

Most of the personnel on these 110 blocks were known to one another. Neighborhoods such as the one described earlier had produced many blocks: so that kinship ties and those of friendship from early childhood were a feature of interblock relations. But the blocks were not associated in any formal sense. Blocks cooperated by the twos or threes to do specific things: making a purchasing trip together, lending money for bail, and in one case, to finance the escape abroad of a brother who faced a seven-year sentence on an assault charge. Few blocks except Darius's had reserve stocks of marijuana large enough to assist another by supplying them in a time of scarcity.

In December 1976, an infant girl was molested in a lavatory of a well-known primary school in San Fernando by someone whom the newspapers described as a "cleanshaven man who looked like a Rasta type" (as "Rasta types" are always hirsute, or resistant to barbers, the description made no sense). In response to the growing hysteria about Rastafari, of which the press report was only the latest example, Botts, Matos, his brother Jerry, Singham,

Doc, and Ramses, a San Fernandian who had begun cultivating marijuana near Toco, approached the police and offered to find the criminal, if he was indeed Rastafari. This group then agreed to meet regularly as the "the Inner Circle of Rastafari." Members made friendly visits in their cars throughout the day among their several selling locations, and Botts and Matos emerged as its primi inter pares.

Stanley was very suspicious of the Inner Circle. Blocks inspired or influenced by him—Jeru, Joseph, Robes, Simba, Henry and his wife, and about nine other blocks—felt themselves, in some imprecise way, to be the "other" to the Inner Circle and its friends. They did not, however, combine into a formal organization. Members from the two opposed camps were cool about each other's protestations of Rastafari orthodoxy. One heated discussion between Stanley and Buen Retiro, over tickets to Matos's Peter Tosh concert, ended with Stanley being slapped in the face—a polarizing event. When Cindy and Richie constructed their apple and food coop at the Library Corner for the 1976 Christmas season, Kuper, Bott's brother, promptly installed one beside theirs, selling apples and Rastafari religious items. Both coops were torn down by the police in 1977. But in Stanley's "camp" there is no evidence whatever of interblock financial cooperation, beyond the preferential rates for marijuana Stanley occasionally offered.

Vim was also cool toward Botts and Matos. He felt strong moral objections to Botts's cars being used to transport high school girls after schools were out in the afternoons. He thought that Matos especially was unimaginative, a mere copycat of Jamaican fashions, rather than a Rastafari by his own privately produced convictions. Vim's influence extended throughout the Cocoyea area and into Pleasantville, where several blocks met fortnightly to share in a feast of worship to Jah. Vim did not attend these meetings because they roasted meat for the ceremony, but he exchanged visits with them on other occasions, and had persuaded them to begin two vegetable gardens. Stanley and his "grouping" also objected to the ceremonial meat-eating and had no contact with these brothers. Another purely vegetarian feast was celebrated weekly by assembled blocks in the Marabella area, to the north of San Fernando and abutting the oil refinery at Pointe-a-Pierre.

At the time of writing in 1978 and 1979, the 110 blocks and the pathways between them, criss-crossed by rivalries and friendships, had made a substantial addition to San Fernando's cartography. The space, marked apart even more vividly by Rastafari taboos and conventions, took on the aspect of a separate, self-sufficient, independently functioning life or nation, existing in the heart of San Fernando. Marijuana smokers had learned its layout, and they associated different types of marijuana and marijuana experiences with the constituent blocks.

This sentiment of a separate nation was one which the Rastafari ideology best expressed.

NOTES

1. Frantz Fanon, Martiniquan author of *The Wretched of the Earth* (*Les Damnés de la Terre*), required reading by radicals during the 1960s and 1970s.

Chapter 4

Religion and Ritual in the Ganja Complex

Economic systems tend to be self-perpetuating. As a laboring population in the informal economic sector (see preface and chapter 8), drug distributors consume some of the product of their labor to reproduce themselves. In the case of the marijuana economy, participants enjoyed smoking the commodity they produced on city blocks, and the beliefs and worldview by which they justified the practice were codified in the Rastafari ideology.[1] The latter reproduced the hearts and minds which worked to construct marijuana—the cultural good, with cultural benefits—and make it available to the wider world.

Additionally, the Rastafari ideology, providing religious sentiments and ritual practices, provided the last remaining requisite element in the successful transplantation of the ganja complex in Trinidad.

Simultaneously as blocks were being molded into a distinct form of socio-economic formation among young, urban, unemployed African youths in Trinidad, block leaders converted to Rastafari. They were quickly followed by their associates and customers. The converts grew their hair in long matted locks by shunning comb and brush, allowed their beards to grow by avoiding the razor, restricted their diets to vegetarian foods and beverages, and refused all stimulants except marijuana, the "holy herb." They proclaimed the divinity of Haile Selassi-I or Jah Rastafari, and believed in the doctrine of redemption to Ethiopia. These preoccupations excited even the ordinary, nonusing San Fernandian, and Rastafari attracted many staunch sympathizers in low-income neighborhoods. They created some sinister enemies too (see chapter 5).

Block leaders converted to Rastafari at the same time that the police were escalating their campaigns against them and the institutions of the marijuana economy they had created. They saved their most ardent verbal assaults as Rastafari for police officers (or "the Babylon") and especially for Deputy

Commissioner of Police Randolph Burroughs.[2] A year of training by the Drug Enforcement Administration (DEA) in the United States in methods of the war on drugs and counterinsurgency had turned him into an indefatigable hunter of "guerrillas" in the southern rain forest, where he liked to spend weeks at a time on safari. On returning to Trinidad, he had formed the Flying Squad, a group of police marksmen he had personally selected to accompany him on these campaigns. They regularly confused Rastafari marijuana growers with "guerrillas," and their exploits are reported in chapter 5. Inspector Randolph Pierre, the commander of the southern branch of the Flying Squad, has already been introduced by the Jaguar in his recollections in chapter 3.

This chapter documents how Rastafari beliefs and practices in San Fernando defined themselves in the process of block consolidation and as the marijuana economy matured despite (and actually in defiance of) mounting police pressure. The coherence of Rastafari beliefs in Trinidad is sought in the symbolism of marijuana and the marijuana traffic. Finally, Rastafari is identified as the ideology of an emergent "development" elite of the informal economic sector which had replaced the Black Power doctrines of the 1970s. This ideology was differentiated from that of the dominant "modernization" elites (Schneider, Schneider, and Hansen 1972).

A review of Rastafari in the Caribbean and in Trinidad is briefly summarized in order to contextualize the steps in the evolution of this belief system in San Fernando. This chapter, however, is not an exhaustive examination of the beliefs and practices of Rastafari. It is not a study of Rastafari primarily, although it does explore a perspective which differs from those usually taken in the literature. A study of Rastafari would be incomplete if it did not locate the movement as a culmination of 400 years of African resistance in the Caribbean, and as a specific response to the contradictions of colonial society in the English-speaking Caribbean (Barrett 1977; Bishton 1986; Campbell 1980; Chevannes 1978; Kitzinger 1966; Lewis 1993; Owens 1976; Simpson 1955; Smith 1960; Taylor and Bogdan 1984; Watson 1973; Plummer 1978). On the other hand, these classical studies have neglected the multiple, nonritual values which marijuana had for Rastafari, and accordingly they have incompletely identified the political and economic agencies of Rastafari in Caribbean societies.

Finally, from the standpoint of one of the major theses of this book, their most serious omission is any appreciation at all of the cultural transmission of the ganja complex across continents, centuries, and ethnicities. Through the ganja complex, the Rastaman ("I-man," dreadlocks, marijuana smoking, cultivation and distribution, blocks, asceticism, vegetarianism, and all) reincarnates not only his African ancestry, but more exactly than any young Indian in the Caribbean,[3] an (essentially Saivite) Indian tradition which had originated 5,000 years before in the Hindu Kush.

A BRIEF HISTORY OF RASTAFARI IN THE CARIBBEAN

In the 1920s, a self-educated Jamaican scholar, Marcus Mosiah Garvey, organized the Universal Negro Improvement Association (UNIA) in Harlem, New York City. He preached that a king would soon be crowned in Africa who would redeem the lost tribes of Judah and call them home to Ethiopia. He recalled for the impoverished Africans of American cities that their heritage had included mighty kingdoms in Africa and the accomplishment of milestones in human evolution. In contrast, Garvey taught, only the lowest instincts of Europeans were reflected and cherished in the "white" civilization of America which oppressed Africans. Wealth had only magnified those instincts, which included greed, tyranny, and genocide. Garvey worked tirelessly to recruit members in New York City and Chicago for UNIA, and eventually enrollment reached 40,000. He solicited donations from the membership and sympathizers and used the proceeds to launch a newspaper and several businesses. After a decade of organizing and struggle, he was convicted in 1927 on charges of financial wrongdoing and was deported to Jamaica, where he immediately resumed sharing his message (Cronon 1955; Edwards 1967; Jacques-Garvey 1967).

The influence of Marcus Garvey on contemporary African American and Caribbean African thought has still to be fully appreciated. Garvey had insisted on economic and cultural self-sufficiency and independence for Africans. This position alienated many other African American intellectuals, who denounced him as a separatist and racist. They later cooperated in his downfall. Programs of concrete self-help, however, have been the enduring legacy of Garvey's ideas—first among American Muslims, and then among Rastafari. Garvey himself had started several enterprises. A major success was the Black Star Line, a shipping company which owned three ships and traded between America, Africa, and the Caribbean. Other successes were his agricultural projects in West Africa. It was on charges of mismanaging them that Garvey was convicted and deported from the United States (Cronon 1955; Edwards 1967; Jacques-Garvey 1963).

Meanwhile in Africa, as though in response to Garvey's messianic prophecy, Ras Tafari was crowned Emperor Haile Selassi-I in Ethiopia in 1930. At his coronation, he was named the King of Kings, Lord of Lords, and Conquering Lion of the Tribe of Judah.

Garvey's followers in Jamaica were impressed by the numerous signs of Haile Selassi-I's divinity. One was the liberation of his kingdom from Italian rule. Soon after his ascent to the throne, Ethiopia had been invaded by Mussolini. The emperor vowed to recapture his land without shedding a drop of Ethiopian blood. After conducting a vigorous press campaign (in a famous photograph accompanying his many appeals in the major European newspapers, he was shown standing on an unexploded bomb), he regained his throne in 1941. Other press photographs circulating in Jamaica showed lions roaming free in his palace (Boot and Thomas 1977).

Garvey's followers also judged that the emperor had fulfilled exactly the prophecies of Revelation 5 (verses 2, 5, 6) and Revelation 19 (verse 19).[4] Moreover, they were satisfied that historians had proven that his throne was the oldest in the world and that he was a direct descendant of King Solomon and the Queen of Sheba. Garvey's teachings were accordingly adapted as the true form of worship of the one true God, Jah Rastafari. Many of his followers, regarding him as the founding prophet of the religion, converted, and the religiopolitical movement soon found its niche in the complex melange of ideologies and interests which composed Jamaican social life (Post 1978).

The number of Rastafari in Jamaica continued to grow, and by 1960 two-thirds of the island's population were thought to be sympathizers, if not actual followers (Smith, Augier, and Nettleford 1956). Until the 1960s, however, recruitment had proceeded gradually and had been restricted to the Jamaican countryside and the urban ghettos. Rastafari grew fond of land, subscribing to the sentiment found in the Old Testament of "everyman dwelling under his own fig tree and in his own vineyard," and they cultivated vegetable gardens or built communal agricultural settlements wherever they could. In the urban ghettos, they lived cooperatively in communes and cultivated vacant lots of land in the outskirts of cities. Most revered marijuana and grew or consumed large amounts of it. Without any central organization or leaders, and with a doctrine infinitely arguable beyond a few fundamental precepts, a variety of orthodoxies and conventions and sects divided them. Eventually dogma was derived as much from the Bible and Garvey's teachings as from the lessons the brethren distilled from their observations and analyses of current events. As Rastafari became more numerous and their message more audible, they attracted the attention of other segments of Jamaican society, such as intellectuals, social workers, journalists, politicians, and the informed public at large. For example, a report by the University of the West Indies in 1956 was among the first published accounts, and states:

> Some are criminals, others are not. Some wear beards, others wear plaited locks of uncut hair;[5] others wear neither beards nor locks. Some brethren seem to live in camps, most live dispersed throughout the city. Most of the brethren are unemployed, many of these for several years . . . many brethren are willing to take employment providing they are not required to shave their hair and beard . . . other brethren reject the idea of wage employment but are quite in favor of cooperative Rastafari group production (Smith, Augier, and Nettleford 1956).

These contemporary Jamaican commentaries and analyses, however, routinely overlooked the connections between Rastafari and the marijuana traffic, regarding use of the "herb" as something quaint or bizarre (and, of course, illegal) or, more benignly, as a sacramental or folk-medicinal substance (Nettleford 1963; Patterson 1964; Simpson 1955) rather than as a medium of economic exchange, or as a source and model of indigenous creation of value, self-sufficiency, and economic survival in third-world countries. And even in the view of marijuana as a sacramental or folk-medicinal substance, its role in the persistence and diffusion of the Asian ganja complex was not recognized. In the 1960s, however, a turning point in the history of Rastafari was reached when marijuana cultivators in Jamaica mobilized, by expanding production and introducing innovative smuggling operations, for the growing export market to Europe, Canada, and the United States. Police raids and corrupt involvement with the traffic intensified, and even politicians used bribes of marijuana to win votes. In response, Rastafari elaborated their belief system, adhered more devotedly to it, and, emboldened by these convictions, grew more outspoken about the grim political situation on the island, thus penetrating the formal political institutions of the country, and adding themselves ominously to the climate of crisis which existed there.

Another turning point came when reggae music was invented. In it, Rastafari musicians, likening themselves to the biblical psalmist David, had blended Jamaican folk-musical conventions with the rock-and-roll styles of marijuana-smoking metropolitan performers (Hebdige 1987). The musical expression also celebrated the confidence Rastafari beliefs had gained from the emperor's visit to Jamaica in 1965, as well as from the experience of practicing them for thirty years. Subsequently reggae music functioned very effectively as a means for propagating Rastafari ideas on other English-speaking Caribbean islands and in the immigrant communities abroad.

The first Rastafari in Trinidad, however, were not merely imitators of a Jamaican fashion. The same breeding ground of colonialism, class conflict, youth rebellion, countercultural lifestyles, marijuana use, and struggle with the police had existed on both islands (and, indeed, on all Caribbean islands). The first Rastaman in San Fernando, or at any rate the first one to grow dreadlocks was Vim's brother-in-law, Ras Chari (see chapter 3). A leading marijuana distributor in the process of becoming a block leader, he had "locksed up" in 1973, two or three years before the majority of San Fernando Rastafari did so. He claimed that he had borrowed the idea for the hairstyle from a picture of Ndebele tribesmen in an article on Africa in *National Geographic*. He never became an outstanding spokesman of Rastafari beliefs and was easily outstripped in this talent by younger followers. Reggae music, replacing African American soul and funk as popular music in Trinidad only toward 1975–1976, confirmed Trinidadian Rastafari in their beliefs but did not create them.

RASTAFARI, BLOCK DEVELOPMENT, AND THE MARIJUANA TRAFFIC

In San Fernando, the popularity of Rastafari coincided with the creation of blocks rather than with the borrowing of a Jamaican fashion. As noted, the first known Rastaman in the city was Ras Chari from the Prince Alfred Street block. He had "locksed up" in 1973, but admits that Rastafari then meant little to him. By 1976, however, the leaders on 108 of 110 San Fernando blocks were Rastafari, as were all their associates. Then working-class members of their clientele and other unemployed persons began "locksing up." By 1979, at least 1,500 had converted.[6]

Rastafari furnished the thematic cues through which individuals were transformed into orators/spokesmen and subsequently block leaders. Just as earlier spokesmen/organizers had used African American music as a rhetorical element in organizing the limes (see chapter 1), block leaders used the Rastafari messages of reggae music as a bond on the block. In addition to the major themes of worship of Jah Rastafari, redemption, and repatriation to Africa, the music explicitly sanctioned marijuana use. In effect, it legitimated the relationship between block leaders and their associates and justified the belief that the Rastafari alone had been "called" to handle the "I-cient herb."

Rastafari had the immediate effects of multiplying the number of blocks, promoting the diversity of their operations, and ensuring Rastafari participation at all levels of the system, including cultivation and transport by taxi along the routes from marijuana-growing areas to the cities.

During fieldwork, these effects were best appreciated in Tobago, or in the smaller Caribbean islands, where the process was actually taking place in 1978. It had been set in motion in those locales principally by San Fernando Rastafari. Diversifying their operations, they sought to smuggle marijuana by air and sea to the islands of the eastern Caribbean. Conversion to Rastafari and block formation followed and quickly took root on these islands. The following extract is selected from field notes made in May 1978 in Tobago, where the researcher had traveled to observe directly the simultaneous, and mutually reinforcing, diffusion of marijuana, blocks, and Rastafari:

> *Tobago*: Although it is the most colonized and dependent of the two islands, Tobago, with a population of 49,000, is in some respects the better-off part of the nation. The island's homogeneously African society is closely knit by bonds of kinship and neighborliness. Although the dominant tourist industry is seasonal and does not provide steady employment for young people, their subsistence needs are readily met.

For example, there is easy access to farming and fishing. More substantially, to make sure that Tobago remains an electoral stronghold, the governing party, the People's National Movement (PNM), has funded the Special Works Program and other relief programs handsomely.

Among the youths on the island, therefore, the traditions of pimping, petty theft, prostitution, arrests, transitory housing, and homelessness have not penetrated as deeply as they have in San Fernando or in Port-of-Spain, Trinidad. An older generation of kinsmen, landed peasant proprietors, government officials, store owners, estate owners, and the operators of services for tourists (hotels, cars, restaurants, and boats) remain firmly in control, and in everyday life, young Tobagonians are more comprehensively constrained by them than their Trinidadian counterparts are by middle-class, middle-aged adults in Trinidad.

At the same time, such benefits are still insufficient to support any of the ambitions their literacy and education have nourished in young Tobagonians. The Special Works Program—paving a road one day to break it up again the next—is nakedly meaningless work, a mere token response to unemployment, and pays very little anyway. Being circumscribed by elders who themselves have a limited life, compared to the one the tourists boast from November to April, is stultifying.

In May 1978, Stanley and two associates of his block in San Fernando hatched a plan to smuggle marijuana into Tobago. The island had recently become a target for Trinidadian marijuana distributors. Many were from San Fernando. For example, on the weekend Stanley and his associates had chosen for the expedition, Kid from Cocoyea had joined Peaches from the Prince Alfred Street block and had gone also. A third party, led by Ras Blaka from the Carlton Lane block, was making an independent trip. The San Fernandians had discovered that the traffic in Tobago was still controlled by three older men in Scarborough, the capital of Tobago. Their own efforts were wresting the traffic out of these hands and placing it in those of younger men, and the circumstance was being attended by a perceptible increase in demand and volume of trade.

In the first place, the three older distributors were Trinidadians who had introduced, solely for the profit, a custom they had observed in Trinidad. None smoked marijuana himself or was Rastafari. The situation therefore resembled the early, pre-block organization of the traffic in Port-of-Spain and San Fernando, where schoolboys, taxi drivers, and itinerant peddlers had enjoyed the limelight briefly, although they had not been marijuana smokers, growers, or enthusiasts themselves.

The first distributor was an Trinidadian African male of fifty years of age. Originally from Cedros in south Trinidad, he was an oil worker who had been living with a Tobagonian woman in her family yard in Scarborough for the past twenty years. He shuttled by air to and from Trinidad each week to work, spending weekends in Tobago. He started distributing marijuana two years ago. Before emplaning in Trinidad on a Friday, he would put a couple of pounds on a boat at the docks in Port-of-Spain. His wife, the childhood friend of Tobagonian dock workers, picked up the parcel at the Scarborough docks the following day. The second distributor, also a middle-aged African male, retailed dress clothes and fashion accessories in Scarborough from three small boutiques. He smuggled in his supply of marijuana among the bales of cloth and readymades he imported from Trinidad. The third was a younger Trinidadian African male, thirty-five years of age, who was a ground employee of the Trinidad & Tobago Air Shuttle service (TTAS) at the Scarborough airport. The three men had no assistants, except the wife of the first. In Trinidad, they bought the marijuana from city distributors in San Fernando or Port-of-Spain rather than from the actual growers in the rain forest.

Under this regime of supply, the Tobago traffic languished. The typical Tobagonian consumer visited the three distributors infrequently. They smoked large joints on weekends and special occasions, such as parties or weddings. Outside Scarborough, it remained difficult to buy marijuana. A typical user was the gregarious Walter, for example, who worked at one of the hotels for tourists as a bartender. His repertoire of mixed alcoholic drinks and his convivial manner attracted many foreign visitors and Tobagonians to the bar. Walter smoked marijuana on rare occasions to add to his glamour at a party and when he wanted to show off his familiarity with a metropolitan lifestyle. But he spoke of being afraid to use too much of it, and said with a smile that he was happier among the drinks in his bar.

The first distributor, the Trinidadian from Cedros, said that he sold marijuana mostly in joints and that his fortnightly turnover did not exceed two pounds. Recently, he said, some customers from Tobagonian villages had bought as much as half of a pound, to be made into joints at home. He felt that demand was increasing, and he put in a bid to buy outright the ten pounds of marijuana which Stanley, David, and Dina had brought.

Thus the status quo had started changing when Rastafari from San Fernando and elsewhere in Trinidad had arrived. The first expeditions by Peaches and Ras Blaka in 1977 had resulted in the sale of their stocks wholesale to the three senior Trinidadian distributors. On that occasion, the first Trinidadian paid $300 a pound for marijuana that was sold in Trinidad for $200. He also bought cigarette papers, at $1.00 a packet (to be retailed for $2.00 or $2.50), which were being sold wholesale in Trinidad for $.50 to $.75. On subsequent trips, however, Peaches and Ras Blaka had bypassed these distributors and had dealt directly with some Tobagonian marijuana smokers who were trying to differentiate themselves as distributors. They helped to foster these individuals as emergent Rastafari block leaders by selling them marijuana pound by pound (thus prolonging their stay in Tobago and increasing their overhead), but fetched prices of $400 to $450 per pound and $1.50 for packets of cigarette papers.

Most Tobagonians had a deep-seated revulsion against Rastafari in 1978. The proprietors of the services and hotels for tourists and the weekend residents or guests have experienced them in Trinidad and speak of them as "being everywhere," like an alarming epidemic disease. They are relieved that they have not appeared in Tobago as yet. They cite it as one of the proofs of the "untouched" beauty of the island. They have not yet taken stock of the fact that they are all saying, with a small face, that they discovered one the other day, "even here." One of their number is a renowned writer who has studied the speech of the Jamaican Rastafari. He allays their fears by remarking that the Trinidadian Rastafari "are only for joke," since (according to him) the key to Rastafari is the lyrical and encoded Jamaican dialect, something Trinidadians generally, and those idlers in particular, could never master. This opinion offers no real comfort: robbed of authenticity, Rastafari then seemed to be only the bearers of filthy hair, spouting ridiculous and probably hypocritical misappropriations of biblical texts and quite capable of arson and raping children.

These suspicions of the Rastafari are shared by the Tobagonian employees at the hotels and gift shops, by the taxi drivers and leisure boat operators, by the government officials and businessmen who find themselves at the hotel bars of an evening, getting to know the tourists. The established heads of landed families, whose matrons spend Sundays straightening their daughters' hair, also give Rastafari short shrift.

The young crews of the fishing and leisure boats, the manual laborers, the sons of subsistence farmers, and other young, unemployed Tobagonians remained, however, a potential pool of recruits. So far Rastafari had had little showing among them, although they were main clientele of the three established marijuana distributors. But the Rastafari movement in Tobago took root and experienced rapid growth in this segment of the population when the Trinidadian Rastafari reached out to individual marijuana smokers among them. The latter started by purchasing ounces of marijuana from the Trinidadian Rastafari to share with friends and often made a small profit while doing so. The arrangement was advantageous to both the Trinidadians, who got better prices, and to the Tobagonians, whose blocks thrived under this system of regular supplies delivered to the door. These neophyte blocks were palpably energized as demand rose, and conversion to Rastafari followed. Soon they were buying pounds of marijuana from the visitors.

By the time Stanley and his party arrived, there was a Rastafari settlement in Egypt, a village near Scarborough. There were Rastafari or "dreads" in several other villages throughout the island. All were eager to do business with visiting Trinidadians and to make business alliances for the future.

The head of the Egypt group is a typical product of the process of conversion to Rastafari which is still going on in Tobago in 1978. A young man of twenty-nine, he is the son of a respected landowner and cocoa farmer. Unlike most of the young adults encountered in Trinidad, he works on the cocoa estate and still lives at home with both parents. But although he is neither unemployed nor dispossessed by migrating parents, he is still the Tobagonian version of the Trinidadian "bad john." A big-built man, he likes liquor and "romancing the daughters." Since income from the cocoa estate is intermittent and small, however, he has been obliged since he was a teenager to find other sources for ready cash. He found the Special Works Program more preferable and accessible than the other options, such as joining a branch of the tourist industry in a menial capacity. It also had hidden advantages. It mobilized a workforce of at least 700 men and women in various projects in Scarborough. He soon took the opportunity to organize gambling rackets among them, and to control their labor. Then last year, he was an accomplice in an armed robbery—he still keeps revolvers—and although he was never brought to trial, his involvement appeared to be a well-known fact to the police and public in Scarborough. During Stanley's visit, a policeman surprised him at a street corner as he was making a marijuana joint and he taunted the officer, inviting him to interfere in what he was doing or to arrest him for the robbery. As the officer turned his back and departed, he shouted that policemen were foreigners (from other islands) and cowards.

The robbery, however, was apparently a step beyond the limit he had himself imposed upon his fantasies of fast cars, money, three-piece suits, champagne, and endless parties. The experience of marijuana smoking had already chastened his outlook, and when visits from Trinidadian Rastafari guaranteed regular supplies of marijuana, he realized that the Special Works Program labor force in Scarborough was a market he could capture all for himself. He started "locksing up." He refrained from the flamboyant outrageous escapades which had made him notorious in Scarborough. At

> length, he started the Rastafari settlement near his father's property in Egypt, installing grass shacks (living quarters), gardens, and enclosures for goats and chickens, and selecting four young neighbors to live with him and to help distribute marijuana. Like their peers elsewhere in Tobago, these block members revered and smoked marijuana themselves. Like other Rastafari, they excluded meat and alcohol from their diets and celebrated religious rituals and ceremonies.
>
> The new life is still an unaccustomed fit for the young man. He sometimes goes around in his three-piece suit, but he has learned that visiting Rastafari from Trinidad do not favor noisy receptions at bars, where offerings of the "best" meat and the "best" drink can be made. As marijuana revenues strengthen the settlement, he has diversified and now imports or retails incense, handicrafts, buttons with the picture of the emperor, and other Rastafari paraphernalia. At the same time, he is genuinely more serious about his beliefs, and makes requests for literature on Rastafari. The settlement already grows food in its own gardens for home consumption, although this is not the novelty in Tobago as it is in Trinidad. Stanley made a lasting impression upon him. He persuaded him to stay for two weeks, although Stanley had allotted only three days to this trip. He flattered Stanley about his resemblance to the emperor, and invited him to lecture at evening gatherings each day during the extended visit. The relationship transformed both men. Stanley grew more thoughtful, skilled, and careful about the theology he teaches, while the other cultivated a more attentive, more studious approach, out of which he was fashioning a new persona.

Block formation and Rastafari are ongoing processes not only in Tobago but throughout the Caribbean. Since the mid-1970s, all of the smaller islands, Guyana, and Belize have been penetrated in the same way as Tobago by Rastafari of Trinidad and Jamaica. In Barbados, for example, Barnes and Pitts from the Cipero Street block in San Fernando import marijuana from Trinidad and Colombia, and have bought hotels and taxicabs in Bridgetown which accommodate their couriers among the other guests. Soon after the trip to Tobago, Stanley, Ras Blaka, and Peaches purchased tickets on a ship for a tour of the Windward Islands and planned to smuggle marijuana into St. Vincent, Grenada, St. Kitts, Nevis, and Anguilla. And, of course, several moves in the direction of New York and London have been taken. Blocks had already been established there, and revenues of American dollars were enriching and strengthening the multiplex, international trading system Rastafari were putting in place. In each place into which marijuana was smuggled, a local network of Rastafari blocks has sprung up.

Another important function of Rastafari was to articulate the pressures within the block to redistribute marijuana surpluses in an approved manner. Since a fundamental Rastafari teaching was self-sufficiency, or material and spiritual independence from the mainstream world, revenues were directed toward the achievement of that goal. Since brotherhood was another valued precept and the ideology through which blocks worked together amicably and smoothly, it had to be safeguarded or strengthened when revenues were redistributed. After Rastafari, therefore, the carefree splurging of marijuana profits on luxury food, drinks, and entertainment, or on "conspicuous consumption," which had dissipated some earlier marijuana fortunes, was replaced by investments which substantiated the religious beliefs and further profited the investors.

Land acquisition was one solution. Ten Rastafari blocks in San Fernando maintained gardens in and around the city, while five others have bought extensive agricultural lands in rural parts of the island. Two of the latter have also purchased pickup vans, as prospective farm vehicles. Some members of four more blocks have transplanted themselves to separate settlements close to the southeastern rain forests, where they are cultivating marijuana. Several other Rastafari groups simply squat on country lands and live by subsistence and by sporadic marijuana cultivation. One group of men, women, and children lived naked in the rain forest iself and supported themselves by gathering vegetables and fruit. They showed up unexpectedly at Woodford Square in the center of Port-of-Spain and were the national sensation during the week they camped there.

A Rastafari block leader who had been crippled by many arrests, but who still kept about six young male associates busy with a chicken farm and kitchen garden in the heart of San Fernando, has tried to interest government officials in his plans for the land:

> *I have a project for feeding de people. I have observed in dis country dat farming is not established as it should be established. I much rather de Canadian approach to farming. De agricultural sector takes care of de animals: you know, you grow corn to feed your fowl and from dere you could grow grain for milling and if you have cattle, you plant grass for de cattle and you don't have to be much buyin' from outside sources, you know. A sort of self-sufficient community.*
>
> *You see de marijuana can provide de revenues for dat. Dis is one a de main problems you will have though. De system will get down on you. My information is dat de police, when dey see shacks on de land, dey does break it down. Probably is because "serious farming" [marijuana cultivation] has been going on in de environment ah dese shacks.*
>
> *So just "rest up" [temporary] shacks is not de idea. De idea is establishing communities where . . . you know, every man will be living under his own vineyard and fig tree in time.*
>
> *What we really need is land, shelter, food, and tools. Is seven brothers involved. Mostly in deir twenties, you know. One brother has a couple of children, but dey have de spiritual motivation. Dey ain't want to be here on de concrete [city streets], in de cinema. You can't eat your cake and have it, you must sacrifice. And dey ready.*
>
> *I have two children myself. And in 5–10 years' time I must be able to provide someting real solid for dem. I just need time and de farming base. In more times I would like to write dis all down.*

The newfound reverence for land, for its spiritual as well as material promise, and its flowering within the marijuana experience, was voiced by another Rastafari block leader:

> *You know what was I first experience in dis new stage of life dat de ganja bring? I garden. I-man have a piece of sweet peppers dey, me and de brothers plant it together. Peppers, eggplant, pumpkin. I sit dong in de hammock, me alone, and I smoke about four joints [of marijuana]. And I-man just gone off on [was absorbed by] de pepper. I-man stan' up by de pepper tree and I-man went off on it. One sweet pepper tree. I nearly black out [lost consciousness]—the vibes [vibrations] was so heavy. I lose about $1500 on de garden. But every week de daughter [my wife] does sell [produce] from it—and it go pay too. For 15 minutes, dread: I just concentrate into dat tree so much dat I nearly black out, I could not hold de vibes. Dat was I first experience in dis [marijuana] stage of life. Develop de land. A complete development. Developing dis man.*
>
> *Plenty people sighting up dis idea, but dey not acting upon it, dey not forwarding in de right procedure of de idea dey sight up. Dey taking it wrong, dey just think about it. Dey should put de idea in different forms. Dah is why dey say weed [marijuana] cracking up people: dey should act. Vegetables is our real food.*
>
> *Dis is a new generation, you know man, and I-man have de power to do things. People in Trinidad don't tink class again: dey tinking only of de standard of living. And de cost ah dat going higher and higher. But poor people can overcome dat high form of life. Is just false ideas. But poor people need togetherness. Dat is what we want. Is obvious two people could do more dan one. From de time we start dat life, it will come easier to de youth dem, because we learning it while dey will be experiencing it.*
>
> *Once people shunned me up here because dey say I was wayward, but in dis stage of my life, as I put forth works, people respect I. Look at dese children, dey does make you human. From stage to stage, the ganja develop. It just revealing itself clearly. And I seeing dat and forwarding it, as de life lead. I gain my knowledge through dat concentration. De ganja lead me to know and win de hearts of my people.*

Reverence and expenditure of marijuana funds were reserved not only for land, but for all the other ways in which "poor people can overcome dat high form of life." In addition to the purchases of land and farm vehicles already listed, Rastafari in San Fernando have also spent marijuana profits on: five taxis, three on one block alone, which provide self-employment for the drivers; four modest-sized chicken farms; two herds of goats; and two dog-rearing businesses. Three other blocks have purchased equipment for making shoes, an activity which engaged all their members; while two others produced marijuana paraphernalia from local materials, such as coconut shells, wood, and leather. Yet another was a brotherhood of woodworkers, sculptors, and carpenters. And then nearly every block, over and above its other investments, maintained a "coop": a shed of wood, wire, and galvanized iron roofing, from which fruits, vegetables, cooked foods, and sundries might be sold.

Thus, Rastafari not only contributed to the multiplication of blocks, and to the reinforcement of social relations which differentiated the block, but also figured very significantly in the redistribution and exchange phenomena of the marijuana economic system.

And finally, the step which some Rastafari brothers have taken in cultivating marijuana themselves was radical not simply with respect to the present functioning of the marijuana economic system; but by the establishment of an African presence in agriculture and in the south Trinidadian countryside, it had upset the ideological bases of the social, cultural, and economic institutions of Trinidad as a whole.

THE COHERENCE OF RASTAFARI BELIEFS AND MARIJUANA

Rastafari of San Fernando believe, first of all, that they are a nation: they reject the idea that they are members of a gang or cult. The Rastafari nation is thought to crosscut the usual national boundaries—witness the growth of Rastafari throughout the Caribbean, in America, Britain, and urban West Africa—and in the Caribbean, where several racial groups are represented, even racial boundaries. Like other nations, however, a great diversity of types, personalities, behaviors, and convictions are held together by a few central conventions. In the case of the Rastafari, they are the conventions of marijuana and the marijuana traffic, actual or metaphorical.

One convention is the worship of Jah Rastafari. Haile Selassi-I is variously considered as God Almighty, his earthly representative, or Jah's most accomplished worshipper. Jah Rastafari is God of the "natural." His enemy is Babylon, the city of "artifice," false gods, and corrupting ideas.

Thus, the reverence for land and agriculture, the "natural" par excellence, is a second convention. Jah will redeem his faithful followers in Ethiopia. Some San Fernandian Rastafari are content to believe that any agricultural land anywhere in the world, producing food free of "artificial" fertilizers and supporting self-sufficient cooperatives of brethren and their families, can be painted in Ethiopian colors, and is Ethiopia. The fact that human existence originated in Africa also, or that the Pangean landmass was once centered around Africa, supports the belief that the whole world is after all potentially a multiracial, universal, Rastafari nation called Ethiopia.

Reverence for marijuana is the third convention. It is the "natural" product of the "natural" earth and was given by Jah for the "healing of nations," as recorded in the Book of Genesis. In the Rastafari symbology, marijuana discloses the inner man, the "natural" man, and inscribes the discipline needed for his evolution into the "I-man," or Oneness with Jah.

Thus, the idea of growth, or "going forward," simultaneously toward "I-man," and through redemption, to repatriation to Ethiopia, is yet another convention. Marijuana grows, marijuana becomes more potent, awareness grows, creativity grows, the I-man grows. Marijuana "builds up" the individual. There are no symbols of death in the Rastafari ideology, only those of going forward into life. Rastafari have never died, but have existed from creation.

Rastafari did not arrive upon these conventions as a logically related whole, but gathered them together from different sources. The first is derived from Marcus Garvey and Ethiopianism, while scholarship has proved that the second is a prevalent African cultural survival in the diaspora of the New World. The third is said to be sanctioned by biblical authority. The fourth is thought of as an extravagant claim. The symbolism of marijuana, however, is the logic which, rooted in the marijuana traffic, unifies them and energizes them into the dynamic, meaningful whole which has electrified Caribbean and minority populations throughout the world.

A central dramatic imagery in Rastafari belongs to the Old Testament story of the liberation of the Israelites from slavery under the Pharaoh by Moses and their subsequent settlement in prosperous lands under a dynasty of illustrious kings. The turning point in that story comes when the Pharaoh, further hardening his heart, denies permission to the Israelites to worship God, and punishes them by stopping supplies of the straw from which they had built the bricks they sold to Egyptians for their livelihood. The prohibition of marijuana was likened to that against the ancient straw.

While the belief in redemption to Ethiopia is expressed in biblical language, the contemporary Babylon where the modern Pharaoh rules is described in the language of the newspapers or is drawn from the daily experience of modern, underdeveloped Trinidad. The Rastaman is usually a graduate of the tremendous theorizing and practice of the Black Power demonstrations in 1970. He knows about police states, paranoia, bureaucracy, terror, terrorism, economic crises, unemployment, malnutrition and starvation, the arms race, and the threat of nuclear disaster and ecological disasters. He hears about communism, oil sheikhs, multinationals, and international movements of capital and labor. He compares the struggle going on or accomplished in Cuba, China, Vietnam, Chile, Angola, Mozambique, Rhodesia, South Africa, Ethiopia, Iran, Nicaragua, Afghanistan, Jamaica, and Guyana and finds similarities between them and Trinidad. More than other Trinidadians, the Rastaman takes an obsessive interest in world affairs. He takes a daily record of the doings of the well-to-do: he notes the corruption among government officers, businessmen, and professionals, their public and private hypocrisies, the disenchantment with the island which they express by their frequent trips abroad, and their oft-repeated desire to migrate permanently—once enough money has been put aside for departure. He notes particularly their sterility and barrenness, their racisms, their inability to produce anything authentic, their slavish devotion to every metropolitan taste.

The Rastaman believes that Babylon will fall and that Ethiopia will rise again. Ethiopia is the earth before Babylon corrupted it: a land of peace, love, and togetherness. The destruction of Babylon through revolutionary action is not directly the Rastaman's concern. Jah Rastafari reserves for himself the right to punish the ungodly and unjust. The Rastaman is to anticipate redemption and repatriation by being peaceful, full of loving-kindness, and cooperative among brethren. The ideal Rastafari policy is the acquisition of land where the brothers may practice their religion undisturbed; this feeling is celebrated in music, painting, and literary composition. These expressions are also encouraged and rewarded with esteem and patronage.

All these beliefs—in marijuana as a spiritual food, land, Ethiopia, Babylon, Jah Rastafari, Haile Selassi-I, "I-man going forward"—and the prescriptions for action which follow from them have an internal consistency when the marijuana economic system is taken as a metaphor for life generally. Whatever their disparate origins, they were like engines idling until synchronized and energized by the marijuana economic system.

Both Ethiopia and Haile-Selassi-I, the nation and its king, are prefigured in the special space and time which the 110 blocks mark upon the San Fernandian topography and in the self-sufficient, ever-resourceful block leader who increases his substance and that of his following. It is a location and a personality defined by the struggle between the police and marijuana distributors, and then shaded more deeply by rituals of exclusion and inclusion.

Agricultural land, a real Ethiopia where fruits, vegetables, and of course marijuana may be grown, acquires its energies as a symbol, not only on account of its symbolic association with the "natural" but from the process of redistribution of revenues and the exchange system in and among blocks.

And finally, the universal applicability of marijuana as the criterion between the "natural" and the "artificial" derives from the opposition between it and money, each being the most general symbols of the opposed systems creating value in the Trinidadian socioeconomic formation. The discovery that "marijuana making" refers to the "going forward" from creation in the life of the inner man has its opposite in the deduction that "money making" originates out of spiritual death. Thus, attitudes, tastes, behaviors, styles of life, deriving either from spiritual plenitude or depletion, can be contrasted.

Marijuana and the marijuana traffic, therefore, are the keys to the understanding of the entire Rastafari experience in San Fernando.

RASTAFARI AS A NEW FORM OF PROTEST AND AS A DEVELOPMENTAL IDEOLOGY

"Marijuana making" and "money making" also differentiated the informal economic sector from the corporate capitalist sector of the national economy. In chapter 8, certain changes in outlook are described as necessary if an underdeveloped region like Trinidad is to prosper economically. Dependence on metropolitan centers has to be reduced, and this means that a revolution in tastes, habits, and expectations has to occur. Indigenous production must supersede imports. Personalities, or the ways in which persons identify themselves, must be altered. It is in effecting these changes that Rastafari has been most successful as protest, and as the basis of a developmental ideology and practice.

First, the Rastafari interest in land and agricultural development must be counted among the most exciting motivational reorientations to have occurred in the Caribbean. The new motivation is the cornerstone of the agricultural renaissance that is actually required before the nation can feed itself.

Then, as apostles of "natural" substances like marijuana, Rastafari have been influential among San Fernandians in breeding distrust for a whole range of packaged foods and meats, most of them imported or produced through foreign methods of processing. They challenged the dietary wisdom, health assumptions, and consumer habits which made them attractive. Rastafari reserved special scorn for the fried chicken and hamburger franchises owned by Kentucky Fried Chicken, McDonald's, and other American companies. Even young middle-class children have been heard protesting that they will not eat "the dead"!

The Rastafari have clearly won an important battle over the use of marijuana instead of alcohol and other drugs. Very many low-income persons in search of a stimulant will eschew the expensive imported Scotches, which had once been status symbols, and choose instead the good produced at the neighborhood block.

The Rastafari have also fostered a preference for locally made shoes, sandals, and other leather goods. Several Rastafari women receive tuition fees from brethren to be trained in clothing design. Studies in nutrition and child-rearing are also funded. Rastafari handicrafts and art works have received recognition, and the market for them is expanding.

In entertainment, reggae or other forms of Caribbean music have completely overtaken American popular styles on radio stations and at parties and dances for all classes of Trinidadians. Rastafari speech conventions, derived from the Jamaican folk language, have also been incorporated into the speech of Trinidadians generally.

Finally, the stereotyping of Caribbean peoples has been turned upside down. The "white–black" color classification of persons and behaviors, handed down from colonial times, had been used to rank the islands whose contacts with one another were less important than those each maintained with the metropolis. Trinidadians were more civilized, that is, more "white," than Jamaicans (or so the Trinidadian prejudice went). Rastafari has broken down these prejudices and offered a new Caribbean identity to replace them. Already, the pan-Caribbean marijuana traffic has effected more interisland economic cooperation than official attempts have done.

These revolutions in tastes, consumer preferences, and habits of thought and behavior were very influential forces in lower-class Trinidadian communities in 1978. They were featured in very genuine personality changes to which not only the unemployed but workers also were susceptible.

These developments have not gone unnoticed. In the next chapter the extreme official reactions to them are reported.

NOTES

1. The word "Rastafari" is used in the text as believers use it themselves. Hence, "Rastafari" may mean: (1) Rastafarianism; (2) a Rastafarian or Rastafarians; and (3) Rastafarian (adjective). The words "Rastafarianism," "Rastafarians," and "Rastafarian" are never used by Rastafari. "Jah Rastafari" means God.

2. "Babylon is the whole complex of institutions which conspire to keep the black man enslaved in the Western world and which attempt to subjugate colored people throughout the world" (Owens 1976). For Rastafari, the police force was one of its incarnations.

3. Darius, in chapter 3 had moved closest to being one.

4. "And I saw a strong angel proclaiming with a loud voice, Who is worthy to open the book, and to loose the seals thereof? . . . And one of the elders saith unto me, Weep not: behold, the Lion of the tribe of Judah, the Root of David, hath prevailed to open the book, and to loose the seven seals thereof. And I beheld, and, lo, in the midst of the throne and the four beasts, and in the midst of the elders, stood a Lamb as it had been slain, having seven horns and seven eyes, which are the seven Spirits of God sent forth into all the earth.

5. The Rastafari explain that they had followed the biblical examples of Samson and Daniel in keeping dreadlocks. Additionally, Jamaican Rastafari had been exposed to the example of Indian yogis among the Indian immigrants, who wore dreadlocks as a mark of their devotion to Lord Shiva, the Great Yogi of Hinduism, from whose dreadlocks the River Ganges had poured to nourish agriculture and life in the vast Indo-Gangetic plain.

6. The number 1,500 is an estimate. During the 1979 Carnival (in February) for example, 150 Rastafari were jailed in San Fernando. Another 400 paraded in a band called "Kingdom of Zion," which had been organized by some Rastafari blocks in Mon Repos. Rastafari participation in the Carnival, which had originated as a Christian celebration, was rejected by many other Rastafari, who stayed at home and off the streets throughout the two-day event. Another 500 Rastafari were among the more than 2,000 vendors who lined the streets during the holiday selling food and drinks to revelers.

Chapter 5

The Ganja Complex, Rastafari, Public Opinion, and Law Enforcement

Argyll: *Once dey place you, once dis society place you on a spot, you ha' to stay dey. Because you know what society is about. Once a society say: alright . . .*

Vim: *You is a Rasta. . . . !*

Argyll: *You is a Rasta! You could do what you want, you ha' to stay Rasta. It ain't make no sense trying to compromise with dem den. Dey say you Rasta, you ha' to stay a Rasta and live a Rasta.*

(from a conversation between San Fernandian Rastafari).

This chapter reports the contradictory nature of the official Trinidadian reaction to marijuana, the ganja complex, and Rastafari during the 1970s. This response was integral to the phenomenon as it was then constructed, sanctioning actions, qualifying the behaviors of users and distributors, intimately informing their experience of marijuana itself, and furthur shaping the adapted ganja complex. Mixed into the substance which San Fernandians consumed as marijuana was the flavor (or potency!) of the block leader's and the block's relation with the community and the police.

Although loud vituperation was the norm in written or oratorical public opinion, large sections of the population were in fact very accommodating of marijuana use. For example, using or nonusing residents of low-income communities, in whose midst marijuana use and trafficking had flourished, sanctioned them. Regular use and experimentation were also commonplace and tolerated among the more privileged classes, who were aware that their counterparts in the United States and other metropolitan countries also approved of marijuana. The government had not treated the widespread adoption of marijuana as a public health matter, as it presumably would have treated a malaria epidemic or the introduction of some virus causing physical and mental damage among citizens: it had appointed no "commission of inquiry" with respect to the novel and striking phenomenon. Indeed, it had concluded that the organ best suited for the management of the "drug problem" was its police. In this approach, of course, it had been encouraged by the U.S. government through the State Department and the Drug Enforcement Administration (DEA).

Before 1970, in the period of the limes, Trinidadians had regarded the use of ganja as an individual failing rather than as a manifestation or symptom of a social problem. The offender, probably already labeled an embarrassment to a family or a neighborhood on account of other criminal behavior, found that this generally poor public regard for himself had been confirmed by ganja use. The substance was at the time being cautiously tested out even by its first users: reports about its properties relied heavily upon hearsay and upon such American sources of information as the film *Reefer Madness*.

Arrests remained few and unpublicized throughout the 1960s. Pot use was reported mainly as a phenomenon occurring abroad among the well-to-do youth of metropolitan centers, especially those astir in that decade's forms of personal rebellion or nonconformism. During the 1970 revolt, however, marijuana was viewed in a new light. Some critics held that ganja use indicated social malaise and proved the incompetence of government. Thus, Desmond Allum, defending the army mutineers (see chapter 1) before the Commonwealth judges, situated marijuana use as a negative effect of adverse social conditions:

> That you find equal measures of dispiritedness, despondency and disaffection in all sections of the community at the same time is no mere coincidence. It is not mere accident that our civil service is inefficient and unproductive, that our foreign service is demoralized, wasteful and inutile, that our medical service is crippled by strikes and walkouts, that our children cannot get into schools, that road transport is strangled throughout the country by mismanagement and that 35 percent of our labor force under the age of 25 is unemployed so that our young men and women roam the streets dazed and maddened by marijuana and narcotics (Allum 1971, 337).

One group which was prominent in the Black Power revolt and which, in the low-income milieu of 1978, vigorously opposed marijuana use was made up of the remaining adherents of the National Joint Action Committee, one of the most influential national associations of limers in 1970. In 1978, they professed an African nationalism which obliged many to wear African dress, to create and observe African holidays, to seek employment, and to lead an anticipatory, but "Africanized," bourgeois life. At the top of their list of ganja's reputed ill-effects was "political apathy." They were passionately opposed to Rastafari, whom they identified as the most "apathetic" of the marijuana smokers. Their disapproval was shared by some members of innumerable small churches and by some older residents. While preachers thundered against marijuana from their pulpits, however, few persons actually condoned informing to the police or facilitating their antimarijuana initiatives.

The Black Power revolt of 1970 stopped the accommodationist trend. Privileged persons were then convinced that marijuana smoking and lawlessness were intimately correlated. For them, the drug was responsible for every social ill: it made its victims idle and rebellious, and those failings explained unemployment, family dysfunction, community disempowerment, and poverty. The attitude persisted throughout the early 1970s and legitimated more police raids, arrests, eradication programs, and other campaigns against marijuana growers, distributors, and users. Of course, the mounting arrests cemented the link between marijuana and lawlessness. The well-to-do, guarded behind strong fences by attack dogs and private police, felt besieged by masses of envious poor, whom marijuana had maddened.

It must be emphasized that the efforts of the U.S. government were not insignificant in fomenting hysteria. Where public opinion wavered, was uncertain, or tended towards indifference, the influence of U.S. agencies over local elites and the leadership of Trinidadian police—through conferences, workshops, and training programs in the United States, at which overall antinarcotics strategy in the hemisphere was decided—reinforced the war against marijuana trafficking and use. A sense of crisis, polarization of civil society, and the breakdown of law and order was thus perpetuated (Nadelmann 1990).

As use spread gradually among workers and in the privileged classes themselves, the assertiveness of the police overtook public reservations on the issue of marijuana. An opinion which gained currency—that marijuana, like every other substance, was detrimental only when abused—helped to discriminate among users, and to justify use among the well-to-do while condemning it among those targeted by the police.

Finally, as the full-fledged ganja complex, now comprising blocks, marijuana use, cultivation, distribution, export, and Rastafari (ideology, reggae music, other cultural output), gained increasing coherence in the new terrain to which it had been transplanted and was being adapted, the public, aided by the police and newspapers, translated it into a sensationalist construction of "drug trafficking, rebellion, crime, cults, guns and 'guerrillas.'" Alarm over this potent package contextualized all further views of marijuana.

Thus, in late 1976, after Rastafari had succeeded in establishing a presence in low-income communities and had won their neighbors' respect for their enterprise and upright behavior, a series of articles in the newspapers assailed them. In the first, the attack singled out unemployed Trinidadian Africans, who were suspected indiscriminately of lunatic, "fringe" behavior. Rastafari were rumored, with no hard evidence, to be responsible for rapes, burglaries, and the arson which destroyed several large department stores in downtown Port-of-Spain in December 1976. Subsequent articles escalated the broadside. Rastafari were depicted as a more insidious urban blight, a sickness of communal will, requiring surgical removal. The authors condemned Rastafari appearance, attacked their authenticity, and ridiculed their dietary practices and beliefs.

In the mounting blitz against Rastafari, other official voices were raised, not to moderate, but to add fuel. A community officer, returning after a three-year course of studies in Jamaica, was dismayed to see so many young Trinidadians sporting dreadlocks: he felt he was back in Jamaica! He urged the government to take strong action against them. San Fernando Borough Council officials delivered an even more serious blow, by refusing to grant food-vending badges to Rastafari for the upcoming Carnival in February 1978. They said that Rastafari dreadlocks posed a health hazard. At the San Fernando General Hospital, doctors were diagnosing all cases of mental disturbance in which marijuana use was mentioned as "cannabis psychosis"; they regarded Rastafari, when it confronted them, as a "drug-induced" disassociative thought formation, and prescribed powerful psychotropic pharmaceuticals, such as Haldol and Thorazine, as treatment for them.

The newspapers continued publishing stories throughout the latter part of 1977, buttressing the putative connection between drugs, crime, and Rastafarianism. The *Bomb* newspaper, a locally financed weekend publication whose racy coverage of the carnal and financial scandals of the powerful or wealthy had made its publisher a millionaire and a staunch defender of free enterprise and America, spearheaded the offensive. In May, it goaded the mayor of San Fernando to revoke her permission to Rastafari groups to build coops, or curbside retail stalls, in the Pleasantville suburb of San Fernando. They would not be emblems of self-employment, as the mayor had hoped. The Rastafari, the newspaper reported, were selling "hard drugs" from them; quantities of "the illegal stuff" had been seized in police raids. The report now challenged the mayor to complete the work of the police, by authorizing their demolition. As a lagniappe, the appeal asserted that the Rastafari had disrupted life in Pleasantville, had molested a young woman, and had trespassed on private property.

This researcher's private investigation of some of these news features, aided by a disaffected member of the police force, proved that many were based on information provided by police officers directly to newspaper reporters. The officers had submitted the stories while the police was advocating for Cabinet approval of the formation of a special squad to target Rastafari in San Fernando. It was to be patterned on the "Flying Squad," the unit in Port-of-Spain led by Deputy Commissioner of Police Randolph Burroughs.

The deputy commissioner, who liked to be photographed in army fatigues and with a submachine gun, his shaven head g style, had been personally leading his Flying Squad in raids aga growers in the rain forests. All the nation's newspapers, but especially the *Bomb*, had been making a hero of him. Trinidad, with its small population of only 1.5 million, boasts two daily newspapers, an evening news and seven Sunday weeklies. The two dailies, the *Guardian* and the *Express*, are well-recognized, award-winning newspapers. The weeklies are the worst examples of yellow journalism. Trinidadians, however, read all of them, or as many as they can get, and are much affected by them. Circulation of these newspapers, and especially the weeklies, numbers several hundred thousand.

Throughout this aggression, several Rastafari groups had been seeking out public figures or professional persons—lawyers, politicians, schoolteachers, this researcher—who could be persuaded to articulate a different outlook on Rastafari and the marijuana traffic. One San Fernando group met with the city's inspector of police to pledge their assistance in tracking down dangerous suspects claiming to be Rastafari. Others volunteered their personal handwritten stories to the newspapers. A few were printed. Of the favorable stories, one featured the conversion of a "jetset girl," who had gone to live in the hills with a man she revered as her teacher: the story stressed the "queer" circumstance that there were no sexual relations between them. Another articulated the ambitions of a coop owner and his wife, who planned to make and sell clothes and disavowed any concern with marijuana. A third was accompanied by photographs of wooden sculptures made by a Rastafari group, whose members explained that their religious faith had inspired the remarkably fine work, as well as their decision to exhibit them on street corners, rather than in banks, stores, and galleries. The report mentioned that some particularly impressive pieces had been broken repeatedly by the police, only to be carefully repaired each time, but the news reporter refrained from comment.

In 1978, another dimension of the war being carried on between the police and the Rastafari made its way into the newspapers. While the latter had focused on urban skirmishes, a continuing battle, waged chiefly by Deputy Commissioner Burroughs and the Flying Squad, raged in the forests. The quarry in this theater was "guerrillas." At first, the latter were widely supposed to be surviving activists from the Black Power revolt in 1970. Thirty-two had been already killed, when in April 1978, the thirty-third was shot "in the middle of a marijuana field." In the photograph, the slain "guerrilla" looked Rastafari, like the more recent of his predecessors at the morgue. Many Trinidadians then concluded that there had never been "guerrillas," only Rastafari, and that the war was against them and marijuana. They thought that, if these were indeed the adversaries, the military-style efforts of

Inspector Burroughs were not justified. As far as Rastafari were concerned, however, Burroughs had made the Old Testament story of the persecution of the Israelites by the Pharaoh identical with theirs.

The *Bomb* newspaper, however, did not withdraw their encomiums of their hero. Under a picture of in him with the trademark dark glasses and machine gun, an unsympathetic text reported the thirty-third killing:

> The leader is dead. Michael Percival alias "Pumpkin" was killed by police bullets last Friday morning, hours after the Bomb issued a call to Mayaro guerrillas to come out of hiding and give themselves up.
>
> Pumpkin, the leader of the Mayaro guerrillas is alleged to have shot old man Frances at Mayaro. Now Pumpkin lies still and cold, his bullet-ridden body tells the story of the hunter, Randy Burroughs.
>
> As I watched Pumpkin's body on the ground in the forest, it made me wonder what it was all about. One man running from the law, killing people, doing what the hell he wants. Now his body stretched out on the ground, stiff and cold and in his chest was a gaping wound. The grass stuck in his knatty hair, his mouth wide-open and the ants and flies moving in and out of his mouth. Flies and other creatures kept crawling in and out of his wounds and there was Randy Burroughs and his men over the body waiting for the ambulance to arrive.
>
> As Pumpkin lay dead, he carried the mark of the Rastas, a red string tied around his waist, knotted in two places. This was his cult, the Rasta cult. He also wore his Rasta hairstyle and as he lay on the ground both hairstyle and red string made no sense.
>
> Yes, it makes you wonder, doesn't it? Just what the hell are these young men trying to prove when they steal a shotgun and declare war on the law? Just what cause are these men fighting for when they rob, beat and kill their own?
>
> Pumpkin was shot just about 50 yards from the Naparima/Mayaro Road. He had pitched camp there in the forest and with him carried one of the deadly five-shot repeater guns. In his sack was a large quantity of ammunition, binoculars and other army-type material.
>
> The shooting took place at about 11:30. According to reports, Pumpkin had gone out to the roadside and there he met a young boy whom he asked for food. The boy, sensing what was going on and who the man was, quickly alerted older people and they in turn alerted the Rio Claro police. From there a call went to the Crime Chief, Randy Burroughs, and in quick time young Pumpkin lay dead, stretched out and cold.
>
> And now it leaves you to wonder what will happen to the rest of these so-called guerrillas who believe in violence. There are now two known men left, Kenneth Sammy and Jude Lobin—and by these standards one of them has to step into the shoes of Pumpkin and it is going to be the same old story again.
>
> Can somebody get a message to Jude Lobin and Kenneth Sammy and tell them that it is not too late for them to come in? Sooner or later you are going to end up like Pumpkin—dead, stiff and cold. Pumpkin's picture did not make a pretty picture and those bullets and bullet holes that filled his body is just what is going to happen to you.

What good was the five-shot repeater that Pumpkin carried with him? Nothing. After the shooting, all Randy Burroughs had to do was move in and pick up the pieces. And those pieces did not look good at all, fellas.

It was not long before Jude Lobin was shot, together with his young girlfriend Victoria Pascall: April 16. On this occasion also, the *Bomb* newspaper praised Chief Inspector Burroughs:

It is easy for us to sit in air-conditioned offices in far-off Port-of-Spain and talk about killing human beings and all that rot. What do we know of the fears of the Mayaro people as they live on the edge of doom?

I don't think the cops who serve with Burroughs like the bush life they have to live. Many of them would like to come home to the bosom of their family, but they feel they cannot leave this job undone.

I hear that one big gunman is still out there in the bushes waiting to gun down anybody who comes his way. I am talking about Sammy who is believed to have killed a few people including the preacher in St. James a year ago. Peaceful people cannot walk the streets until this man has been captured and put away. But will he give himself up? I do recall that last year I made a call to the guerrillas to give themselves up, or face the guns of Burroughs.

Some of them called me, one was Jude Lobin, who is now dead. He said he wanted to come in and he in fact came to my home one evening. He hijacked a taxi and tied the driver up and kicked him out of the car near my home.

Is that the behavior of a man who wanted to talk peace? More like he wanted to get me too.

At this point, I myself would not trust any guerrilla who says he wants to give himself up. I feel sure that those fellows are playing the jack and they have become kill-crazy.

We have been hearing of the behavior of crazed guerrillas in Ireland who spend all their time thinking how to kill innocent people.

I think our boys in the hills see themselves as some sort of tribe who will shoot first and take any action against the peaceful population just to perpetuate the kind of life they chose for themselves.

There was a time when a man who was disaffected from society would leave the country or some such thing. Now they go to the hills and get guns and try to kill others who don't want to live like them.

Like the people of Mayaro I hold Randy Burroughs in the highest esteem and I think if these bush folk want to kill peaceful people then they must take the consequences.

To pussyfoot and talk about police persecution is a lot of hogwash. This is a problem facing us and we must tackle it strong, not to bow to the wishes of the guerrillas.

If a guerrilla knows that he will have to face trial for the acts he has committed, will he really come in? Unless, of course, those who suggest turning-the-cheek feel we should take these men back into society and forget all their past misdeeds? If that is so, I would not mind becoming a guerrilla too, do my thing, and then just come out and beg.

That would not be a bad idea. In the meantime, I would settle for Randy Burroughs and his men. Let them clean up the hills. I up to that.

The *Punch* was the only Trinidad newspaper to carry an editorial line, for a few weeks, condemning the killings. The *Punch* editor wrote (April 23, 1978):

Jude Lobin, the "guerrilla" who was shot to death last weekend by the Police in the Mahoney Forest of Guayaguayare wanted to come out of hiding and give himself up. But he was afraid the police would not give him a chance to live.

This is the story his father Donovan Lobin gave after he received the news of his son's death. And I believe Jude Lobin's father because the same thing is happening to several other young men who are in the hills and forests of Guayaguayare. They want to come out and give themselves up, but they are afraid they will end up like Lobin. I know, because I received calls for assistance on behalf of some of these young men. But there seems precious little I can do for them.

Even before Lobin was killed, the Punch received its first call for help. According to the spokesman on their behalf, most of them admit freely to being guilty of any and all kinds of marijuana offenses which they might be accused of.

But when it comes to the more serious charges of murder, shooting, and robbery, they are denying that they know anything about these crimes.

"Some of these men I am talking about have grown up in Mayaro-Guayguayare," said the contact. "And they would never think of bringing harm to the people they have known all their lifetime," he pleaded. On yet another occasion, the incidents surrounding two brothers taking to the hills were related to me. The police raided their home on Maloney Road two years ago and found some weed [marijuana] in the house: as a result they were charged. But after this, they were terrorized and fled to the hills, not to become guerrillas or anything like that, but out of frustration. They want to come out and face the charges they know they are guilty of. And there are others in the group like them but they are afraid they will be killed and they need help.

I do not doubt for a minute that crime-ace Randy Burroughs and his Flying Squad are after some killers in the Maloney Forest. But I know for sure that there are other young men in the hills who are not in this class and they find themselves like Peters, paying for Pauls.

This country has become so accustomed to "guerrillas" being gunned down by the police that it is no longer front-page news in the newspapers.

In fact it is hardly even a talking point anymore. We are just dismissing these deaths as though it was a movie we had seen or heard of. But it isn't a movie and those young men in the hills need help or they too may end up on slabs in the mortuary.

To make matters even worse for these young men, there is a businessman in the area who is doing a thriving business out of the labor in the hills of these unfortunate and misguided young men. And while he struts around, unmolested and enjoying the finer things of life, his "employees" are now facing the barrels of police guns.

The messages I received all indicate one thing: they would accept any man of any choice to act on their behalf to work for their safe exit from the hills.

The *Punch* followed up this article with reports of their investigations in the "battle" area. "Jude was cornered and killed by the cops" was the title of the first (April 30, 1978):

> Jude Lobin, the "most wanted" man who was killed by the police, did not try to ambush the police, as original reports indicated. In fact, it was the police who waited on Lobin that night in an effort to capture him.
>
> These are the conclusions a Punch Team of investigators have come to after spending several days in the area where Lobin and his girlfriend Victoria Pascall were killed. And after speaking to several residents in the Guayaguayare districts.
>
> Lobin and Pascall were confronted by the police just 50 paces from where Lobin's family lives at the corner of Maloney Road and Guayaguayare Road.
>
> According to the Punch investigators, the drama really began on Friday night of that weekend when police spotted 21-year-old Victoria Pascall in a taxi heading along the Guayaguayare Road. Realizing that she was on her way to see Lobin who was hiding deep in the Maloney forests, they waited for the couple at the Maloney/Gyaya Junction. At around 8 pm on Sunday night, Lobin and Victoria were seen walking towards the junction where Victoria was to get a taxi to carry her back to her home in Pleasantville, San Fernando. Lobin was armed with a sawed-off shotgun.
>
> They stopped to say their farewells on the Maloney Road, about 50 paces from Lobin's home at the corner. And at approximately 8:15 pm the shooting began.
>
> One resident in the area said: I heard one shot first of all and this was followed by a burst of shooting from what sounded like machine guns. Then the police started shouting in the street for everyone to stay in their houses and not to come out until they were told to. In the morning, when we came out, we saw signs where Lobin had died.
>
> Residents all confirmed that Lobin knew the Maloney forests like the back of his hand as he had lived in the area for most of his life. But they all confirmed that he met his death just yards away from his home which would have been most unlikely place to lay an ambush for the police.
>
> One of Lobin's brothers Martin was at home at the time of the shooting. "I lay flat on the ground and did not move when the shooting started," he said. Another brother, Tony, says he was "down the road when the shooting started." I remained down there and did not go home for some time," he said, "then I learned it was Jude who was killed with Victoria."
>
> The Punch also learned the new identity of the new head of police's "most wanted" list. He is known in the area as "Brothers" but the villagers refuse to give any more information about him other than to say that he is a man who has vowed never to be taken alive.
>
> It is widely believed in Guaya that "Brothers" was with Jude Lobin on the night of the shoot-out. But he was waiting for Lobin some fifty yards behind on the other side of the Maloney Road. One resident said: this would account for the police shouting that night that it was three of them they had caught.
>
> The villagers all agree that Lobin was on the scene of the three murders for which he was wanted. "But why should the reports say he tried to ambush the police," they ask. "He certainly would not have tried such a stupid thing at the spot where he was killed."

San Fernandians were asking these questions with particular urgency in taxis, shops, bars where persons drink after work, at the market, and on the streets. Victoria Pascall had been a San Fernandian, as Jude Lobin had been once, and both belonged in the circle of Rastafari on the city's blocks. The latter felt that it was no longer useful to hunt for differences between "true" and "false" Rastas as a defense against the police: the latter would not discriminate.

Parents in low-income neighborhoods, the parents of the Rastafari, thought that, even if they disapproved of marijuana and an unusual hairstyle, their censure certainly stopped short of murdering their children. Even lower middle-class persons—elementary schoolteachers, nurses, clerks—who had always considered themselves immune from such police attacks, could not accept the silence and complacency of their role models in the middle classes. There had been the murder, after all, of Keith Cumberbatch on April 8. The *Bomb* had reported this story on April 14:

> A young widow is calling on Security Minister John Donaldson to clear the air on the shooting of her husband, by one of his policemen. She is Betty Cumberbatch, wife of the late Keith Cumberbatch, shot by police on Saturday last.
>
> Cumberbatch is the 29-year-old Texaco pipefitter who was shot outside a Siparia fete last weekend. Police say he was smoking marijuana and when they went to arrest him, he pulled a toy gun on them. But Betty Ann, a trained nurse, is not buying their story at all. She's charging that her husband was slaughtered like an animal in cold blood. "If this was not the case," she's asking, "why were there so many strange developments afterwards?"
>
> Betty Ann is charging that her husband was shot in the back. A midwife at the Couva Hospital, she told the Bomb she was at the post-mortem of her husband at the San Fernando Hospital. And the post-mortem showed that the bullet had entered his back, piercing his lungs.
>
> If we can take the nurse's word as correct, then there is need for a full investigation into this case.
>
> Another point she is raising is that the police did not tell her about the toy gun when she went to the Siparia station to inquire about her husband's death. She said: "Keith's brother Steve is also a policeman and when he went to the station he was told about the gun. But nobody could produce it for him to see."
>
> Betty Ann reported that her hospital contacts reported that on the following day after her husband's death—Sunday last—a party of policemen went to the morgue and tampered with the body. She said one of the policemen had a parcel, with something which looked like a gun. And she feels that it was at that time they skillfully placed the deadman's fingerprints on the toy gun. She said there was fingerprinting ink all over the dead man's hands afterwards.
>
> The young widow from Plaisance Park San Fernando is building a strong case against the police, for she is no fool. She said: "A doctor told me that there was no evidence of dope in Keith's body." Betty Ann is also talking about the matter of the dead man's keys. "Why did they want the keys? Evidently, they had not known he drove the car. Did they want to take something out, or put something in is my question to the Security Minister.

"The whole thing about him having a toy gun is a big joke among all who knew him. Keith joined Brinks in 1970 and worked as a security officer until 1973. He left the job because of his dislike for guns. And that's how he ended up working as a pipe-fitter at Texaco."

The Bomb is of the opinion that Security Minister Donaldson should check on his policemen about this one. For underground investigations have revealed that there were intoxicated policemen at the Siparia fete, on that tragic night.

The events of April were not dismissed in the public mind as resulting from drunkenness on the part of a few police officers. It would not be extravagant to claim, indeed, that Babylon had acquired a corporeality for a population far more numerous than its Rastafari component. Babylon included all those who were keeping silent: the lawyers, the government officials, the businessmen and their lackeys, other professionals, and people too "blinded by their religion to see reality."

The cleavage in San Fernandian society which had expressed itself in the demonstrations of 1970 grew deeper as a result of these more recent events. Henceforward, wherever San Fernandians gathered, the issues of ganja and the Rastafari were viewed from opposed structures of class prejudice.

The newspapers continued to view the "guerrillas" as political activists and expressed the view that the police were not adequate to the situation. Trevor Millett had written in the *Express* of April 30:

Nobody calls them guerrillas anymore; they are just plain bandits. Their intention is to terrorize the country and get something for nothing. At least that's what people say. And who can prove them wrong?

But if the guerrillas of this country are waging a war, it seems to be a war of self destruction because nobody but themselves are the losers. Their deaths no longer stimulate concern but only passing interest which soon melts to indifference.

Yesterday it was Beverly Jones (September 1973): today it is Victoria Pascall. Both were young, black females who were sent away quite abruptly into eternity. How many will suffer the same fate, only time will tell. And what is being done to prevent it? Nothing, absolutely nothing.

And yet one cannot help but be troubled by this shameful waste of human resources. It is said that our human resources occupy an important place in the national economy. If that is so, shouldn't we do something to conserve it?

There is no question about the necessity of punishing criminals but even "The Son of Sam" has been accorded the opportunity to face a court of law. No instant death. If instant death were an effective deterrent then the guerrilla war would have ended long ago. Why does it persist? "Guerrilla activity is first and foremost political activity of the most sophisticated and technical nature. Criminals give up, guerrillas cannot," writes Bukka Rennie in "Revolution and Social Development." He advises: "To eliminate such activity, its causes must first be removed." And he goes on to explain that the causes lie in the contradictions of capitalism. Perhaps he is right, perhaps not. True enough, one cannot help but believe that social conditions have something fundamental to do with the persistence of this kind of activity. And possibly because they are convinced that they have the solutions to the problems of the country, the guerrilla/bandit continues to fight even though he suffers the most.

Nevertheless, one wonders whether in fact they do have any sort of feasible economic and social programmes planned for the country if they should ever take over. Or are they going to plunge us into darkness, into an even greater chaos than we are in right now. Can they eliminate the scourge of unemployment, which in 1974, according to the Central Statistical Office information, claimed 61,800 victims? Will they make it easier for middle and low-income groups to buy lands and homes? In short, do they have workable plans to improve the quality of life in Trinidad and Tobago? Surely they know that a revolution based on guesswork and haphazardness is doomed to failure? Maybe that accounts for their non-achievement so far.

Say what you will, but there must be some reason for these people, branded bandits, to appropriate funds and weaponry and live in the hills. Why the hills? Why not the towns where they can spend their money and enjoy life? If nothing else, their way of life shows they are disenchanted: the roads are bad, the telephones do not work, the education system leaves much to be desired, insanity is on the rise among young adults and daily the society is growing more vicious. But whatever the causes for this type of activity, it is destined to face constant suppression. And probable defeat. "When disaster strikes an island," wrote the late Tobagonian poet, Eric Roach, "there is simply not enough room for maneuvers and time to manipulate forces to contain it. In the limited space, one's back is immediately to the wall and one has either to annihilate or be annihilated."

Let us hope that something miraculous happens soon to bring a halt to this annihilation of young citizens which is taking place.

An article in the *National Target* of May 27 gave further expression to the unhappiness the whole development had brought:

A ceasefire between Government and the misguided youths in the bush, seems to be something out of the question. These guerrillas or whatever they truly are, will keep on the run, frightening villagers. Crime Chief Burroughs will pursue, relentlessly killing one of the hunted here and there. And this is how matters will be next week, next month, next year, most likely in the year after that.

Christmas, Carnival, cocktail parties, billion-dollar industrial dreams at Point Lisas; business as usual notwithstanding, the Burroughs pursuit will continue. Burroughs may not be getting any younger. But he does not appear to be tiring also or any less enthusiastic in his grim and seemingly unending chore. The hunted do not seem to have lost heart, and are just as elusive, no less tenacious, or for that matter any smarter. It is now more than six years that these youths have taken up arms against the Establishment, and there seems to be no letting up, although Burroughs has been doing a fairly efficient job in wiping them out. But each fallen comrade apparently serves to strengthen their resolve to remain in the bush and fight a hopeless battle, gaining recruits all the time.

When will it all end? Government does not seem to be too concerned about it: after all Burroughs is still there. And, to which Government do these youths really pose a threat? Aren't they more of a nuisance value. They are on the run all the time, so why bother to call a truce or have a moratorium: why should the government step down and have dialogue with common criminals. This appears to be the Government's attitude in the whole affair.

In the legal sense, government is right, since this would be interfering with the due process of law. Unfortunately, this has been quite often the barrel of Burroughs's gun.

On the other hand, a government must show some public concern for alienated youth, especially those who have opted for the extreme of violent revolutionary activity. These same youths are the sons and daughters of the PNM—23 years ago their parents invested their hopes and dreams on this national movement, expecting a brighter day for themselves and their children. If only for this reason, Government should have a moratorium on the matter.

The grim reality is that thousands and thousands of graduates from secondary schools are not going to get jobs and are going to trip out on drugs or be hostile to the powers-that-be. They will, in the long run, pose a greater threat to the Establishment as prices soar, as land and housing slip out of the reach of the average Trinidadian, and as food shortages continue. This is something for Dr. Eric Williams to think about.

As the second half of 1978 continued, more bombs rocked Port-of-Spain, more raids on marijuana growers and dealers were reported, and more complaints were raised against the police. But the same assumption continued to hold: people were either going to be "doped out" or be against the "Establishment"; and if not the police, who would deal with these alternatives? The *Bomb* editor, champion of the police force, had to admit in an article on August 18:

My files are bulging with complaints made against senior and junior officers who have taken bribes, beaten up women, bought and sold weed, seized money in raids and converted it to their own use. I know of a top cop who himself went illegally down the main and brought back contraband liquor for himself and friends. What about the cop in the infamous Pampallone affair brought to light in Parliament? Nothing was done to him. He was just given his pension and told to go home.

When junior officers see this sort of thing happening, who can blame them for feeling that if the officer could do it, who is we?

In the September 29 issue of his paper, the same editor wrote, on the question of search warrants and the registry of prisoner's property in the Property Book at police stations:

Today I want to discuss with the man I admire, Police Chief Randy Burroughs two aspects of the police work that would clear the air for many citizens who have been calling me to get the damned thing settled.

First is about these fast Flying Squad-type raids all over the country, like the one last weekend when at least twenty persons were rounded up by keen cops in this drive to keep the country free.

Let me say first that this little nation of ours is riddled with too much crime and brutality and I am one hundred percent in support of any move to check it. But let us make sure at the same time that in trying to stop one sort of crime we do not create

> a bigger monster—the brutal police officer who will invade the rights of citizens to make his raid.
>
> Have these policemen got the right to search the homes of citizens by just swooping down on them or must they get a search warrant? I myself find it difficult to believe your cops, Randy, can get search warrants for all these people and their homes in these lightning raids. A Trinidadian home, like the Englishman's must be considered his castle no matter at what level, and it is wrong of policemen to swoop down like that on the home of anybody no matter at what stratum of society, just like that.
>
> It could have the makings of a police state. It could make our citizens in this democratic nation very uneasy and that stage could be worse than the first stage.

Throughout 1978, the battle between the police and the "guerrillas" raged and claimed another six lives. Then it escalated to another level of complexity with the new year. The action returned to the city, where some groups of Rastafari had been favored over others and had been given carte blanche by the police to sell marijuana.

On January 9, 1979, a feud began between two Rastafari blocks in San Fernando. During the four days it lasted, five men were severely wounded with blows from cutlasses. The newspapers reported that the fracas had resulted from a quarrel over meat-eating and the correct Rastafari attitude toward it. In fact, the dispute resulted from the unprecedented straits in which the marijuana supply had found itself.

In December 1978, the price of marijuana had been $300 per pound from the planter. Two weeks later, at the time of the dispute, the price had risen to $600, and marijuana was extremely scarce. Blocks were idle, and some were planning to close down. In February, the price rose to $850, and the entire San Fernando supply fell into the hands of one man. Cultivators turned back their clients, promising that fresh crops would be available by early April if they were not destroyed.

The effects of the "lightning raids" by police and army during the previous year, and especially in the latter half, when helicopters and light airplanes were used for the first time to search for plantations in the rain forest, were finally being felt. The feud reflected the difficult times. Blocks had been staking out turf for their operations, and in the case of these two blocks, boundaries had been violated. The situation was unprecedented, the feud was unprecedented, and so was the violence.

The police in San Fernando, under Inspector Randy Pierre, immediately formed a "Rasta" Squad and supplied several stories to the press. "Rastas are on the move in San Fernando and surrounding areas following the formation of a special squad to deal with them," said the first, on January 29.

> At the start of the new year a series of break-ins and larceny at houses and business places led top police investigators to believe the Rastas were behind the crimes, a po-

lice source said. He stated that scores of complaints from other citizens about adverse activities of the Rastas led to the formation of the squad.

"Rastas have been accused of molesting both old and young women in the areas, and trafficking and selling marijuana, especially to schoolchildren," he said. "Following a full investigation into the complaints we believe the reports are true. As a result, a squad of 10 constables and a corporal has been formed to deal with the situation."

Over the weekend, 15 Rastas were held for questioning in connection with possession and trafficking of marijuana. Since the squad hit the street last week, over 50 people have been arrested, the majority Rasta, charged with offenses ranging from whe whe [a gambling game] to larceny.

During last week's drive by the special squad, a number of Rastas have abandoned their shacks and fled the areas.

On February 5, another story declared, "COP KILLERS being trained in South":

A bloodcurdling story of killer dogs being trained to jump at the throats of policemen has been revealed and is now being linked to the disappearance of over 25 dogs in South Trinidad. The report has put a group of Rasta-styled men under close scrutiny, following confessions by deserters of the group. The dogs are being trained to attack policemen. "Dummies dressed in black shorts and grey shirts, the colors of the police uniform, are the targets used for the dogs to jump at," said one former member of the group. According to his report, "the dogs are given daily intensive training and are programmed to attack the targets and reach for throats. The result is snarling, spitting, vicious dogs who are just out for blood," he said.

The aim of this killer dog project, it is understood, is for the men to have some sort of defense should their group be attacked by the lawmen.

A recent situation where a "Rastaman" terrorized some Port-of-Spain schoolgirls with fierce dogs, led to a decision by the school's board to start classes at Whitehall today. This morning parents and uniformed children will ask Prime Minister Eric Williams to discuss security at the St. Francois Girls School in Belmont.

"Don't move. Don't scream. The dogs are trained to attack," he told them as they cowered in a corner. He moved off as a group of boys approached. South police have expressed concern over the rash of dognapping in the area. The canine thieves are very choosy and go after pedigree breeds like Alsatian and Doberman.

On February 16, front page news was that Kenneth Sammy, the "guerrilla" who had accompanied Jude Lobin, had been killed. The news reports said that he had been killed "in the middle of a marijuana plantation."

On February 16 the *Bomb* carried a long article called "Naked War on Cops by South Rastas":

Rastas in the Southland have launched a frightening and vicious war on policemen. In surprise night attacks over one week, Rastas have wounded five cops, all in separate incidents. The Bomb has learned that the Dreadlocks men mean deadly business and within the past two weeks have held two meetings in the Roy Joseph Scheme, San Fernando planning an attack strategy.

So far they have agreed to use sulphuric acid in eggshells and small phials for pelting the cops, trained Alsatian and Doberman dogs and cutlasses. The Bomb learned too that the Rastas are keeping the cops under observation and in surprise moves have cast aside their differences and banded together.

The attacks on the cops who were all in plainclothes at the time, began last week Thursday (8th) when PC Matthew George who is now on suspension was bombarded with a barrage of bottles. At the time he was in a bar in La Romain and he had to be rushed to the San Fernando hospital for injuries to his face, chest, and head.

Then next night, PC Hillary Brereton (No. 8766) who is attached to the St. Madeleine Police Station was chopped behind his head and received seven stitches. PC Brereton was walking along a back street on patrol duty when a car pulled up and a Rasta swung a cutlass at him and the car sped away.

Then, on Saturday night, PC Smith (No. 9382) of Benson Street Station was badly beaten by three Rastas while he was at a party at the St. Louis Commercial School in Chase Village, Chaguanas. He was warded at the San Fernando hospital.

On the same night PC Humphrey John (No. 6925) of the San Fernando Special Squad was chopped seven times while he was walking along Chaguanas Main Road. The Rastas were in a Datsun 120Y and the car passed him, turned around and when it was alongside him the Rastas leapt out shouting "Look, a Babylon from the South" and rained chops on the surprised cop.

And on Saturday too, at the Clash of the Giants in Skinner's Park, San Fernando, PC Francis (No. 8774) of the St. Margaret's Police Station was injured on his face and head.

Apart from these attacks, two women have also been threatened, one being WPC King of the Special Squad whose husband was WASA's acting PRO Patrick King who recently died in a motor accident. She had been walking up High Street when some Rasta told her "So you in the Special Squad too . . ." and left on that puzzling note.

The other woman was Marilyn Charles, an employee of Barclay's Bank, Lower High Street. She is the wife of PC Allen Charles of the Special Squad and she had just left the bank after work last week when some Rastas approached her. "If we can't get your husband, we'll get you," they threatened and went off.

Rastas in strange cars have also been driving around the homes of some cops, like Inspector Randy Pierre (who resumes duty today) and PCs Joel Shepherd, Robert Dash and Desmond Renne. In fact, the situation has created so much concern in the Southland that senior police officers have advised cops to be very careful. On Monday, ASP Peter Richards held a meeting with San Fernando cops and warned them to be on the alert against attack, particularly for the upcoming Carnival.

Within the last two months 25 Alsatians and Doberman dogs were reported stolen to police, five at one swoop at Coconut Drive in La Romain. Reports that the Rastas were training the dogs with dummies on the San Fernando hill leaked out to police following a split in their camp. But when the cops raided the Hill two weeks ago, the Rastas had abandoned their camp—but there were traces of their activity there.

The Bomb learned from store owners that Rastas in San Fernando waged war against each other and the cops were frightened to break it up. And with deadly at-

> tacks against them and other frightening ones planned, the cops are going to need a hell of a lot of back-up.

These articles, appearing as San Fernandians got ready for Carnival on February 26, caused a great deal of alarm. The Rastafari blocks made several individual attempts to contact journalists who could be persuaded to print more truthful information. One police officer, a marijuana user and familiar on the blocks, supplied proof that Rastas had not been involved in any of the incidents reported in the *Bomb* article, but that the information had been given to the newspaper by the Special Squad, as part of a massive campaign they were preparing against San Fernando Rastafari.

Persons in the middle classes did not ask whether sulphuric acid could in fact be contained in eggshells, or whether the huge demand for cutlasses was not a yearly occurrence, coinciding with the sugarcane-cutting season. Messages were passed from senior police officers, magistrates, and others to prominent businessmen, professionals, and other well-to-do people that the Carnival would be a violent one. Many made plans to spend the holiday at beaches or out of the island.

The calypsos of 1979 were a very definite ingredient in the turmoil. Four Rastafari calypsonians had hit songs, including Black Stalin, whose "Caribbean Man" won him the Calypso Monarch Crown. The music had become very sophisticated: there were soul and calypso blends, as well as reggae and calypso ones, which astonished Trinidadians. The lyrics represented a complete turnabout from previous years: they were "message" calypsos, in which the Rastafari voice was outstanding and predominant. The "guerrilla war" was the topic of many songs, as was the economics of marijuana and the police infiltration of it.

Further excitement was caused by the announcement that there was a yellow fever outbreak which required the island to be sprayed by light airplanes in the week before Carnival and perhaps on the Carnival days also. There was a mass inoculation effort, and it was rumored that Carnival would be postponed. The unprecedented state of the marijuana supply was also a serious inconvenience to the thousands of lower-class users. Of the 110 blocks in San Fernando, only 42 had remained in operation. Planters had no more marijuana to sell, as Darius had bought out what they had at $450 a pound. He was now selling his hoard from his country location, and all the remaining 42 blocks were compelled to buy at his price, or $850 per pound. In the city, the price of a joint doubled, from $1.00 each to $2.00, and then settled at $1.50 each. It was an odd, unsettling figure: the $1 unit is a worldwide one in the marijuana traffic. Ten days before Carnival, Darius was arrested, and this supply too was threatened.

Throughout the week before Carnival, marijuana-using and -distributing circles were baffled by yet another mystery. Two Port-of-Spain blocks put out for sale large quantities of what they called "Colombie" (Colombian marijuana). In a few days, the remaining San Fernandian blocks who could afford the price—$1,100 per pound—had bought some to retail at $2 a joint. It was widely believed that this was "police" marijuana and that it was pressed local marijuana rather than an import from Colombia. According to this interpretation, the purpose of the mounting police campaign against San Fernando Rastafari had been to stamp out their independent relations with planters (or Darius, as it turned out) and to bring them under control, in the allegedly police-dominated, "Colombie" supply chain. Port-of-Spain blocks, it was argued, were not being harassed in this organized manner, because they had already been brought in line.

On Friday, February 23, in the mid morning, police and army armored trucks rode along the main street of San Fernando and arrested Rastafari in Navet, Pleasantville, Mon Repos, and other low-income neighborhoods. The raids continued throughout the weekend and over the two days of Carnival.

On Monday, February 26, rumors that these police actions were taking place were confirmed in the Express. The headline said, "150 held in South Raid":

> Surprise raids by a joint police/army party are continuing in San Fernando and its environs. So far over 150 people have been detained for questioning and several Rasta shacks demolished. Several cutlasses were found in one hut.
>
> The raids started Friday at La Romain and the combined force has since visited Pleasantville and Marabella. A party of Regiment soldiers have set up camp in San Fernando and unconfirmed reports state that Police Commissioner Randolph Burroughs will be in San Fernando for the Carnival celebrations.
>
> The moves followed reports that an Inter-Rasta "war" is to take place in San Fernando. Tensions have escalated since mid-January when there was a free-for-all fight in which several Rastas received chops and were warded at the San Fernando General Hospital. The incident is said to have arisen after a dispute over some Rastas trespassing on others' "territory" to peddle marijuana. Then early this month Marabella Rastas had their fight during which five shacks were razed and several men were chopped. One of them is still in a serious condition at the San Fernando Hospital.

Later on Monday morning, a bomb exploded at Skinner Park. It had been placed in one of the steel drums used to support a parading platform, under the area where the Carnival Development Committee judges sat. No one was hurt. But for the rest of Monday and all day Tuesday a police light airplane circled over the Carnival crowds, and news flashes reported that Deputy Commissioner of Police Randolph Burroughs of the Flying Squad was in it. The news flashes discouraged many spectators and revelers from coming out, but a few hours after the event, San Fernandians in the park were wondering whether the police were not the ones most able to plant the bomb, and whether the incident had not been engineered to justify the surveillance.

As usual, the Carnival celebrations in San Fernando were not marked by any violent acts whatsoever. On both days, the masqueraders, who are drawn nowadays almost exclusively from the ranks of white-collar workers—from clerks and secretaries to their employers—paraded undisturbed; while other San Fernandians, and hordes of visitors from surrounding areas, bought and sold foodstuffs and drinks, looked on, and "jumped up." On Tuesday evening, a Rastafari band of about 400 dreads, as well as other dancers, paraded with a steel band. The newspaper reported two shocking crimes for the season—a rape and a murder—which had both taken place in Port-of-Spain.

On Wednesday morning, San Fernandians learned that in the future, government purchases of arms for internal security purposes would be made in secret. Many Rastafari read the announcement in the newspapers as they hurried to arrange bail or engage lawyers for their arrested comrades. Crowds of Rastafari gathered near the courthouse.

A secondary school teacher, heir to a thriving Lebanese clothing store, was very upset by what he saw as a definite upsurge in racial feelings. He had played "mas" himself, but felt excluded by Stalin's calypso, which said of the "Caribbean Man" that he belonged to "the same race, from the same place." Abroad, where he had been a student, he had been active in West Indian organizations, and felt that there, other West Indians would have rejected the "racial" appeal of such a calypso. He felt, if people were going to be "racial," that he was an Arab, that he had had nothing to do with the white man and slavery, and so he would fight for his rights. He had already admonished his wife's family, who were Indian, that it was up to the more numerous ethnic groups like the Indians to take action in this deteriorating situation.

Asked whether he had experienced any racial animosity during Carnival, he said he didn't think so. Asked whether he felt the police were not being allowed unnecessary license, he thought, yes; he even volunteered the information that people he knew were wondering whether a "police state" was not in the making. "But is dem Rasta fault."

A marijuana-using accountant said that he felt two "cultures" had divided Trinidad: one, using and trafficking in marijuana, welded together by police oppression, comprised up to 30 percent of the population. Rastafari was their voice. The other, based on fear of the first, craved more police.

In summary, it may be said that the ganja complex had created, in the decade since its revival, a climate which has enabled opposing class feelings to expose themselves. The Carnival events illustrated how much of San Fernando's middle-class opinion rests on irresponsible journalism, hearsay, naive belief in the police, and prejudice. There were no institutions to remind journalism of its responsibilities, to critique abuses by the police, or capable of finding out facts in an objective manner; at least, they had not been deployed when it came to issues concerning the unemployed and the low-income classes generally.

Thus, while marijuana itself was accepted fairly generally as innocuous, the multifaceted ganja complex and its adherents were repressed. Vagrancy laws were reinforced, empowering the police to pick up "suspicious" persons. Mental health authorities made marijuana the cause of a wide variety of psychosocial maladies referred to them. Squatters faced demolition squads. These measures all targeted Rastafari. The announcement in the newspapers soon after Carnival, stating the government's intention to buy secret weapons for national security purposes, thus appeared ominous, indicative of the direction in which events are likely to move.

In the ten years during which the ganja complex was being diffused, the police had emerged as a right-wing force in Trinidad, much favored by businessmen, professionals, and their government employers. On account of their fight, first against Black Power and striking workers, and then against ganja and Rastafari, they had acquired enormous powers over the working classes as a whole.

Official police operations in the matter of marijuana may be briefly summarized. In 1966, there were 18 arrests, and only 17 pounds of marijuana were seized; in 1971, 210 convictions and 3,500 trees destroyed. By the first six months of 1974, arrests and seizures had surpassed total figures for 1973 and 1974: 545 men, 32 women, 440 pounds of cured ganja, 581,960 trees. After 1974, as Rastafarians began to appear, arrests, raids on Rastafari communes, and raids on planters were daily reported. Rastafari discovered in the countryside were shot: by February 1978, the total dead of these "guerrillas" was 25. (At least 33 men, however, have been shot in connection with preventing marijuana cultivation and sales.)

Unofficial police operations with respect to marijuana were more difficult to uncover. It is difficult to decide, for example, whether the police battle against guerrillas, who are more often than not marijuana cultivators, is motivated by a desire not to eliminate planting or revolutionary activities, but to control planters. What is known is that individual police officers have had arrangements with planters whereby the latter were protected in exchange for money, marijuana, liquor, and game. Trinidadians consider it a sign of status (wealth and connections) to put a variety of game on the dinner table: agouti (a forest hare), tatou (armadillo), quenk (wild boar), manicou (a tree-dwelling marsupial, and deer. These meats are usually prepared in fiery curries, flavored with coconut, habanero (Scotch bonnet) peppers, and thyme.

Again it is difficult to prove whether the police persecution of some blocks rather than others rests on chance only. It is known that some of the officers who receive marijuana from planters also have city operators who sell it for them.

It is difficult to gauge how extensive these abuses were. In San Fernando, there were eight policemen who dealt regularly with marijuana raids and were members of the new Rasta Squad, formed before the Carnival to deal with an anticipated insurrection. Complaints of extortion had been heard against all of them; block leaders reported being propositioned by all, to sell their ganja. What seemed verifiable among these charges, was that the officers act piecemeal, if at all: they formed no organized unit to control supply and distribution.

For the San Fernando Rastafari, these events speak for themselves. They are wondering how best they might circumvent the police in turn.

RASTAFARI AND THE PEACEFULNESS OF THE MARIJUANA TRAFFIC

While the target of so much public vituperation stirred up principally by cynical police officers and an irresponsible press, Rastafari had in fact curbed tendencies inherent in any illegal business toward the settlement of disputes by violence, and had replaced them with an ideology, derived from the Old Testament, which enjoined circumspection and patience, and surrendered judgment and punishment to Almighty Jah. In Trinidad, the injustice of the police campaigns was not lost on many residents of low-income neighborhoods. Indeed, they provided protection for Rastafari marijuana distributors and their selling locales, protection without which these businesses could not have survived.

Of course, there were a few occasions when Rastafari marijuana distributors resorted to violence. Perhaps in a lesser proportion than in the general population, some Rastafari were still jealous of unfaithful wives or filled with hatred against their lovers, and acted violently. The single example described in this chapter, however, had been fomented by the police.

Many of the puzzles posed in this chapter were solved in 1986, when the report of a commission, appointed by the government to investigate drug trafficking in Trinidad and Tobago, named Deputy Commissioner of Police Randolph Burroughs as a major drug distributor, who had been heavily involved in cocaine smuggling and trafficking since 1980 (Scott 1986). It now appears that some of his pre-1980 activities, recorded in this chapter, were attempts to wipe out marijuana cultivation and use, to weed out several targeted marijuana-selling blocks and locations, and to prepare the scene for the introduction of cocaine trafficking, which he then apparently dominated. He was aided by certain persons described in this research, although to further identify them would be to violate the confidentiality they had enjoyed with the researcher. Perhaps affected by the special animus against marijuana which the

Reagan administration and Nancy Reagan bore, Burroughs had not engaged in the marijuana traffic before 1980 except as executioner and scourge. Although the commission had blamed him for the extent of cocaine and crack use and distribution in Trinidad, he had resigned and migrated to the United States before the report could be presented in Parliament. His was a grim legacy. In the 1980s, cocaine smoking virtually supplanted marijuana. Addiction to crack became widespread. Blocks disbanded, and Rastafari was enervated and diminished. Finally, the ganja complex, fearsome perhaps because of its very antiquity, or because it had stimulated social, cultural, economic, cultural, and political passions in human hearts across a span of at least 5,000 years, was undermined and once again (temporarily) disjoined.

Chapter 6

The Ganja Complex in Brooklyn: The Rise and Fall of the Marijuana Complex and the Advent of Cocaine

All roads in the Caribbean—of individuals, capital, resources, political power, and value generally—lead to the United States of America, the core nation of the world system of which Trinidad and Tobago is a peripheral part (Wallerstein 1974), and it was in Caribbean immigrant communities in the United States, such as Brooklyn, that the ganja complex and Caribbean marijuana economy, portrayed in their provincial forms on the home islands in the preceding chapters, attained their fullest flowering. It was in the United States also that this researcher witnessed the hemispheric waning of the marijuana economy after 1981, although by that time the ganja complex had become a permanent addition to American metropolitan culture.

A BRIEF REVIEW OF THE CARIBBEAN DIASPORA

Persons of Caribbean ancestry have been settling abroad since the 1500s, when the islands were reached by Europeans and colonized by them. The first migrants were European, or the islands-born children of the European officers, merchants, farmers, adventurers, and indentured laborers who had migrated there.

The migration of Africans from the Caribbean began in the very first years of slavery, when Africans were forcibly brought to the islands to labor in agriculture. Sizable communities grew in London, Bristol, Paris, and Amsterdam.

In the eighteenth and nineteenth centuries, English-speaking Caribbean Africans crisscrossed the Caribbean Sea restlessly, and communities grew in Panama, where the immigrants had gone to build the Panama Canal, and in Honduras, Venezuela, and Colombia. English-speaking islanders settled in distinct enclaves in the Dominican Republic and Haiti, while Martiniquans and Guadeloupeans (together with white French estate owners) fled to the English-speaking islands during periods of revolution and unrest in France. Eventually, kinship ties united families throughout the archipelago. Particularly close bonds grew in the eastern Caribbean between such islands as Trinidad, Grenada, St.Vincent, and Barbados.

Caribbean islanders had been migrating to the United States in steadily increasing annual flows since the 1960s. Indeed, migration to the United States from the English-speaking Caribbean islands had been noted since the early 1900s. Before the Depression, about 250,000 had settled in Harlem and Brooklyn and had earned a reputation for hard work and entrepreneurial ability (Thomas-Hope 1976). When the Depression came, however, many returned home. During the 1940s and 1950s, migrants traveled to Britain and Europe, where the postwar recovery absorbed them readily as workers, and only a small contingent arrived in this country. They were mostly professionals.

In the 1960s, however, migration to the United States resumed, and its scale surpassed the earlier migratory waves. Twin factors accounting for the high tide were the achievement of political independence by many islands and the Hart-Cellar Immigration Reform Act of 1965. The provisions of the reform legislation improved the balance of migration between the eastern and western hemispheres, and allowed up to 20,000 islanders from each independent statehood to migrate annually. At the same time, high rates of unemployment and inflation, resulting from the implementation of U.S.-directed modernization and development plans in the region, sparked abundant motivations to migrate (Hamid 1980; Koslofski1967). U.S. Immigration and Naturalization statistics show that more than one million West Indians arrived in the 1960s alone (INS 1970). Many others settled in Canada (Chaney and Sutton 1979).

The events to be described before apply not only to New York City and Brooklyn, but throughout the Caribbean diaspora, or wherever there were sizable Caribbean immigrant communities.

MARIJUANA IN NEW YORK CITY BEFORE THE GANJA COMPLEX

It should be noted that the ganja complex, in taking root in the contemporary Americas and Europe, had supplanted nascent home-grown cannabis cultures. For example, in many of the low-income minority neighborhoods of New York City where Caribbean migrants settled in the 1970s, many circles of African Americans and Latinos smoked marijuana, but distribution had not been organized systematically until the new culture bearers of the ganja complex, the young Caribbean Africans featured in this book, accomplished this task. Thus, Malcolm X described how he bought loose marijuana in the 1940s from merchant seamen and sold it as reefers (tiny cigarettes) to an esoteric coterie of musicians and clubgoers in Harlem. His daily profits exceeded $50:

> *Both Sammy and I knew some merchant seamen and others who could supply me with loose marijuana. And musicians, among whom I had so many good contacts, were the heaviest consistent market for reefers. And then, musicians also used the heavier narcotics, if I wanted to graduate to them. That would be more risky, but also more money. Handling heroin and cocaine could earn one hundreds of dollars a day, but it required a lot of experience with the narcotics squad for one to be able to last long enough to make anything.*
>
> *I had been around long enough either to know or to spot instinctively most regular detectives and cops, though not the narcotics people. And among Small's veteran hustler regulars, I had a variety of potentially helpful contacts. This was important because just as Sammy could get me supplied with marijuana, a large facet of any hustler's success was knowing where he could get help when he needed it. The help could involve police and detectives—as well as higher ups. But I hadn't yet reached that stage. So Sammy staked me, about $20, I think it was. Later that same night, I knocked at his door and gave him back his money and asked him if I could lend him some. I had gone straight from Sammy's to a supplier he had mentioned. I got just a small amount of marijuana, and I got some of the paper to roll up my own sticks. As they were only about the size of stick matches, I was able to make enough of them so that, after selling them to musicians I knew at the Braddock Hotel, I could pay back Sammy and have enough profit to be in business. And those musicians, when they saw their buddy, and their fan, in business: "My Man!" "Crazy, Red!"*
>
> *In every band, at least half of the musicians smoked reefers. I'm not going to list names: I'd have to include some of those most prominent then in popular music, even a number of them around today. In one case, every man in one of the bands which is still famous was on marijuana. Or again, any number of musicians could tell you who I mean when I say that one of the most famous singers smoked his reefers through a chicken thighbone. He had smoked so many through the bone that he could just light a match before the empty bone, draw the heat through, and get what he called a "contact" high.*
>
> *I kept turning over my profit, increasing my supplies, and I sold reefers like a wild man. I scarcely slept: I was wherever musicians congregated. A roll of money was in my pocket. Every day I cleared at least fifty or sixty dollars. In those days (or for that matter these days), this was a fortune to a seventeen-year-old Negro. I felt, for the first time in my life, that great feeling of* ***free!*** *Suddenly, I was the peer of the other young hustlers I had admired.*

Claude Brown described a slightly brisker marijuana traffic in Central Harlem in the 1950s (Brown 1963), while Oscar Hijuelos identifies Latino musicians as the marijuana smokers and distributors of Spanish Harlem (Hijuelos 1991) in the 1960s. Thus, marijuana-using variants of "deviant" subcultures had thrived among New York City's "invisible" populations.

Yet other variants of a marijuana-using culture emerged as a dramatic turn in the history of the plant in the Americas was taken from 1965 to 1970, when the proportion of youths smoking marijuana rose from under 5 percent to over 50 percent in the continental United States alone. Young European Americans accounted principally for the precipitous increase. Several factors enabled them to do so. If unemployment, political instability, migration, and cultural erosion in countries like Trinidad and Jamaica (or areas such as the American inner cities) were one side of the coin of modernization and development initiatives (see chapter 2), the other side was the longest uninterrupted period of unchecked economic growth for several social classes in the United States. Consumer spending grew, and a spirit of consumerism, attaching great status value to the range and luxury of belongings, flourished. More than 76 million babies—almost one-third of the current population—were born between 1946 and 1964; indeed, more babies were born between 1946 and 1952 than had been born in the previous thirty years (Jones 1981). These privileged American youths entered college in record numbers in the 1960s, at the same time when college campuses were being polarized by the civil rights movement and anti–Vietnam War protest. Indeed, unrest across the globe—independence movements and occupations by the U.S. military in every region—added to the radical dispute in academia. Targeted on the one hand by merchandisers and advertisers attempting to draw them through their sizable disposable income into the world of American consumerism, these young Americans were confronted on the other hand by a knowledge of the tremendous costs by which that world was being supported. In response, many mapped out countercultural lifestyles which signified their discomfort or disassociation. Of course, the novel lifestyles generated new products and businesses, including intensified trafficking in illegal drugs. Countercultural lifestyles from which young persons in the 1960s borrowed were those of the bohemians of the 1950s, among whom the use of drugs (alcohol, amphetamine, and marijuana) was an aid in heightening the senses, gaining self-transcendence, and creating artistic work. When the style of the bohemians was reworked to include political stances and activism, marijuana emerged as the predominant symbol of protest (Gitlin 1987; Polsky 1967).

The enormous demand for marijuana among European Americans, and the fact that it could be grown anywhere, stimulated the emergence of a wide range of distribution arrangements. Young European American individuals forged all kinds of contacts with citizens from many foreign nations to secure supplies of marijuana, and satisfied a large part of their demand through these idiosyncratic efforts. Although organized crime groups in New York also imported and distributed marijuana, the snatch of Arlo Guthrie's song,

Coming into Los Angeles,
Bringing in a couple of keys [kilos]
Don't touch my bag, if you please
Mr. Customs-man.

described the method by which plenty of marijuana was supplied.

By 1970 the typical marijuana smoker was likely to be an urban college graduate in his early twenties (Goode 1970), and a survey in 1979 indicated that 68 percent of those aged eighteen to twenty-five had used the drug (Fishburne et al. 1979), including 69 percent of European Americans, 62 percent of other ethnic groups and 73 percent of those who attended college. Thus, not only had marijuana use undergone a precipitous increase among youth in the 1960s and early 1970s, but the demography of use had also shifted considerably since the 1930s when minority populations comprised the bulk of users. Indeed, the increased risk of arrest for affluent young European Americans was a critical element in the passage of laws decriminalizing marijuana in several states during the 1970s (Galliher et al. 1974; Galliher and Basilick 1979).[1]

Young middle-class European American marijuana users contributed to several countercultural complexes without developing a distinctly marijuana-using subculture in the 1960s and 1970s. A principal reason might have been their failure to form a self-supporting system of production, distribution and exchange of marijuana. Meantime, the ganja complex, supported by just such a system which Caribbean African youths had created, flourished, invaded the other subcultures, and dominated them. In this book, the struggle in Trinidad between ganja and madi-juana in chapter 7 represents the kind of political and cultural struggle which was fought to vanquish these other marijuana use-complexes.

THE GANJA COMPLEX IN BROOKLYN

In the preceding chapters, frequent mention was made of the increasing migration of San Fernandians to the United States. In particular, several block leaders who traveled abroad, or maintained regular business contact with both legitimate and illegitimate enterprises in the United States, were identified. For example, in chapter 2, Constable recalled Phyliss, who had migrated with her entire family in the 1960s. In chapter 4, Gentleman Slim was mentioned en route to New York, where he had established a marijuana-selling "gates" in 1973. These San Fernandians were only a few of the many who settled in Brooklyn.

As Caribbean communities were established in such places as Brooklyn in New York City, the opportunities for illegal migration grew (Kasinitz 1992). Many Caribbean islanders now regard Brooklyn as the largest Caribbean island.

Daily contact with the islands is maintained, and many stores and groceries are Caribbean-owned and specialize in Caribbean goods. Caribbean voluntary or political associations abound. The undocumented visitor is thus absorbed quickly by friends, employers, and other support which screen him from detection. By 1970, neighborhoods on the Caribbean islands were experiencing the catastrophic impact of the continuing legal and illegal migration to the United States. In some Trinidadian neighborhoods, for example, such as the one described in chapter 1, the entire generation of productive adults (those born in the 1930s and 1940s) had gone abroad in search of work, leaving behind aging grandparents and unemployed, delinquent/truant adolescents. Houses had fallen into disrepair, while hardship and hard feelings tore occupants apart within them.

At the same time, in the United States, the migrants themselves were struggling to settle into the host community. While a few had achieved success in the professions and business, the majority adapted to the changing post-1965 New York economy, making significant inroads in the burgeoning low-paid service sector (Kasinitz 1992) and the informal sector. It would take them until the mid-1970s to make the remittances and the annual return trips necessary to salvage what remained of neighborhoods on the home islands, and to improve their lives materially in the United States (Thomas-Hope 1976; Chaney and Sutton 1979; Hendricks 1978).

An early sign of the gradual accommodation of migrants to New York City was registered when they began sponsoring the immigration of younger dependents to the United States (Immigration and Naturalization Service 1980). The latter were frequently the identical young persons who had been occupying neglected family property in the Caribbean, and their removal from that unhappy situation introduced them to another here (Chaney and Sutton 1979). A parent who had finally managed to secure permanent employment, and who was saving to afford a home away from Brooklyn and to renovate family holdings on the islands, had little patience with a young man or woman who had been a school dropout at home, was destined to be a dropout in New York, or was too old for school and had no employable skills. From grandparents' disapproval at home, therefore, young people plunged directly into conflict with parents in New York.

As a result, many young people were disillusioned about the worth of family ties altogether (Hamid 1991a). Gradually they constructed a life of their own which featured a migratory experience quite different from their elders'. In addition to yearly visits to the islands, they charted a unique migratory itinerary which included residence in the U.S. Virgin Islands, California, Florida, Texas, Montreal, and Toronto. At each stopover point, they found short-term employment as messengers, store clerks, or unskilled manual laborers. Later, the unique itinerary and work experience were put to lucrative use in the marijuana economy. In New York, several locations—abandoned lofts and buildings—served as lodgings and meeting places. In some locations the young migrants formed communes which lasted several years. Participants were from the pan-Caribbean region, and they shared food and the costs of upkeep of the dwelling places. A variety of interpersonal and sexual relations obtained among individual members. At the same time, relationships were marked strongly by individualism, competition, and violent struggles fomented by joblessness and the struggle over petty, income-generating "hustles." The groupings of young Caribbean males and females in unauthorized housing soon excited curiosity and hostile attention from the police (New York Police Department 1985).

For many other young West Indians, the Vietnam War served as the bridge into American life. Shunted out of school by poor grades, many who retained educational ambitions were lured into the armed forces. Their first taste of America was savored in the jungle combat zones of Southeast Asia. They were simultaneously introduced to marijuana and other drugs. Patron's account, given below, is typical of several reported in this research by veterans. In the end, as Patron indicates below, they too did what their siblings, cousins, and friends on the islands and in New York City had done: they turned to marijuana not only for recreation, but also as work and self-definition.

BLOCKS IN BROOKLYN

Blocks formed in New York City in the same way they had in San Fernando. The major difference, of course, was that the amounts of money to be made, in top-valued U.S. currency, were vastly greater. Other critical differences were that Caribbean marijuana distributors served a polyethnic clientele in New York City, and that they were becoming rich and powerful in a milieu in which several ethnic groups vied for wealth and power. The belief, however, that marijuana-selling in New York City was different because it was dominated by long-lived criminal organizations, is not supported by any ethnographic evidence. For example, exactly the same period of experimentation among neophytes in the traffic culminated in the formation of blocks. Patron gave the following overview of marijuana selling in Flatbush from 1971 to 1991:

> *I am 48 years of age today, and hail from a small village in north Trinidad. When I was growing up, church, school, and community controlled your life, and if you were outside of them, you were a renegade. My three older brothers and my sister excelled in those areas: one brother is today a senior administrator at Baruch College [City University of New York], my sister owns her own farm in Florida, all of them are doing well. Because I was the youngest, I think I got estranged*

from all of that. I loved to play pan [the steel drum], and would be out of the house after school from an early age. My mother used to beat me a lot for that, but then she gave up on me. When I was doing well in marijuana, I sent money to her in Trinidad, and those big barrels [100-pound containers used by exporters] full of goods. I think I am still trying to prove to them that I am not the nobody they had me down as.

Anyway, I was isolated and have always remained a loner. Now when my mother says that she wants to see me settled down and married, I think to myself that "you never trained me up for that, you never bothered to see that I was educated, you gave up on all of that."

I first started dealing in marijuana after I had come to this country, and while I was stationed at the army base in Texas during 1969 to 1971. Texas was where we were mostly, but we moved around to bases in other states too. Mexico was close by, everybody was smoking at the base, so I started selling it. Guys were into all sorts of drugs then, and especially acid. In fact, I was in a CID (or Intelligence) unit, and we used to have gallons of cheap wine spiked with acid, and fellas used to trip all day long. We would smoke marijuana and trip on acid. It was a racial thing too, because the white boys wouldn't let us hang with them, and those places [Texas and the other southern states] were pretty prejudiced so we couldn't leave the base, so we kept to ourselves and got high.

I came back to New York in 1971, and at first divided my time between Harlem and Brooklyn, because I had close friends in both places. But all the people I used to smoke marijuana with in Harlem were now into heroin, which the Italians in East Harlem were supplying to blacks and Hispanics. It was an overnight thing, a really rapid transformation, just like crack today, except that crack is more of a nighttime thing, while people got off on heroin during the day. But suddenly people were either robbing and stealing and sticking up, or they were selling the dope, or they were using. Three ways to go, and all three full of violence and distrust, because people's personalities had changed. Lots of guns were around. So eventually I decided to settle in Brooklyn completely, to get away from that scene.

I didn't have anything to do with drugs from 1971 to about 1975. I was more into family then. I never married, and I have a lot of children by different women, but I was close to this one and the one child we had so far. I was into buying the first car, and improving our quality of life, and by 1975 I was looking for a house, and she found one in Florida. Later, when the marijuana money was running, I helped her to buy it. I explained to you that I value that independence, but it's my house and I'm always welcome there. But then, I had a good job as a clerk at Morgan Guaranty, and on the side lines, I used to throw West Indian parties. I was more into family and the West Indian community you could say. I used to rent a basement for about $60, pay a DJ another $60, and put in about $150 worth of food and drink. Then I'd print up flyers and distribute them to people in the street, or leave them in shops. And I would take away $800 the night of the party.

I got back into marijuana around 1977. I had lost touch with Harlem, but now I saw the same sort of heroin scene—with the guns, the stickups, and violence—beginning to happen on Fulton Street [Brooklyn] to West Indians. A whole lot of little shops had sprouted up there, selling smoke [marijuana], dope [heroin], coke [cocaine], whatever.

Then I made contact with some Jewish kids who lived in Park Slope [a nearby section of Brooklyn] and who were getting bales of smoke from Florida. Panama Red, Colombian Gold at $200 a pound. I think they were the children of people who had moved from here earlier, and now the children were coming back, and they knew how to deal with black people. Or they knew how to get along with West Indians, because American blacks [African Americans] were largely cut out of this marijuana thing. So they were giving me smoke, and there were all these shops I could sell it to.

By this time, it was all about stores [blocks] in selling marijuana. Mostly Rastafari. Apartments had died out, because nobody could be bothered to go up to somebody's apartment for marijuana. It was more professional with stores, and since everybody had their stuff out there, you had to get your stuff out too. I had no thought of the police then, and I used to travel around with 30 pounds of marijuana in the trunk [of a car], dropping some off at this store, picking up some of the money and setting a date for the rest, leaving more in the next store, and then on to the next store. I was living good, I sent lots of money to my brothers and my mother, I sent her lots of goods, I helped out my children and their mothers.

I was living luxuriously, but the real money flowed in during the four months when I had my own store with a partner. You remember I had said that the white boys had drugs all along on Parkside Avenue. Well, there was one white boy with a ceramics store on Church Avenue, and he was going to sell me the store and all the stock but then he OD'ed on Parkside Avenue. Must have been dope. But finally we got a store on Parkside Avenue.

But you know, money changes people and it spoils friendships. It brings about evil. "Bosses" develop out of it. So I got out of that business after falling out with my partner, and I stayed out of stores and did a more discreet, wholesale business from my apartment. To stay in the store would have turned me into a gangster, into violence and death, and I didn't see myself going that way. It was less money because you are dependent more on fast turnover, and when selling in pounds, you only made $25 or $50 on the pound. But you always had money in your pocket.

In San Fernando, it was to avoid the same temptation of gangsterism (which had frightened Patron) that copartnership in marijuana distribution evolved into blocks, and submitted to the guidance of Rastafari. In those forms, copartners endured and prospered. The same path was followed in Brooklyn. Blocks (or gates, as they were eventually called in New York City) operated from a greater variety of locales in New York City than was possible in the Caribbean. As earlier European American residents migrated to the suburbs, they left behind not only apartment buildings and homes, but also commercial stock. For retailing marijuana, therefore, distributors could choose not only among apartments, but also from a wide assortment of storefront operations (grocery stores, candy stores, clothing boutiques, record stores, and crafts workshops). Rastafari revived these properties in Brooklyn and sought them out in the other boroughs of the city.

At first, Rastafari were dependent on EuropeanAmerican suppliers. Buying marijuana at $350 to $500 per pound (from individuals like Patron), they resold it in "nickel bags" (3.5 grams sold for $5), clearing at least $300 in profits per pound. The typical block sold more than ten pounds in a week. As Rastafari became richer and more powerful, however, and as they practiced their religion more strictly, they sought to restrict the traffic as much as possible to Rastafari alone. They thus succeeded in "Caribbeanizing" a sizable corner of the trade. Several brethren made return trips to Grenada, Trinidad, and Jamaica, stimulated cultivation on these islands, and then assumed roles as exporters—importers to the United States, Canada, and Europe. The exclusive reliance on European American suppliers, or on anonymous cultivators in far-distant corners of the world, was broken.

Sinsemilla, introduced in the mid-1970s, boosted profits enormously. A pedigreed female plant, it required complete removal from males, or from pollination. Plants were carefully nourished as a seedling, then transplanted in the ground, a few roots spaced apart over a wide acreage. A regime of daily irrigation and exposure to bright sun followed for nine months. Denied pollination, the female plants produced buds and flowers so concentrated with perfume and delta-9 tetrahydrocannabinol (THC) that crystals of the latter were plainly visible, twinkling, to the naked eye. Protection from pollination also increased the weight of the dense buds and flowers and prevented weight loss to seeds. Planters manicured the mature buds, snipping off supernumerary leaves without THC content, and fetched $1,400 to $1,800 a pound for the finished product, which was packaged and sealed in polyurethane bags (Boyle 1984).

Young Caribbean Africans, in their unique itinerary up the archipelago and across the United States (see above), were on hand in California and Oregon as plentiful harvests of domestic sinsemilla were reaped for the first time in the early 1970s. Some eventually apprenticed themselves to "hippie" (European American) growers in those states, and when they received in-kind payments of marijuana or preferential rates, liaised between the West Coast growers and Brooklyn gates where $2,800 to $3,300 per pound was willingly paid for the aromatic, superpotent marijuana. Others returned to the islands to teach eager coreligionists the methods of intensive cultivation. Fewer plants of sinsemilla earned more than many more plants grown commercial or plantation-style, and they were also easier to conceal from police surveillance. The outcome was a successful transplant of the techniques on the islands, and from Jamaica, Grenada, and Trinidad especially, supplies of local sinsemillas were soon forthcoming. In Brooklyn, retailers sold a gram for $10 (a "dime bag".) Not only was the greater return attractive, but so was the accounting: a pound, or 454 grams, was to be sold for exactly $4,540. The greater ability to foresee and manage revenues enabled Rastafari to engage in more effective financial planning.

Although Brooklyn Rastafari preferred to distribute supplies grown on the islands by their coreligionists, their love of marijuana impelled them to collect exotic cannabis varieties and preparations from around the world. Sinsemillas were home-grown in every state of the United States. Some were grown indoors in the coldest states, using innovations on the basic cultivation techniques. For example, hydroponics, which utilized indoor space, artificial lighting, and a water-borne nutrition system, produced potent strains. Rarities such as purple Hawaiian kona buds, or the black buds of West Africa, were highly prized. Rastafari also sought out the dozens of shades of color and potencies of hashish and hash oils which were produced in the Middle and Far East, and the fabled marijuanas ("Thai stick") of Thailand and Vietnam.

REINVESTMENTS IN BROOKLYN

In Brooklyn, Rastafari found many more ways to invest their marijuana revenues in accordance with their religiopolitical beliefs. The most obvious was renovation of the selling location itself. Not only did they revive conventional locations like groceries and candy stores, but they installed new ones like health-food stores. Indeed, the health-food movement in Brooklyn, and in low-income minority neighborhoods throughout New York City, which in 1978 featured seminars, workshops, and myriad informal consumer groups, was pioneered by the health-food stores Rastafari opened. Several outlets for cooked vegetarian food (restaurants, snack bars, and curbside stalls) followed, which provided a training ground for Rastafari women eager to try out an evolving Caribbean vegetarian cuisine on the public.

Stores from which marijuana was sold also displayed other Rastafari novelties produced by talented coreligionists. Matos's associate Opinion had been expert at leather crafting in San Fernando, and after emigrating to Brooklyn, had sold marijuana from a store where he also displayed his creations, such as bags, belts, and boots. In 1994, the store has been greatly expanded and renovated, and he also sells Rastafari paintings, reggae albums, and T-shirts handpainted with Rastafari designs. On a busy commercial avenue, it stands next door to a jewelry store, where Shark, cofounder with Patron of one of the earliest Brooklyn blocks, carves earrings in the shape of Africa or Nefertiti from fourteen-carat gold. Smoking paraphernalia, such as chalices (water pipes hand-crafted from coconuts), roach clips, and Rastafari insignia of cloth and leather were also sold. Stores also displayed the work of seamstresses and tailors—African gowns, quilts, wall-hangings—as they were made, or commissioned them.

Homes and real estate in Brooklyn were also purchased. Before migrating from San Fernando, Botts (see chapter 3), who later entered cocaine and crack distribution successfully, had declared that his ambition was to buy a property in the $300,000 to $350,000 range for each of his thirteen children. In 1991, he had purchased eleven properties in Trinidad and Brooklyn and was looking for a twelfth in Manhattan.

A lot of money was diverted to the Caribbean islands, where agricultural projects were launched. The best-known of these brought 1,600 acres under cultivation in St. Anns, Jamaica, and offered employment to many Rastafari families. Rastafari directly and indirectly invigorated lines of trade with the islands other than marijuana. For example, as health-food stores and restaurants offering Caribbean–vegetarian fare multiplied in New York City, suppliers of island-grown foodstuffs flourished. At that time, tropical produce well known in the United States, such as bananas, pineapples, and mangoes, was handled by the giant multinational food corporations, including United Fruit and Del Monte. Smaller-scale entrepreneurs now bought shipments of the more ethnic agricultural goods like nutmeg, allspice, and other spices, seamoss, cocoa, Spanish thyme, Scotch bonnet peppers (habaneros), pigeon peas, okras, callaloo (the greens of a tuber, the dasheen, which are puréed), Jamaican yams, and pumpkins from the primary producers on the islands, airlifted them to Kennedy Airport in New York City, and distributed them in a few days throughout shops in the region from U-Haul or privately owned trucks. The early import and distribution of fresh coconuts remained another exclusive Rastafari domain, until Latino entrepreneurs began airlifting them from Spanish-speaking islands such as Puerto Rico and the Dominican Republic.

Finally, marijuana revenues were spent on a weekly newspaper and two schools, one of which remains in operation and is top-ranked among Brooklyn primary schools. Reggae bands were sponsored. Tuition for Rastafari women who studied nutrition, seamstressing, or education were paid.

RASTAFARI IN BROOKLYN

The greater wealth enjoyed by Brooklyn Rastafari enabled them to offer lavish praises to Jah Rastafari. Several congregations with large memberships were formed. As each elaborated its own orthodoxy, debate and controversy were never in short supply in the Rastafari community at large. Some ideological divisions in the community were indicated in chapter 4.

Among the congregations, the Ethiopian Coptic Church, founded by Brooklyn Rastafari but transplanted to Miami and Jamaica, is to be remembered for the case it is continuing to pursue in the U.S. courts, to legalize the use of marijuana as a Rastafari sacrament. Implicit in the plea is legal recognition of Rastafari as a bona fide religion.

The Twelve Tribes of Israel emerged as another beacon of Rastafari arts and cultivation near Fulton Street (Lewis 1993). An Inner Circle of Rastafari (Brooklyn) was also established in Crown Heights. Dreadlocks, reggae music, the unique intonations of Jamaican speech, made even more impenetrable in the deliberate attempt to invent a separate Rastafari dialect, and, of course, the message of African identity and self-sufficiency formed a package of symbols which proved irresistible to young African Americans in New York City's inner-city neighborhoods. Young males loved to affect these diacritics, while young women fell in love with the brethren. Although African Americans were effectively barred from the least involvement with marijuana distribution, and functioned only as consumers, their warm regard for Rastafari and reggae music would eventually have such outcomes as rap music in the 1980s, when African Americans did enter the drug trade as cocaine distributors.

The marijuana economy demonstrably restored vitality and prosperity to neighborhoods which had suffered disintegration on account of modernization and development initiatives. Embittered relationships among the young distributors and users were healed, and a new religion enfolded them; while the relationship between them and their parents improved when marijuana revenues bought Mom and Pop stores and other property for the latter.

In Brooklyn, at the level of interethnic relations, marijuana use and distribution also served an integrative function. Rastafari conformed well with and provided influential symbols for the thrust which Caribbean politicians, power-brokers and entrepreneurs ("Babylon!") were mounting to develop a Caribbean constituency or market. Rastafari, its roots in marijuana cultivation, distribution, and use barely concealed, was a rallying point in the search for a distinctive Caribbean identity in the multiethnic milieu.

DECLINE OF MARIJUANA/ADVENT OF COCAINE SMOKING (FREEBASE AND CRACK)

For most of the 1970s, apartment buildings were maintained by tenant rolls of low-paid African American and Caribbean African workers. At first they consolidated their position, and marijuana distribution advanced them further toward that end. Rastafari marijuana distributors, encouraged by their religio-political ideology as well as by the prudence which often accompanies arrival at middle age, bought the stores from which they sold marijuana and the many other storefronts from which they had launched various forms of cottage industry. They also bought homes for themselves, their conjugal families, and their parents. They lent a mighty shoulder, therefore, to the task of renovating property and retarding abandonment.

In the 1980s, however, another stage of deterioration forced new upheavals in the local population. The demographic characteristics of Flatbush residents changed again. On the one hand, many apartment buildings were rescued from abandonment and converted into coops and condominiums for middle-income investors. But the remaining buildings were further devalued, and an increasing number of displaced families, in-migrating from ruined proximate sections of Brooklyn, was crammed into the habitable ones, where they were forced to double-up or treble-up. Their next step, to be taken in the mid-1980s, would be toward the shelters or into the streets, as the city's homelessness crisis escalated.

It was as neighborhoods of apartment buildings throughout minority Brooklyn and the city suffered greater decline that marijuana was replaced by cocaine hydrochloride powder. As Rastafari marijuana distributors were drawn into experimentation with cocaine distribution and use, the important function they had served as preservers of real estate was lost.

The example of Flatbush, a section of the borough of Brooklyn, illustrates these transformations. It was the site of several research undertakings by the author. It is not very different from many other low-income neighborhoods in cities across the United States, such as those named above, certainly not in the gross parameters of inner-city deterioration. Evolving from a village of prosperous farmsteads in the 1600s, when it was home to the first church and primary school in America, it has accepted successive waves of immigrants continuously to the present day. Irish, Jewish, and Eastern European migrants came until the 1940s and established stable communities of merchants, professionals, skilled, and manual laborers. Spacious seven- and eight-room apartments in solidly appointed apartment buildings, none more than six floors high, as well as luxurious family mansions, standing in extensive manicured grounds along street after street lined with leafy elms, sycamores, and oaks, sheltered them. These mansions are today the homes of European American federal judges, prominent doctors, and the heads of prestigious institutions in New York City and State. Many politicians who represent Flatbush in the City Council and the State Senate live here.

Three blocks eastward to Flatbush Avenue, however, a different fate overtook neighborhoods where most of the imposing apartment buildings stood. During the 1970s, large numbers of migrants arrived from the Caribbean and the American South (principally the Carolinas), as European tenants moved out rapidly for New York's more affluent suburbs, taking their businesses with them. By the 1990s, there were few local employment opportunities in Flatbush (chiefly in the commercial strip which runs the length of major avenues, such as Flatbush Avenue and Church Avenue, and at the local hospitals or other state agencies), and none at all in the study site, where the bodega was owned by Yemenis and the pizzeria by Italian Americans from Bensonhurst.

Patron, the forty-eight-year-old marijuana and cocaine distributor introduced above, has successfully survived two decades of drug distribution. After dramatic reversals of fortune and some brief periods of continuous good luck, he has on balance maintained himself with a constant fund of the independence and modest means he says he finds indispensable to his personal style of life. About Flatbush, he recalls the following:

> *When I moved into Brooklyn in 1971, it was still white—mostly Jewish and Italian. White doctors and nurses lived in the building I moved into, near Kings County Hospital. Where I live now, on Ocean Avenue [Flatbush], was all white too. All the shops on Church Avenue and Flatbush Avenue were Jewish or Italian: vegetable stores, liquor stores, and so on. The white kids used to do drugs near Parkside Avenue: they had acid, mescaline, coke, and marijuana there. There were very few blacks: lots of West Indians had settled in Crown Heights, on this side of Nostrand Avenue, while black Americans went down towards Fulton Street [Bedford-Stuyvesant].*
>
> *The neighborhood really began to change around 1974. The whites started moving to the outskirts, further across Nostrand Avenue, or towards Sheepshead Bay. A lot moved out to Long Island. And blacks [West Indians] started moving in from Crown Heights, where buildings were being abandoned. A lot of West Indians bought up property, and then in the late 1970s, they too would start moving to Long Island, or to the nicer houses going towards Coney Island Avenue.*
>
> *While all of this was happening, services were being cut. When I lived near Kings County Hospital, we had a doorman, two porters, an electrician, a super, painters, and we had access to the landlord. Things got repaired faster and more professionally. When I moved to Ocean Avenue in 1975, we had the same sort of staff. There was someone who washed and buffed the marble floors every day, so the place was cleaner and smelled sweeter. Today, we have an untrained, low-paid super and none of the other workers. Before, there was a tap-room next to the incinerator on each floor, for you to wash up the garbage pail before taking it back into the apartment, but the taps and sinks have been removed or are broken down, and no one has replaced them. The place is a lot dirtier. After 1975, I think the city went into bankruptcy under Mayor Beame, and that's when parks, sanitation, fire services, and so on suffered too.*

The substitution of marijuana by cocaine offers further superlative proof of the argument that drug prohibition approaches to the drug problem—interdiction, crop substitution, and street-level enforcement—make matters worse, even in the rare instances when they happen to be successful. Drug prohibition damaged marijuana distribution, but the end result, brought about in the context of urban decline, was to deliver users over to cocaine.

In 1981 the plentiful supplies of marijuana flowing from every corner of the world to America were interrupted by DEA-inspired campaigns (DEA 1981). In the White House, the Reagan administration continued to target marijuana as the nation's number-one drug problem, although a "blizzard" of cocaine had already blown in, and its intranasal use had become more in vogue. On becoming prime minister of Jamaica in 1988 (on a pro-free-market conservative ticket which had defeated opponent Michael Manley's socialist prospectus), Edward Seaga rushed to Washington, promising in Kingston and at Kennedy Airport in New York to advise his mentor, President Reagan, that marijuana had made significant contributions to the island's economic life, and about the benign effects users experienced in the Caribbean. After his arrival in Washington, however, no further mention was made of the brave plan, and joint U.S.–Jamaica army raids continued to uproot the island's marijuana fields. In Pakistan, joint military operations, coupled with attractive crop substitution programs, effectively reduced cultivation, but diverted both cultivators and marijuana users to heroin production and injecting.

In northern California and Oregon, raids were made on the farmers who had pioneered sinsemilla cultivation and other innovative agricultural techniques. Victims of the raids have described how full-scale military operations, involving ground troops and helicopter backup, were waged against them.

At the street level, distributors faced stepped-up police surveillance and harassment which began with Operation Pressure Point (Zimmer 1987). Each precinct formed its own antidrug initiative (ranging from SWATs to drug education programs in the precinct's schools). In the Flatbush study site, a favorite tactic was to arrest marijuana distributors en masse on Fridays, no matter how "strong" the arrests. Prisoners could expect to be incarcerated until at least the following Monday. Even if the case was dismissed, the weekend sales—the heaviest of the week—would have been lost. If officers, while making the arrests, had also "inadvertently" destroyed costly equipment like bulletproof glass partitions, store gates and locks, deep freezes and refrigerators, or grocery stock, losses could be prohibitive. Seizures of marijuana and arrests reached record levels.

In Patron's account below, the police, like the Reagan White House and the DEA campaigners against marijuana in Colombia, were curiously blind to the steeply rising production, distribution, and use of cocaine. He continues his overview:

> *In 1981, I got an art store near Fulton Street. But then I got frustrated with the busts, and jail and losing money. By that time, the police were coming down hard on marijuana. Lots of coke shops were starting up—one started up right next to my marijuana/arts shop—but the police didn't touch them. They sold half-grams and grams, for $50 and $100. It made me feel that they were running the cocaine, that they were*

trying it out to see how people would like it. And that's how they created a market for another product. That's how we moved from smoke to coke.

In 1981, all that Panamanian red and Colombian gold [commonly available "commercial" marijuanas] dried up, and up until 1984, Jamaican smoke and local sinsemilla, selling at around $2,400 a pound, made up the market. Then the price dropped to about $1,200. And now [1991] it's mostly American. We get it from New Mexico and Texas, not from the Florida side anymore, and the cheapest grade is about $1,600 a pound. Better smoke sells for up to $5,000 a pound. Nowadays, it's only a small set of people who use marijuana. Some who used to use it were messed up with cocaine and don't touch any drugs whatsoever. And the guys who are selling it are into it just like a business enterprise. They are the few, in a few communities, who stuck it out until this time, by avoiding jail and death. You know, in this business, it's just one little mistake for you to be sent up for twenty years, or to lose your life.

Well, you know me and my half-brother had worked for the past eight years to build up his health-food store and the marijuana he ran through there. In 1988, I went down to Florida for a long visit and came back to find that people who worked with him had ransacked my safe-boxes. Over $100,000 was missing. Then my half-brother got killed in 1989. Some little coked-up [African-] American punks robbed the store and shot him dead. There was nothing I could get from his family. So now I am really a little broke, business is pretty slow, and I'm down to moving no more than a couple of pounds a month. That's why I'm in college today, trying to come back up. I think I am still proving to my mother and family that I can make it. When the marijuana money was running their way, they patted me on the back and said I was being a success my way. Now it's back to "we always knew you couldn't make it."

Over the years, I have had dealings with cocaine, but marijuana was my principal thing. At one time, I think it was in 1978, we had an after-hours club, with naked dancers and stuff, near Fulton Street where we sold coke too. But I never liked the glitzy side of coke. It changes you, it attracts people to you, the most beautiful women come to your apartment, but you know it's not for you but for the coke. So it's a false thing and I didn't like it. Then again I use it too, and I still like to take a hit [smoke cocaine] to this day. So I know I would be sacrificing that pleasure if I wanted to sell it, because it is a very easy drug to mess up on, to mishandle. I would have to do some soul searching, and build up a fence, and say this is money and product, and not for use. Because it could get sweet, but it always centers inward towards the self, not outward. And then I see what it does to people: how the most ambitious and the prettiest crumble. So I sell cocaine by the kilo whenever I see the connection. But since I made that $1,000 I told you about last November, I haven't done a coke deal. I know where to get some, I could phone up people to get rid of it, but I wouldn't go looking, it would really just have to happen, like that last kilo, for me to be involved.

INCREASED PRODUCTION OF COCAINE

World cocaine production before the 1980s had remained small and did not exceed fourteen metric tons. Cultivation was concentrated exclusively in the eastern Andean provinces of Bolivia, although varieties of the shrub (*Erythroxylon coca*), with extremely low cocaine content, grew wild in lowland areas and in the Amazon Basin. In Bolivia, cultivation had been undertaken by various traditional Andean highland nations in whose society and culture coca chewing had served important functions for several centuries (Antonil 1978). They sold surplus coca leaves in markets organized by Ladinos (Bolivians of European extraction), who then supplied laboratories in Medellin and Calli, Colombia (Craig 1990; Antonil 1978). Processed into cocaine hydrochloride powder, it was transported out of Colombia and distributed in illegal markets in Europe and America.

For most of the 1970s, intranasal cocaine use in America had been restricted to the very affluent. Among minorities, only celebrities and rich professionals could afford to use it; and in low-income, minority communities, only the most successful, the criminals, and the distributors of other drugs. For heroin distributors, for example, intranasal cocaine use was an item of conspicuous consumption, which indicated their status and style.

In the early 1980s, however, cocaine became more easily available in the United States. Displaced by policies recommended to the regional governments by the World Bank and the International Monetary Fund, more farmers had relocated to the Eastern Andes, where they began to cultivate coca. As more cocaine was being manufactured in South America (Morales 1989), a new breed of middle-class European American criminal organizations surfaced in the United States, to bring it to the noses of their fellows (Adler 1985).

AFTER-HOURS CLUBS

As cocaine hydrochloride powder became more plentiful in New York City, locales for its more widespread appeal and glamorization were furnished. In the late 1970s, the chief recreational venue for affluent adults who favored night life in low- to middle-income minority communities was the afterhours club. They responded to the need for social outlets for an expanding immigrant populations, which also served as a vehicle of capital accumulation and political maneuvers. A demimonde which attracted dominant personalities from both the legitimate and illegitimate worlds, after-hours clubs were places where a successful heroin distributor could meet musicians, businessmen, and professionals. In his account, Patron had included in his club's ambiance "sex shows and gambling."

Heroin distributors of those days recalled that in their circles, although the price of cocaine was prohibitively high, it was usually bartered, or exchanged as a gift, rather than bought and sold. The clubs, however, provided one of the few markets existing at the time for intranasal cocaine, demand for which was slowly growing throughout the late 1970s (Hamid 1992).

Intranasal cocaine users recalled that the heavily adulterated drug was sold from table to table by distributors who visited the clubs. They would place dollar bills on the table, onto which the distributor measured out quantities worth $20 and $50. Although distributors excused themselves from time to time to smoke cocaine (freebase) in the bathrooms, their clientele was uninterested in this method of administration, and the distributors indulged it as a private, very restrained and esoteric practice.

A Love Story

Landing a job as a corrections officer had ushered Bruno, a twenty-nine-year-old (1990) African American, into a luxurious world. When he cashed his check on paydays, he never ceased to marvel at the hefty package of $50 and $20 bills he received from the teller. He liked cashing his check just to feel that fistful of money, and his wife Alice had given up the campaign to introduce him to the modern conveniences of the banking system. She was content that at least some of his money was direct-deposited in the credit union. She deposited her own salary in an account at the bank in Manhattan where she had been working for the past fifteen years, and she issued checks against it to pay the rent, the utilities bills, and the car repayments. Bruno, Alice, and their daughter lived in one of the newest housing complexes in Crown Heights, and owned a souped-up 1979 Pontiac Grand Prix.

The family hadn't always lived this comfortably. After Bruno's return from service in Korea, a couple of years had passed before he was accepted for this job. Those had been years of struggle while Bruno went to college, when they were supported by only Alice's income. Bruno's childhood had been less stressful than these years. Then, his mother had kept them in good clothes, fine food, and excitement from her earnings as a madam.

Bruno had learned to appreciate the good feeling which holding large bundles of cash conferred while he was searching for work. He once organized a welfare fraud scheme in which several female relatives collected checks in the name of fictitious women. Until he got scared and discontinued it, the scheme paid him $50,000 in cash every month. With the money, Bruno bought stolen cars through a friend's repair shop, for reshipment to the South. He also bought two "Mr. Softee" ice cream vans, but his cousins ate up both ice cream and profits.

Bruno worked hard at his job. He was determined to become a captain in corrections, and enrolled for classes at the John Jay College of Criminal Justice, City University of New York, Serpico's alma mater. On Saturdays, he regularly attended seminars conducted in the five boroughs by the Police Academy. On the job, he won awards for punctuality, responsible conduct, and initiative, and was recommended for several promotions. In 1979, with overtime, his biweekly take-home pay exceeded $1,500."

Lots of disposable income provided the family with many of the conveniences thought indispensable in an American home. In both Alice's and Bruno's extended families, there wasn't another young couple who boasted the well-serviced apartment, the car, the home appliances, the computer for the daughter, the summer trips to the Carolinas or Florida, the clothes and jewelry. Members of the extended families visited often, and feasts of fried chicken, baked ham, potato salad, macaroni pie, greens, and Bruno's "secret recipe" banana pudding were prepared for them, with ample stocks of beer, liquors, and—the current family favorite—homemade pina colada (concocted with heavy doses of Bacardi's Gold Reserve Rum) to wash them down. Respecting the tastes of elderly mothers or aunts, staunch members of their churches all, a few of the cousins slipped out now and then, to smoke marijuana in the stairwell or in the playgrounds of the complex of apartment buildings.

Alice and Bruno also partied a lot. Their extended families supplied baby-sitters aplenty, leaving the couple with nights, weekends, and holidays free. In Bruno's extended family, there were many cousins of their age, and he had grown up inseparably from them. He had even gone into the military and overseas with some male cousins. Although a few had married and had families, and were rising, if less rapidly, in the way he was, many female cousins were supported on welfare payments, and were heavily involved with companies of similar women in their neighborhoods. They drank abusively, smoked marijuana, and there were a few who had been heroin injectors. Alice and Bruno accompanied them to house parties and to drinking parties which lasted the whole weekend, or visited bars and bar parties. They danced a lot, and listened to the popular music: Lionel Richie, the Commodores, Michael Jackson, and Diana Ross. These carousals ended when everyone was totally drunk and blacked-out.

Over time, Bruno found that the appeal of these leisure hours was wearing thin. Maybe the romantic music, about love and sex as a total preoccupation, had been making him restless. He supposed that he wanted to be somehow exalted in his experience, and felt that his success and increasing affluence entitled him to it.

In 1980, Bruno was seconded from the Brooklyn House of Detention to Rikers Island for a short spell of duty. Since public transport to the prison is unreliable, Bruno used his Grand Prix to travel to work. Within a week, his car was fully booked by fellow officers for rides to and from work. His passengers were all women. And it was not long before Bruno was invited by one of them, Katie, "to come party with her."

Around midnight on a Thursday in November 1980, Bruno took Katie to an after-hours club at Nostrand and Maple Avenues in the Flatbush section of Brooklyn. Both were splendidly dressed, and out of uniform or the casual clothes she wore to and from work, Katie was transformed into a slender, amiable woman. She had been to the hairdresser's earlier that day in preparation for tonight, and was full of anticipation. The club was housed in a cleanly scrubbed storefront, whose windows had been tinted a heavy shade of blue. A single young man, dressed in a fresh, dark suit, sat at a table just inside the street door, and nodded pleasantly as visitors moved to an inner door which opened upon a bar. Glowing lanterns were strung along the length of it, shedding a steady but soft light upon rows of tables with red upholstered chairs on one side, and rows of liquor bottles on the other. Beyond the bar area, in a second, very dimly lit room was a dance floor and a DJ's booth. Both rooms were full of elegantly dressed people, and there were many lovely women showing plenty of sheathed legs and exposed bosoms. There was a low roar of excitement, laughter, and sophisticated good times which enveloped Bruno and Katie the moment they walked into the bar. It absorbed and enlivened Bruno at once, bringing the blood to his skin and animating his manner.

Katie took Bruno by the arm and drew him to the bar, where she introduced him to Margaret, a tall, handsome African American woman who owned the club. They chatted brightly for a long time, as Margaret served them complimentary drinks. Margaret had a long-standing job as a personal secretary at a Park Avenue firm, and had an extensive network of similarly placed friends. She had tried for years to organize congenial milieux for them to party and had rented bars and halls or private homes before opening the after-hours club. As she continued to work during the day, she came to the club mainly to relax and mix with the crowd, but since her husband, Corvette Shorty, was at the time in prison for distributing cocaine powder, she was currently doing his job of managing it. She made an expression of annoyance when she mentioned the cocaine charges, and confided that there was still good "blow" on the premises. She exchanged smiles with Katie and moved down the bar to greet a newly entering party.

From a table in the area before the bar, two women had been waving to Katie, over the crowd of people sitting down at tables and getting up, and mouthing her name above the noise of conversation and the music pounding from the rear. Katie and Bruno joined the two, who were together with another woman and two men. The two women were introduced as college classmates of Katie's who worked at a theatrical production company, and the other woman was a coworker; one of the men, in his late forties, was the company's manager, the other man was a lawyer, engaged to Katie's classmate. A waitress took their orders.

When the waitress returned with their drinks, a young man came over and hugged Katie. Everyone except Bruno knew his name, and called out to him to pull up a chair. After he had placed an order with the waitress, he asked Katie for a dollar, which she placed on the table. The young man drew a plastic baggie out of his jacket pocket, and poured from it onto the dollar a portion of cocaine powder. He pushed the dollar before Katie, who scooped up a quantity of the powder in the long nail of her little finger and snorted it. She scooped up another amount for the other nostril, and passed the dollar along to her classmates. They snorted from a bit of straw the lawyer had produced. Their coworker took out of her pocketbook a small bottle and used a tiny spoon that was attached to its lid to scoop up her portions. The men snorted. Meanwhile Katie had tipped a little tobacco out of a cigarette. When the dollar came around to her again, she filled the cigarette with cocaine, pinched it at the top and shook and tapped it, then laying it aside, snorted two fingernails full. She licked her fingernail with the tip of her tongue, lit the cigarette, and inhaled deeply from it.

Katie leaned over to Bruno and asked whether he had ever "done blow." She urged him to try some. Bruno did as he had seen the others do, using the bit of straw that lay on the dollar bill. He felt immediately uplifted. The blast of the powder swept away the fog that the afternoon's beers and tonight's drinks had settled in his brain. He could feel the heat and wildness of the alcohol, but the cocaine had sharpened his perception. The splendid features of the people around him suddenly swept into focus, and he felt powerfully attracted to them. His feelings of well-being and goodwill made him seem to glow. He took more helpings of the powder, and although he continued drinking a lot, he didn't feel in the least bit drunk. To Bruno, a practiced drunkard, this result was very surprising.

His companions at the table were each producing dollar bills, onto which Katie's friend poured quantities of cocaine. He collected $20 bills from them. Angie, the coworker, poured her dollar bill's amount into the small bottle she carried in her pocketbook. Bruno's gaze was riveted on her face and movements. It seemed to him that her beauty was another animal, teemingly alive and embracing her real body. Her black skin shone like diamonds and dazzled him.

Later, when they were dancing closely together at the rear of the club, Bruno told Angie that her mouth bloomed in her face like a giant tropical orchid, and that dewdrops lined the petals. He said her wide eyes led him through paths among tall, noble trees showing expanses of open skies. He spoke with a fluency which surprised him.

Bruno loved Angie for the remaining winter and in the spring and summer of 1981. Angie took so much time off from her job that eventually she lost it. Bruno's job allowed him days off during the week. He spent those in Angie's apartment. He would let himself into her apartment with bottles of liqueurs, brandies, and wine and with eighths [3.5 grams] of cocaine. They would undress and lie on Angie's bed, with the alcohol and cocaine within arm's reach. Snorting the drug stimulated them sexually. They daubed the cocaine powder on sensitive parts of their bodies, and got "freezes" when they applied their tongues there. When they made love, they remained locked together for hours. Although extended over such long periods of time, their lovemaking was continuously innovative, and never boring to either one.

By spending some evenings at after-hours clubs in Brooklyn's growing network of them, Bruno filled his telephone book with the numbers of other snorters, whose homes he and Angie visited to use the drug. In this way they made contacts to distributors who sold cocaine from their apartments, and could be reached at any hour. Eventually, they bought their supply from a single distributor in Brooklyn whose company they enjoyed, and in whose apartment they liked to linger. They had learned to beware of cocaine that had been adulterated too much, and found this distributor's product to be consistently superior in this respect, and reasonably priced. They drove to his apartment two or three times a week and bought eighths for $250. At home, they ground into it as much as two grams of a sugar, sold in healthfood stores by the brand name Inositol. Paraphernalia, such as bottles, miniature scoops, mirrored serving trays, grinders, and precision scales they bought as souvenirs of late-night jaunts in Greenwich Village.

The distributor was a Caribbean African painter and sculptor whose conversation and corpus of work impressed them. He invariably invited them to sit with him, and they would talk as he worked. He would invite them to share from his little glass dish of cocaine powder. In their presence, he often prepared batches of smokable cocaine, or freebase. He would measure out amounts of cocaine and Arm and Hammer baking soda and pour them into a test tube with a little water. Then he cooked the mixture over a Bunsen burner set at a low flame. When a crusty substance frothed up at the top of the water in the test tube, he cooled it by rotating the test tube in a cupful of cold water. A pale white ball was then formed in the test tube. This was fished out with a lancet and cooled until it became hard. The distributor then placed crumbs of it in the bubble stem of a glass water pipe. He heated the bubble with the low flame of a Cub torch, and when he pulled at the mouthpiece, a steady stream of smoke would pass down the stem, through the water and up through the mouthpiece into his mouth. The smoke brought sweat to his brow. He would then work (paint and sculpt) or talk with a ferocious energy.

> Although Angie and Bruno were always invited to smoke freebase by the distributor, they showed no interest in it. Once Bruno tried it, but felt no describable effect. Only toward the end of the summer of 1981 did they become attracted to it, and that curiosity ended their romance. They became more absorbed with freebasing than with each other, and drifted apart.

After-hours clubs, of course, were the just the places which Rastafari marijuana distributors scrupulously avoided. In their biblical worldview, these clubs, with their sex shows, gambling tables, pimps and prostitutes, and clienteles of high spenders, such as (often corrupt) off-duty policemen and corrections officers, were the very "vice-dens of Babylon." The popularity of cocaine, a drug Rastafari initially associated with unbridled sexuality and ill-gotten wealth, had been another deterrent.

In 1981, vast stands of *Erythroxylon coca* which had been planted from 1975 to 1978 in Colombia, Ecuador, Peru, and new areas of Bolivia had matured, and an estimated seventy metric tons of cocaine hydrochloride powder were produced in that year alone (Morales 1989). These Colombian distributors, seeking new markets for the extraordinary amounts of the drug, looked to the Caribbean islands and the United States. Several entrepreneurs, like Pablo in Rasta Musa's story (see below), arrived in Caribbean capitals offering attractive deals to islanders and diffusing also the practice of preparing freebase from "basuca" paste (a less refined product than cocaine hydrochloride powder).

The choice of Caribbean capitals was fortuitous. Marijuana distributors both on the islands and in the United States were then suffering the worst shortages of their preferred product in several years. Word of the availability of cocaine on the islands reached New York through the extensive links it had with the Caribbean. The Rastafari in both places, with the uncomfortable conviction that they were violating cherished religious principles, began to experiment with intranasal use and the distribution of cocaine hydrochloride powder.

EARLY DISTRIBUTORS OF COCAINE HYDROCHLORIDE POWDER IN THE INNER CITY

In New York City's low-income minority communities, there were few Caribbean African or African American distributors of cocaine hydrochloride powder in 1981 who had established selling locations outside the after-hours clubs. Rastafari, however, who disdained such places, sought out the few which existed. As focus shifted more directly upon intranasal cocaine use than upon their other attractions, after-hours clubs were losing their appeal anyway. The rash of storefronts, which Patron recalled on Fulton Street, offered cocaine powder which had been so heavily "cut" (adulterated) that they failed to secure a loyal clientele.

Like the distributors at after-hours clubs, the few existing neighborhood cocaine distributors had modest lifestyles, in which cocaine selling was not the dominant feature, although it may have provided the sole income. They also freebased cocaine in a very restrained fashion and were, therefore, the first cocaine smokers of the epidemic described in this book. As Rastafari and other recent initiates to intranasal use sought them out, however, they were swept from what had been a bywater, as it were, in their community's drug universe, into its mainstream. But their brief steerage there did not last beyond 1982. The case of Tomkin, the Caribbean African artist who had supplied Bruno and Angie, is illustrative:

> Tomkin (age 29): While a student of sculpture and painting at the Parsons School from 1979 to 1980, Tomkin, a Tobagonian who had been residing in New York City since his early teens, was introduced to intranasal cocaine use by fellow students (mostly European Americans) and friends in Greenwich Village, Manhattan. Reputedly discouraged by the white art establishment, he moved to Flatbush. After striking up contact with a Colombian cocaine supplier from the Bronx, he accepted weekly consignments of an ounce of the drug (at $1,800 per ounce) for retail from his apartment. From 1979 to 1980, he managed very well: he reserved some of the cocaine for his personal use, he "cut" the rest, and made at least $2,800 per ounce by reselling it, in half-grams and grams [at $50 and $100 respectively], to his former Village acquaintances and to an increasing number of employed Caribbean migrants (office workers, professionals, nurses, cabdrivers, and a few prostitutes). He thus cleared a weekly profit of at least $1,000. He was able to complete an impressive corpus of paintings and sculptures; and kept up a tireless schedule of social events (parties, concerts, openings at art galleries, video, theater), through which he introduced Brooklynites to Greenwich Village, and his friends there to Brooklyn. A "hot" [stolen] BMW from California, purchased for two ounces of "straight-up" cocaine [unadulterated, and in "rocks" or "chunks" rather than fine powder], was the fast, useful shuttle between Brooklyn and Manhattan.
>
> In 1980, Tomkin was introduced to freebasing by some of his Greenwich Village companions and presently stocked the salesroom in his apartment with a bewildering array of paraphernalia (pipes, stems, mouthpieces, grommets, screens, cooking bottles, lighters and torches, baking soda, rags, Q-tips and other cleaning materials, cleaning alcohol, Bacardi 151). Now, between receiving customers and applying himself to new art projects, he prepared batches of freebase for his personal use, and confined intranasal use to testing his "cut," or to sharing among customers. Although he offered freebase to favored customers, they were mostly uninterested in this method of ingestion, and Tomkin continued freebasing alone and in a very controlled manner.
>
> In 1981, a fresh wave of customers/intranasal users greatly enlivened Tomkin's apartment. These were Rastafari marijuana traffickers who had recently relaxed their religious prohibitions against cocaine. Business in Tomkin's apartment quadrupled,

and the demand outstripped his Colombian supplier's capacity. As a consequence, Tomkin had to bestir himself to find other suppliers. In addition, Tomkin had entered the marijuana traffic sporadically: a Rastafari importer might leave several pounds of marijuana with him as a payment for cocaine, which he then resold to other Rastafari customers. In the company of so many Rastafari, he "locksed up", and his new art projects featured biblical motifs and portraits of Emperor Haile Selassi-I.

Nevertheless, the increased flow of customers, the mingling of marijuana and cocaine monies, and the swelling throng of hangers-on lingering around to share Tomkin's freebase brought an atmosphere of confusion. In the midst of it, Tomkin's personal use of smokable cocaine or freebase skyrocketed.

RASTAFARI EXPERIMENTATION WITH SMOKABLE COCAINE

Having relaxed their religious injunctions against it, Rastafari were delighted by the energy and "peachiness" with which snorting cocaine rewarded them. One very wealthy distributor explained during the marijuana scarcity that the nightlong searches for marijuana to sell left him bone-weary. Producing a foil wrapper containing cocaine hydrochloride powder, he snorted a few lines and declared that the stuff provided him with the energy to overcome his fatigue. An activity which Rastafari marijuana users and distributors enjoyed was to visit nightclubs to listen to concerts given by coreligionists who sang reggae and calypso: Tramps to hear Jah Youth, Bonds International for Burning Spear, Brooklyn College for Peter Tosh, My Father's Place for Steel Pulse, the Beacon Theatre for Dennis Brown, the Renaissance Theatre for Gregory Isaacs, CBGB's for Third World, and SOB's and the Boys and Girls High School and other locales for calypsonians. Musicians were frequently the houseguests of the wealthy distributors. In the informal setting at their homes, the singers confessed that they believed, as Italian singers once did, that cocaine strengthened their vocal muscles.

Thus, Rastafari enjoyed cocaine hydrochloride powder as an aphrodisiac and tonic and, using it, redoubled their efforts in Rastafari and marijuana distribution and in making themselves acceptable in the community. When, however, they wished for a psychoactive drug, or for "I-ditation" (meditation which was their way of getting high), they chose marijuana. Although cocaine hydrochloride powder was then being sold at $1,800 to $2,800 an ounce, they appeared not to mind the heavy expense.

While Rastafari marijuana distributors in New York City experimented with intranasal cocaine use, and were developing dependent chains of supply to an ever-increasing street-level clientele, their cofreres on the islands were taking a further step. They were accepting an introduction to freebasing by the many Colombian cocaine suppliers with whom they had come into regular contact. The same wealthy distributor, returning to his home town in Trinidad, reported:

> *I-man live with the Colombians and dem, and dey have their way of doing business, which is dat dey don't mix cocaine business with pleasure. Business is business and pleasure is after, and dat is the way I feel a lot of the poor people get tie up, they trying to do the two. Because this Gestino, this Colombian fella live with me and my family and everything, and he been smoking [cocaine, or freebase] since he was sixteen, and he smokin' every day, and he is one of the healthiest men I ever see.*
>
> *You see, I-man did know Gestino for a few years since he first started coming to Trinidad, and at first it was the weed [marijuana] he had. He used to arrange to get the weed through to Trinidad and then all the way to New Jersey. But then he started coming in with four or five kilos of cocaine.*
>
> *You see, he don't run down [crave] the cocaine. If he smoking, he don' pack, he have somebody packing for him. When he was living at my house, he use to make me pack for him. You know, parcel out the stuff for him.*
>
> *And when he smokin', he smokin' like a witch doctor. Because same like a witch-doctor does light a candle in a glass, or some of them may drink a whole set of puncheon rum, and then start telling everything [soothsaying], he use it in dat form. He use it to "see" things, to offer advice, to tell you who people are to you, to tell you if you going to lose certain things.*
>
> *Now when he smokin', he would smoke for this whole day or for two whole days and den the third day he don't smoke again, he just drink water or soup and build himself up again. He lets it go for about a week. Then, come again [thinking about it], he says he is a weekend smoker in Bogota in Colombia, and the only time he use to really smoke during the week was with we in Trinidad, because he was more like on a vacation than on business.*
>
> *And den I started to smoke. Well, leh we say he bring in a portion ah cocaine and we selling like four, five kilos. Like from the time he reach, he does say "that is for business." And it have about a half-ah-key [kilo] in bazooka [basuca: a gummy, intermediary form in the isolation of cocaine powder]: well, he does say, "this is for your high [using] people dem and for you to smoke." So out ah dat we use to smoke, and give ounces [of the smokable basuca] to the brethren who pushing off the keys [kilos of cocaine] for us. Because we use to send some to Brooklyn, but a lot use to sell right here in Trinidad, Tobago, and Barbados too. We use to sell $50 piece right here.*
>
> *You see, is in New York that the business really see difficulty. Because the U.S. dollar is what they [the Colombians] really want. So there was a pressure to send it to New York to get the U.S. dollar. Because when we put out TT [Trinidad and Tobago] dollars, we put out more money, like in a lender way, and that is ah work [hardship], you understand. Because the kinda prices you getting the coke for in Trinidad, when you get the U.S. dollar, it come like you doubling and trebling your money when it come back down to Trinidad. So when you spend Trinidad money, it come like you paying double and treble. So that use to kill we. The money was slower in Trinidad too because it look like everybody had two or three kilos in the bush. The islands got stock up with cocaine. It come a time when we was holding 25 or 50 bundles of 100 straws [cocaine was packed for retail in containers made from drinking straws], selling at $20 each, and we couldn't move them.*

When the news (and "pressure") of this recent conversion came up the islands to the marijuana distributors in New York City, they too stepped up their demand for cocaine hydrochloride powder, to be converted to freebase for smoking. Distributors like Tomkin, who were already struggling to cope, were now completely submerged by the droves of customers seeking the drug. Tomkin's story continues:

> By late 1982, Rastafari and the rest of Tomkin's clientele began demanding cocaine hydrochloride powder for conversion to freebase rather than for intranasal use. The change in consuming preference placed a fresh burden upon Tomkin. It meant that more customers were demanding more cocaine per person. Now he was obliged to suffer a large crowd of them to remain in his apartment while he, like a crazed apothecary, cooked up their purchases of powder into freebase. Very often they remained in his apartment to use it, sharing with him as he had shared formerly with them. A bevy of females—including a number of European Americans, presumably from Greenwich Village—settled in permanently.
>
> The period from 1982 to 1984 shot by quickly in a freebase haze. By the end of that time, Tomkin had quarreled with his suppliers and had to rely instead on his former Rastafari customers who were now heavily engaged in the import of cocaine from the Caribbean islands, Panama, and Florida. He quarreled also with customers who could no longer make good their debts. Oftentimes he found himself without product or cash. Finally, in fall 1984, he was unable to pay his rent. Together with three of his former customers, themselves reduced to penury by freebase use, he moved to cheaper lodgings near St. Paul's and Flatbush Avenue. Tomkin now assumed low-return cocaine distribution roles. Unable any longer to receive consignments, he acted as a runner between supplier and customer. He took the money from the latter, and returned from the former with the drug. He could not be trusted with both.

The following account of Rasta Musa's block summarizes the highlights of the marijuana economy and its replacement by cocaine:

> *Rasta Musa's Block*
>
> Musa was thirty-five years of age when he settled in Flatbush in 1981. It was rumored that he was well educated, widely traveled, and had held an important government position in Trinidad, his home country. In New York, he had worked for a number of years at various low-paid, freelance, literate jobs: as contributor to a pornography magazine, as an occasional columnist in a Caribbean magazine, and as a data processor for an advertising firm in Manhattan. Then, in 1976, while working on a reggae music project in Jamaica and New York with a video production company, one of his Euro-American coworkers introduced him to an Euro-American marijuana grower from Oregon. The grower assured Musa that he had hundreds of pounds of the fresh high-grade sinsemilla he had given him to smoke. He offered sinsemilla to Musa at $1,200 a pound, which Musa knew he could sell in Brooklyn for $2,800. He asked the grower to entrust a pound to him and assured him that he would return with the money in about an hour. He returned, paid the grower $1,200 and kept $1,600 for himself. A few weeks later, the grower introduced Musa to several Euro-American suppliers of

Colombian "commercial" [the staple of the booming street-level marijuana traffic, sold for $300 to $500 per pound], who also stocked "exotics"—high-grade marijuanas, hashish, and hash oils from around the world.

(Middling Prosperity)

In this way Musa became established as a mid-level marijuana distributor, who "moved weight" [sold pounds or more] from importers and cultivators to street-level sellers. A few Rastafari blocks [distributing organizations selling marijuana from one or several street-level locations] depended on him to supply them. He sold three to five pounds of sinsemilla a week, making a $300 commission on each pound; and twenty or more pounds of "commercial" marijuana, at a profit of $50 to $100 on the pound. He soon accumulated a substantial fortune, and bought property in relatives' names in Trinidad and California.

(Middle-Age Political and Ideological Development and Commitment to Community)

Musa had been an ardent Rastafari since 1974, and had been among the first Caribbean Africans from other islands than Jamaica to embrace the ideology, and to wear dreadlocks. He had expert knowledge of the Scriptures, and of the writings and worldview of Marcus Mosiah Garvey, a Jamaican Pan-Africanist who had stimulated the spread of Rastafarianism in the 1930s on his home island, and is revered as a prophet of the religion. The Garveyite tenet which Musa heeded most exhorted Africans at home and throughout the diaspora to develop their independent economic institutions. In the 1920s, Garvey had raised subscriptions in the United States of $5 each for the organization he founded, the Universal Negro Improvement Association, and had invested in a shipping company, the Black Star Line, whose ships traded between West Africa, the Caribbean, and the United States. He also founded newspapers, restaurants, and other businesses. In Musa's mind, the nickel bags [small brown envelopes stuffed with about four grams of commercial marijuana and sold for $5] into which his marijuana was packaged by street-level distributors were subscriptions, identical to Garvey's, which he was asking from this generation of Africans.

Adapting Garvey's prescriptions, Musa encouraged midlevel Jamaican distributors like himself to stimulate cultivation in Jamaica. Rural Jamaicans were taught to grow, cure, and export sinsemilla to the United States in quantities sufficient to meet their demand. They were then independent of Euro-American or Hispanic importers of Colombian, Mexican, or Far Eastern product, and of domestic growers. On a smaller scale, Rastafari eventually expanded marijuana production in Trinidad and introduced it to Grenada. Musa was thus an early founder of a movement which eventually "Caribbeanized" a sizable corner of New York's marijuana market.

In New York, Musa reinvested a lot of his marijuana revenues in conformity to Rastafari principles. He helped some coreligionists to establish their own gates [street-level marijuana distributorships]. He gave seed money to others for a health-food store and a vegetarian cookshop, and earned the affection of many Rastafari daughters [young women] for his financial support of their efforts in seamstressing, making Rastafari artifacts, parenting, and education. Many midlevel Rastafari marijuana distributors followed his example.

(Middle-Age Spirituality)

As guaranteed in the Bible, another principal source of Rastafari beliefs and ritual, Musa was recognized for his good works. Personally, he lived an austere and even ascetic life, exercised a lot, and played ball in the park. He lived alone, had no motorcar, dressed casually, and had a modest manner of speaking. His many coreligionists visited his home regularly but briefly. Apparently his affairs with women were respectful and discreet, and in the neighborhood of both gates and residence, he was mostly seen by himself. On Marcus Garvey's birthday, he welcomed guests to a vegetarian feast and an evening of drumming and Rastafari chants. The event became an institution in Rastafari Brooklyn and demonstrated the high esteem in which he was regarded.

(How Interdiction Destroyed the Marijuana Economy and Promoted Cocaine)

When cocaine for intranasal use was introduced to Musa in the late 1970s by a young Puerto Rican marijuana distributor, he refused it and explained that it was contrary to his religious beliefs. In the winter of 1981, however, his attitude changed. Vigorous, street-level interruption of the marijuana traffic by law enforcement agencies, international seizures of large shipments, and successful crop eradication and substitution programs had made marijuana scarce. Musa had been spending a lot of time at a candy store in Harlem, from which nickel bags of commercial and dimes of sinsemilla were sold by a coreligionist, Rafi. He had been using the store as a base for searches for marijuana among Hispanic importers and distributors in upper Manhattan and the Bronx.

Tired and dispirited one night, he was approached by two young Puerto Rican women of mixed African descent who were regular customers at the candy store. Although in the past he had politely ignored their smiles and other signs of favor toward him, this time he stepped out from behind the bulletproofed partition and walked with them out of the store. The young women, sisters named Joanna and Nancy, confessed that they were very attracted by Musa's graying dreadlocks and his kindly manner. They wanted to know him better. They were strangers in the predominantly African American neighborhood, and made their living through discreet prostitution.

Musa accompanied them to their apartment on Adam Clayton Powell Boulevard, and perhaps spurred on by the sisters' genuine friendliness, snorted some of the cocaine they offered him. The drug relieved the anxiety and fatigue which had overcome him. He stayed the night at the sisters'.

Subsequently, Musa was seen often in their company. In Brooklyn, he made enquiries and was soon introduced to a cocaine powder distributor from whom he bought eighths [3.5 grams sold for $275] several times a week. The marijuana traffic showed sudden bursts of activity which provided him with the money. Having be come a cocaine user, he discovered that many of the persons he dealt with in marijuana distribution also used cocaine intranasally. When they visited, mounds of cocaine were shared and exchanged.

(Overcoming Misgivings about Cocaine)

Although the intranasal use of cocaine was becoming more prevalent among Rastafari, they were still distrustful of the practice, which violated their religious beliefs. The first page of the Bible had declared that "Jah had given all herb bearing seed to thee, as thy meat." Marijuana use and distribution (as well as vegetarianism) were therefore divinely justified. But where was the justification for cocaine? Rastafari rationalized that it was a tonic with merely physical effects: it toned up the body, it stimulated and prolonged sex, and it induced wakefulness which marijuana distributors valued in their frustrating recent searches for marijuana. It was an extraordinary food rather than a drug. When "I-man" wanted to "get high" or to "I-ditate" [meditate] or to "speak with the Father," "I-man" still used marijuana.

(Learning to Smoke Cocaine from Colombians in Trinidad)

Musa's doubts about cocaine were removed during a trip he made with Joanna and Nancy to Trinidad early in 1982. Marijuana had been impossible to find in New York, and he had needed a holiday and to attend to business he maintained on the island. Both women traveled with several ounces of cocaine strapped to the insides of their thighs. In Trinidad, they went to Rafi's father's house in Central Trinidad. Rafi, the Rastafari marijuana distributor from Harlem, had also returned home. He had started a very popular reggae discotheque which his father managed.

"Taking coals to Newcastle" is the quaint Anglo-Caribbean phrase Musa used to describe their import of cocaine into Trinidad. Several Colombian distributors were conspicuous in inner-city neighborhoods in Port-of-Spain and San Fernando, Trinidad's largest cities. Each had a few kilos of high-grade cocaine to sell, at prices well below those in New York. Rafi and Musa befriended one in Port-of-Spain and took him home to Central Trinidad.

Rafi's discotheque was a well-known drug distribution locale, and many intranasal users of cocaine in Trinidad, a growing legion, started going there to buy the drug. Pablo the Colombian produced five kilos which were quickly sold. Pablo also taught Musa and Rafi how to smoke freebase. He had brought with him half of a kilo of basuca [cocaine paste preceding crystallization], which he cooked into freebase with baking soda.

Long weeks followed before Pablo's return to Colombia—or Rafi and Musa's to New York City—when the three men, their friends, Joanna, Nancy, and some women from the discotheque, would seek out a shady spot to continue their tutelage in preparing and smoking freebase. Central Trinidad is mostly rural, and there are rice paddies, mango and orange groves, stands of bamboo, sugarcane fields, and country lanes which offered the group many secluded, bucolic settings for the purpose.

Cocaine smoking was unlike any experience Musa had ever had. He said that it seemed "as though his world had been in shadow, and that it had suddenly emerged into brightest day." His senses, thoughts, feelings, and emotions had been transferred in midcourse to another plane, where they moved at a dizzying speed. When he trained himself to be still in the midst of the motion, "a wonderful peace shone from him." He felt that he grew masterful in speech sure in his movements and effused wellbeing.

Freebasing was a curiosity in many other respects. It turned the day upside down. The company awoke late in the afternoon, and after bathing and eating and putting on fresh clothes, sought out that day's retreat. Sometimes they remained under the father's house. Pablo would cook freebase from his store of basuca, inviting them to observe how round and how white the ball of freebase he produced was. He used such equipment as was available, and could even cook in a beer bottle without breaking it. While they smoked, he fashioned pipes from bottles, lengths of glass tubing, and rubber joints. He continued cooking basuca throughout the evening and into the night. If they remained at home, they introduced visitors to the pipes. They talked and joked a lot, and listened to reggae. Toward morning, couples separated themselves and by dawn, had sought out private places for lengthy lovemaking. Then they slept until late afternoon again. This daily schedule absorbed them and differed from any other they had known.

(Colombian–Caribbean Cocaine Connections)

What most encouraged Musa in freebasing was the high regard he had formed for Pablo. This allayed somewhat the religious misgivings Rastafari continued to have about cocaine. He learned, through Joanna and Nancy as interpreters, that Pablo and he were very alike. Like himself, Pablo came from a poor family in which he was the achiever. He had been active in Colombian politics and had been imprisoned for it. Exporting marijuana to Panama had ushered him into an easier life and into a new frame of thinking. What he had done, others could do. He had thus become a leader in his neighborhood, in the same way as Rastafari had done in theirs. When cocaine became plentiful in Colombia, it proved a more lucrative way to augment the community work he had begun.

Musa and Rafi responded positively to Pablo's love of the indigenous. Rafi had brought US$100,000 from New York, and paid Pablo a $10,000 down payment against prompt delivery of several kilos of cocaine. When the shipment arrived, Musa returned to New York City with four kilos strapped as before to Joanna and Nancy. One of his first duties upon returning was to send two "daughters" to Trinidad to pick up more cocaine. Through the use of women or families as couriers, Rafi was able to send frequent shipments of cocaine to New York City until late 1984.

(Development of the New York City Cocaine Market)

Cocaine hydrochloride powder kept arriving from Trinidad regularly at prices several thousand dollars cheaper per kilo than New York's. To sell them, Musa and others to whom Rafi sent supplies worked around the clock. Very quickly, an extensive network of midlevel cocaine distributors who bought several ounces at a time fell into place. Telephones rang constantly. Buyers drove up from Washington and Maryland who were willing to double the local prices.

(Freebase Parlors)

Musa's New York apartment was transformed into a freebase parlor as he sought customers for smaller quantities (half a gram sold for $50) of cocaine—or as they crowded to his door. He converted many Rastafari to cocaine smoking, and through Joanna and Nancy, attracted a sizable Hispanic clientele for the first time in his drug distribution career. The scene was greatly enlivened by the arrival of a succession of entertainers and singers from the Caribbean, who had musical bookings in America and Canada. Many were freebasers and claimed, like the Italian tenors of the early 1900s, that cocaine strengthened their vocal cords. With them came throngs of women admirers, well-wishers, musicians, and agents in the entertainment and recording businesses. Last of all, Musa admitted several African Americans who lived in his apartment building or in the neighborhood. A street-level clientele who bought nickels and dimes, they had never suspected that he sold marijuana or other drugs.

(How Cocaine Smoking Unraveled Fortune, Morality, and Politics)

In the dense crowd at his apartment, and in the midst of continuous smoking and attending to business, it was a while before Musa realized that for him, a generous person, the cost of freebasing was prohibitively high. Personal use and gifts to his company sharply reduced his cocaine profits, and he had depleted previous marijuana savings to make payments to Rafi. But he felt compelled to smoke freebase himself, and when there was company, he was obliged to share it. He and others were puzzled by this compulsion. At first, they felt that it was caused by careless preparation of the drug or its improper ingestion. They experimented with a variety of techniques—constructing pipes, measuring out exact amounts of the drug and baking soda, altering the cooking process, finding new heat sources, controlling their breaths—but to no avail. The compulsion to prepare and smoke freebase remained, and continued to siphon off substantial business profits.

By this time, Musa had a number of sexual partners. In addition to Joanne and Nancy, there were several African American women from the neighborhood who spent the better part of a day at his apartment. When he tried to introduce controls on the amount of cocaine he gave away, they quarreled. Since they spent all their money buying cocaine from Musa and were providing him with sexual services, they felt entitled to more freebase. In the end, he always donated it. One of his company discovered a passage in Revelation which read: "I know thy works, and where thou dwellest, even where Satan's seat is. To him that overcometh will I give to eat of the hidden manna, and will give him a white stone, and in the stone a new name written, which no man knoweth saving he that receiveth it." Musa concluded that cocaine and freebase were indeed divine. The "new name" referred to a new discipline. The drugs posed a test, by which the weak were weeded out, and the strong prepared to prevail in the future Armageddon. Musa felt that he was failing the test. "Many shall be called, but few are chosen."

(Escape to Ethiopia [Africa])

In 1983, Rafi discontinued supplies of cocaine to several coreligionists in New York City who could not pay for consignments. Musa was one. To find cocaine to support his own need and for business, he was obliged to network among distributors for whom he had been formerly a major supplier. Many were receiving their own bulk shipments from the Caribbean or Florida. Personal use, however, prevented Musa from making any profits. Convinced that he had been a false prophet in advocating the use and distribution of cocaine, especially smokable cocaine, Musa tidied up what remained of his business interests in early 1984 and flew to Central Africa, where he works on a farm managed by a Rastafari colleague, another former marijuana distributor from New York City.

THE PERSISTENCE OF THE GANJA COMPLEX

Throughout the 1980s, the "cocaine-smoking epidemic" rapidly overtook major cities in the United States and the several islands and territories of the Caribbean region. At the end of the decade, as its use declined in those areas, it thrusted into rural America, Western and Eastern Europe, Africa, and the Far East. In contrast to the previous decade of marijuana ascendancy, which was a period of capital accumulation, building up, not only cash reserves and property but neighborhoods, persons, their relationships and associations, moralities, ambitions, and outlooks, cocaine smoking was one of capital depletion, in which all were "emptied out" (Hamid 1992, 1998).

Despite the decline of the marijuana traffic in the 1980s, however, the ganja complex has remained as the interface through which individuals continue to learn of marijuana and to experience it. After the cocaine economy and cocaine-smoking epidemic had wreaked havoc during the 1980s, young residents stopped the destruction by eschewing cocaine and heroin use, returning to "blunts" of marijuana. At the same time, Rastafari orthodoxy, strained during the cocaine era, has also returned with a new crop of young religionists and reggae musicians.

NOTES

1. Lempert has identified the preconditions of decriminalization as emanating from the "moral dissonance" that occurs when deviant law-violating behavior is identified in an actor simultaneously possessing both high social status and low moral status. This "moral dissonance" induces pressure for decriminalization. However, while in this instance the reforms of the 1970s resulted in eleven states reducing criminal penalties for possession of small amounts of marijuana, some prominent criminologists got carried away in predicting that "In the next 10 years marijuana will be virtually decriminalized in this country" and were even confident that heroin and cocaine would be made legal in some states.

Chapter 7

The Ganja Complex versus Other Marijuana Use-Complexes: Ganja versus Madi-juana

The anthropological research reported in this book aimed to contribute to the scientific understanding of the effects of marijuana on human beings. Accordingly, it documented the impacts the drug has had on Caribbean Africans on the Caribbean islands of Trinidad and Tobago and in the Caribbean communities of Brooklyn and Manhattan in New York City. The investigation of patterns of drug distribution, use, and misuse in these populations is of great value. Although they are under researched and under served populations, they provide insights into unique person–drug interactions which substantially enhance the cross-cultural record on the drug in question. While illuminating important issues such as initiation, patterns of consumption, differentiation of specific effects, modes of administration, drug switching, careers in distribution, income generation, expenditure on drugs, the redistribution of revenues, and public opinion, this book has encapsulated the use and distribution of marijuana within a broader political economy.

This research touched upon several of the questions which had preoccupied Americans in the 1960s about marijuana. Just as in the United States, marijuana use in Trinidad in that decade signified youth rebellion, a provocative countercultural life—style, hedonism, radicalism, permissiveness, critical attitudes to authority, issues of law and order, the generation gap, intercultural conflict, and a general concern for the place of drugs in society and individual lives (Kaplan 1969). Comparing how these points of intersection of the drug with major developmental and sociocultural issues were differentially configured or resolved in the United States and in the postcolonial setting of Trinidad and Tobago illuminates how drugs function in political and symbolic discourses.

Two patterns of marijuana use were identified among the Trinidadian users encountered in this book. The first, or the ganja complex, which blossomed stafari or Rastafari-influenced use of marijuana, formed the topic of ıng chapters. The second use pattern, derided by one Rastafari block ; below) as "'madi'-juana use," will be described in this chapter, which seeks to summarize and explain the differences between the two.

MADI-JUANA VERSUS GANJA

Research on marijuana has concluded either that the drug is relatively harmless or that it is a "deceptive weed," behind the mildness of which lurk multiple serious hazards to physical health and psychosocial well-being. Drugs, however, have a Janus face and the potential both for great good and great harm. In this, they are no different from the host of human gratifications.

When smoked, marijuana produces a state of intoxication for two to four hours; when eaten or drunk, the effects last for up to twelve hours. Psychological set and social setting determine how the intoxication is experienced (Zinberg 1984), but the main common effects are feelings of euphoria and exhilaration, with heightened sensitivity to sights, sounds, and touch. Since it somewhat delays reaction time, reduces short-term memory, and impairs attention and coordination for several hours after use, marijuana use can be dangerous in some workplaces. The main physiological effects are increased appetite, accelerated heartbeat and pulse rate, and slightly bloodshot eyes; but a toxic delirium may be induced at very high dosages, in which the user may experience confusion, agitation, disorientation, loss of coordination, and hallucinations. Anxiety and feelings of paranoia may also afflict inexperienced users (Grinspoon and Bakalar 1985).

Researchers who are not convinced that marijuana is a more or less benign drug, which is never lethal and seldom a personal or social problem, have reported that its long-term use causes a cannabis psychosis, characterized by chronic confusion and disordered thinking. Long-term users are also thought to be amotivational and to suffer chromosomal damage, reduced production of sperm and testosterone, and psychological dependency on the drug. Finally, marijuana users are also prone to escalate their drug usage and to try out "harder" drugs. In the main, these findings have been based on laboratory and clinical studies.

Ethnographic research has been a useful corrective to these studies, which frequently employ captive animal and human study populations and investigate the effects of unusually large dosages in artificial, often hostile settings. Following the pioneering work in Jamaica, in which heavy marijuana smokers were observed in their everyday, natural settings (Rubin and Comitas 1969), ethnographic research has been undertaken in Costa Rica (1980) and

Greece (1983). Work in the same anthropological tradition in Trinidad and Tobago is reported in this book. Ethnographic research demonstrates amply how marijuana use may be integrated uneventfully in the round of a normal (i.e., nonpathological) life.

An arresting proof of the benignity of ganja is provided by a recent ethnographic study which compares the educational outcomes of the children of Rastafari women in Jamaica, who were prenatally exposed to marijuana (the oldest having been subsequently initiated into personal use through teas and eventually smoking), with those of a nonexposed control group of children of abstainers. The Rastafari children not only exceeded the school performances and test scores of abstainers' children, but displayed intelligence and proficiency which were outstanding in their age grades altogether.

In the research reported in this book, the effects on human behavior of even chronic, heavy use of marijuana (when users smoke five to ten joints, or up to fourteen grams, daily for several years) have been found to be demonstrably benign. Permission to assay the THC (delta-9 tetrahydrocannabinol) content of marijuana locally available in the study sites was not sought, but knowledgeable and well-traveled users say that it compares well with the best available anywhere. An examination of more than 300 case histories collected in the various stages of fieldwork in the Caribbean and New York City, of the tape-recorded interviews of several of the study participants, and of field notes reporting multiple interactions with them has not revealed evidence of any physical or psychological ill effects directly attributable to marijuana which can be grossly detected. Long-term damage to the lungs, chromosomes, or brain was not clinically tested; but study participants have continued to produce children, and appear to lead healthy, vigorous, responsible lives. There was abundant evidence instead of a very positive personality change, or of significant cognitive and normative reorientation, occurring in an influential part of the using population, which the affected persons credited to the therapeutic and educational properties of the "wisdom weed." In the rest of the using population, marijuana is smoked without such an expectation of dramatic self-transformation.

When marijuana was introduced in San Fernando, Trinidad, paranoid and disassociative effects were experienced by some of its earliest users. Brought to medical attention at the San Fernando General Hospital, they were treated with antidepressants such as the phenothiazines. A function of the early using groups was to screen out persons (for example, epileptics or those with a history of psychiatric problems) who were more likely to experience those effects. In chapter 3, the Jaguar reports the bout of "laughing and carrying on" which had followed his trial attempts at becoming a marijuana user. Eventually, however, two distinct bodies of effects, or use-complexes, were differentiated among marijuana smokers. Observing this outcome, the Rastafari and their sympathizers claimed that, while they used ganja or "I-cient herbs," non-Rastafari smoked marijuana, or even "madi-juana." A block leader remarked:

> *If you call it marijuana, you could get lock up. Dah is how definitions does ha' . . . vocabulary does ha' . . . You see how words is really terrible! Is a very important thing to study. Words ha' a form of pollution in it and thing you hear thundering and beating this man mind, it ha' to unfold.*
>
> *What, marijuana? Dat ain't marijuana, dat is herbs, I-cient herbs. Dem [non-Rastafari] does smoke marijuana—"madi-juana": dat does make dem mad and make dem go off [do unconscionable acts]. "Madi-ijuana!" All [the only thing] dem Rasta does smoke is herbs. You see, dem [non-Rastafari] believe in smoking dat: madi-juana. But de good "kalli" [Hindi word used in Jamaica for "flowering bud"], Rasta smoking dat, I-cient herbs. With de seed. You want to see de One with itself within itself, with itself is itself, that is One? Just as how de man is, right? Self within self, and de self is de self. Well, dat is what de man does use. Not madi-juana.*
>
> *To go and pick pocket and chap people. Dah is madi-juana work: get mad vibes [ideation].*

At the same time, non-Rastafari users or those not impressed by the Rastafari ideology, especially in those privileged classes most removed from the low-income milieu of San Fernando's inner-city and workers' suburbs, attribute the same "mad vibes" to the Rastafari themselves, allowing that, when misused, marijuana may prompt wrongful thought and action. Of their own use, however, they have no ill effects to report.

The distinction between ganja and madi-juana, however, is a substantial one, the extremes of which are recognized also by the local marijuana traffic. For example, Caribbean European San Fernandians, or the population farthest removed from the low-income context of use in the city, are served by two blocks or selling organizations exclusively. These two blocks are the only ones of the 110 identified in San Fernando which are not operated by Rastafari. The first is operated by an Indian husband and wife team, who have prospered handsomely from the exclusive, well-to-do clientele. Showing similar signs of prosperity, the other is also operated by Indians. Although three associates are Rastafari (although of Indian parentage, they identify themselves as Rastafari and are so regarded by San Fernandians), the leader and two others are not.

At the extremes of the difference, therefore, ganja is sold separately from madi-juana.

What are the differences between madi-juana use and ganja use?

Madi-juana Use: A madi-juana user uses the substance either as other working class/unemployed users (five to ten or more joints a day); or else, especially in the case of most middle-class users, occasionally, on weekends and at parties. Whether use is daily or occasional, heavy or slight, however, the feature which marks madi-juana use is its occurrence in a pattern which often includes the use of other drugs: alcohol, mandrax, LSD and (especially in the case of middle-class users) cocaine, mescaline, and whatever else is available. Also, madi-juana use does not oblige users to exclude cigarettes and meat (or other foodstuffs proscribed by Rastafari) from their diets.

Madi-juana users do not have excessive views about their experiences with it. Unlike Rastafari, who reserve honorific names for the substance (I-cient herbs, ganja, kalli, kaya), they call it by any of these names, as well as pot, grass, weed, dope, shit or drugs with utter lack of discrimination.

One madi-juana user, a young man of thirty-two who is forever nattily dressed, heir to the real estate fortune of an ex-government minister, himself very comfortably ensconsed in government employment, a man of impeccable manners and generous ways, smokes marijuana and drinks whiskey daily, both to excess. Usually, he "tamps" (completes and moderates) the smoke with a drink.

The young man claims that he is unable to distinguish between the effects of alcohol and marijuana. He feels the latter gives more of a "head trip," and enjoys the drugs best while quietly listening to music. Possessing also a restless sexual appetite, he believes that in this matter, alcohol had more "zes" (gusto). He didn't like to make love while he "had his head" (was high) from a "hit" (smoking marijuana), but he liked it a lot when he was just "coming off de head" (the effects of marijuana were wearing off somewhat).

An Indian oil refinery laboratory tester at Texaco, offered the following account:

(Extent of Use)

Every day I does smoke . . . is hard to check. . . . Today, I done smoke 4 . . . 5 . . . 6 . . . I done smoke 7 joints. I smoke 4 by myself, and 3 with friends. And den I go smoke about 3 more before tonight.

Well, I could smoke about 10–15 joints a day, you know. And I never been in de trade, eh. So all of dat I does buy. So sometimes I does put out $14 a day. Dat is why I was telling Vim [a Rastafari distributor: see chapter 3] to give me 3 for $2. If I come with $5, I want 8 or 9 joints, or I want a little piece [4 or more grams of loose ganja, not rolled into joints], you know. Dat is a normal arrangement, but is still costly.

(Expenses and Social Context of Buying Madi-juana)

I figure in a week I does spend . . . say on average about $8 a day. Seven days a week: about $240 a month. Good ting mih wife don't really know I does smoke: ah suppose to stop smokin' by now, right? She ain't know dat I still carryin' on. But look, *me ain't never suffer no ill effect. I wukin', I married, I lookin' after mih wife and children.*

So is roughly $170 a month really I does buy. And mostly I does buy right here in de neighborhood, unless I outside. Say I outside and need something . . . well, I will know where to go look and I will get someting.

Dah is someting, eh? With de ganja, as a Indian, I find I could communicate plenty with the opposite race—dah is de Negro [Caribbean African] race. You find before you couldn't find dat. It still have someting remain, you know [reference to rivalry between East Indian and Caribbean African politicians in the period of nationalist struggle, 1955–1961]: some people still very racial. Especially on de job. At Texaco . . . leh we say I smokin', right? Leh we say dey [Caribbean African workers] smokin' too, right? Well, I does smoke very hard too, right? You find when dey come and dey sit dong and dey smoke, you communicate better with dem. But otherwise, some ah dem does stay racial. Myself, I don't see nothin' racial, you know. Neither black nor white: just people.

Mostly, I don' score in de ghetto though. I does go by Vim, by Mody, by a Negro [African] fella—well, he and I growin' up together, you know—he push someting too. So I don' go much in de city. I use to go dong to de ghetto in Roy Joseph Scheme and dey use to treat me good. Sit dong, talk, smoke with dem. Laugh and ting. At dat time, dey wasn't on no Rasta scene or nuttin'. Dat have to be about four years ago [1974].

So is really less dan $200 I does spend a month. Because sometimes I does go by de pusherman early in de morning, you know, and he does run [gives away] three or four joints. I might buy one. Den I might buy two. But on average most ah de times, is about $5–$6 a day. Den again you ha' friends: friends does have weed to smoke, so is no problem. De weed does pass around . . .

A time [once] I went to a party and mih brother run [gave] me a smoke. Dah is the start: when I was about 18. I 26 now. I started to smoke marijuana at de wrong time, I would say. I started to smoke dis week, leh we say: and de same week come and I get a job at Pointe-à-Pierre [site of Texaco Oil Refinery, about ten miles from the San Fernando city center]. So den I didn't have to look for money anywhere to buy it: money always dere, after I get turn on to it more and more and more. And it goin' in eight years now I smokin'. From November '70. Dah is a salary ah $590 a week, plus cost of livin', shift bonus: everyting come up to $630 a week before tax. I does live at home; same house with my parents but downstairs. So dat is a help.

(Comparing the Effects of Marijuana and Alcohol)

Now de first time I try it, I like de feelin's. You know. Now, I never had what you call hallucinations, eh. Never happen! Once it happen but dah is because I wake out whole night and I get up in de mornin' and I start to smoke. De sun was too hot and . . . but I never freak out or nuttin'. I just like de feelin'. Now I feel is even de habit more dan anyting. That is all.

For me to get a real good feelin', I ha' to stop smokin' for a day, or a day and a half. And den go and look . . . you see de piece ah weed Vim ha' now? Go and look for someting like dat to smoke. Just smoke, smoke, smoke. But when sayin' so, me ain't ha' no plans to stop smokin,' eh.

I prefer to stop drinkin'. I drink plenty. I been drinkin' since two years before I leave school, when I was sixteen. I come to realize I cyant do de two things at de same time, and if push come to shove [if I am forced to decide], booze goin' to ha' to go. Day and night I does be drinkin', you know. Because with shiftwork, I does be out all de time. Say when ah lime of about seven friends get together, is about six cases ah beers we does drink. Dah is six by twenty-four [144 12-ounce bottles]. Now dis wasn't one day, you know. Dis was regular, everyday. Sometimes three of us does sit dong and drink a bottle [26 ounces] of rum . . . by the end of de day, when everybody done pass [has stopped to visit and drink], we drink six bottles. And dah is among de whole lime, about 10 of us.

Well look, I did some heavy drinkin' dis week gone here. Saturday, six to eight men drink four [26 ounce] bottles—four and a half bottles of Johnnie Walker Black in de mornin'. Den we come and we smoke about an ounce [of marijuana]. Went back in de night and drink about half [bottle] a Johnnie Walker Black again. Dah was Saturday. Sunday mornin', we went by de—dong Esperanza dey [a nearby village]: six ah we drink a bottle ah Johnnie Walker Black and four bottles of Buchanan's [an imported Scotch whiskey]. Mody freak out. He drive de car home from de inn [a bar], he reach de house, take off he shirt, come in de gallery, sit dong, just bend over he head and start to vomit and dah is it. Drop asleep right dey.

Now if you see I workin' on a alcohol head [affected by alcohol], you find I go break up de apparatus. Ah go drop it dong too hard. All dese kind a tings. Ah walkin': de flask might bounce [hit against] de desk and break because you walkin' careless and ting. But de marijuana effects does be different. You could concentrate on what you doin' and even like doin' it sometimes.

De ganja does make your head race [stimulate mental activity]. But mos' ah de time I don't be followin' dat. Most ah de time we sittin' dong smokin', playin' cards, playin' pool, cookin' some kind a ting . . . you know. Nothing really constructive, right. Just havin' a good time. Dah is what does be going on with de lime dat I does be limin' in. I, my brother, Mody, he three brothers, Tax—well dis guy from Canada here on holidays, so he ain't really in dat: about nine of us. But every man workin' for pieces [good money]. Mody married, but he get a divorce last September. Den three ah de fellas married too, and ha' children, I married, ha' a child, and expectin'another one nex' month.

(A Result of Combined Alcohol and Madi-juana Misuse?)

We ha' about four cars between we. I sell mine. I had an accident with a man who die a week after. De matter still pendin', so I ain't want to play fast and go and buy a car and lorse my license. Dah was mih father car you see me drivin' today. We ain't really know whether de man death have to do with de accident, because he didn't want to press charges de night: is was he fault. He had no injuries other dan a bruise on he head: he couldn't walk though, was me who carry him to de hospital. And den he died a week after, I don't know how. So I waitin' to see what happen.

Ah liable to get seven years for manslaughter. Accident—man dead within a year: dey could charge me for manslaughter. Is for de coroner to decide.

(Madi-juana, Religion, and Diet)

In some ah dem Indian prayers [Hindu prayer meetings or religious ceremonies] dey does use ganja in a drink too: you know when dey give you a little drink? Get a nice feelin'? No, I is of Muslim origin really. But I believe in God, eh. I gone to Presbyterian, Open Bible, Seven Days Adventist.

I attend all dese churches. I went to Seven Days Adventists de mos'; but I never get baptize. De Open Bible and Seven Days. You know, is a mixed congregation: Indians and Negros [Caribbean Africans]. Same with pastors: Indians and Negros. But de Presbyterian is mostly Indian. I was brought up in de Open Bible Church. Never use to cook from sundown Friday to sundown Saturday. Just sit dong, cool yourself whole day, read de Bible. De majority of the family is Presbyterian: two sisters turn Hindus. Dey don't eat no meat period. Me, I could sit dong and eat meat alone whole day. I love meat. De ganja ain't stop dat. I does eat everyting. Only I don't go off too much on pork. Brought up so [Muslim taboo against pork] . . . never use to go heavy on de pork. Brought up so . . . so I stay away from dat a little bit. But I like everyting: fish, meat.

I start smokin' ganja when everybody start. Around '70. All ah we up here who limin' today, we together from den. But through de ganja, I get to know plenty people. Mostly Negros [Caribbean Africans]. De majority. And dah was a good experience: nobody don't treat you in a violent or racial way or nuttin'. Dey always move with love towards you. I really find dat so. A lot of Rastas move good with we, talk good with we, treat we alright. Not so deep conversation: some ah dem not so deep in dey Rastafari, dey just sportin' locks and pushin' de weed, you know. So dey don't ha' no deep talk with dem, dey really not on dat. But dey ain't on no criminal scene or nuttin.'

All ah we up here does smoke and drink, is why we lime together. You find you ha' some fellas who don't do neither, so we don't lime with dem. Den dey have dose who gettin' off on alcohol. And den deh have dose who only limin' with you if you smokin'.

The foregoing account marks off the main features of madi-juana or non-Rastafari usage: marijuana together with alcohol and other substances, consumed in private recreational circles (limes), without the expectation of any significant life- or consciousness-altering effects. Madi-juana smokers belong to conventional churches and share the conventional outlook on life. Although Rastafari find these uses of marijuana objectionable, regarding them as typical of Babylon, or more domestically, of the derivative culture of Trinidad's moneyed classes, it is clear that workers and other unemployed persons enjoy marijuana in this manner.

The effects of madi-juana are described as mild and benign and, according to this informant, far preferable to those of alcohol. It increases various appetites; and of the two stimulants, it is the one which induces greater sociability, peacefulness, and satisfaction. Cerebral stimulation is seldom reported by madi-juana users: they feel drowsy instead.

Ganja Use

The Rastafarian experience of ganja or I-cient herbs, has been explored more fully in the preceding chapters. Identified as a natural substance, it had inspired confidence in items similarly identified—fruits, vegetables, nature cures, and the "natural self"—leaving hostility toward "artificial" things such as alcohol, other drugs, and the wide spectrum of "vanity"—

personas to whom meat eating, pharmaceuticals, medical science, and money attach themselves. Among Rastafari, ganja use is expected to increase thoughtfulness, creativity, and positive motivations and is credited with the rehabilitation of wasted lives. Rastafari regarded ganja as one of the sacred pillars of their religion.

Matos, a leading Rastafari block leader who was introduced in chapter 3, said in summary:

> *De herbs is really for man I-ditation [meditation, communings with self]. It come like if one's I-ditation is in wickedness, and one use de herb, he and all [even he] could further he meditation too. But I and I [Rastafari] a-deal with goodness. When I and I use de herb, it does put I and I on a higher I-ditation ah goodness. I-man a-deal with de Father, and I-man use de herb to reach to a higher plane to vibes [be in communion with] de Father. Because it real corrupted in dis here time.*
>
> *Well den, de herb does help I to stand more firm [uncorrupted]."*

Explaining the Differences between Madi-juana and Ganja

A puzzle generated by this research, therefore, is the contrast between the two different sets of effects. Ethnicity is only a rough marker between the two, and indeed, it should be noted that similar contrasts in the use of cocaine and of other psychoactive substances in other cultures are reported.

For example, many indigenous Mexican peoples (Huichol, Tarahumara) distinguish between "good" or "bad" peyote (*tsuwiri* versus *hikuri*) or mushrooms, although identical substances are used (Myerhoff 1974; Furst 1986). When peyote is collected and consumed according to traditional regulations, it has benign effects; otherwise it induces psychosis. In explaining the differences between Rastafari use and non-Rastafari use of marijuana, or the contrasts in other cultures, the agency of purely psychopharmacological factors is obviously muted. Drugs identical in form, dosage, and potency are administered to the same human stock, but with strikingly dissimilar results. Thus, the sociopolitical identities of the users, and the social and economic circumstances in which the drug was used, assume prominence.

Becker, for example, dismissing studies which purport to show cannabis-related brain damage or chromosome damage, has argued:

> Sociologists are unlikely to accept such an a-social and uni-casual explanation of any form of complex behavior, whatever the findings of pharmacologists and others. . . .
>
> What interests the social scientist is the problem of the drug-induced experience, taken in its own right. This interest reveals the following facts: (a) that "drugs" are accompanied by a wide variety of effects, only one or few of which the user may choose to experience. Thus the same drug may induce different experiences

in different populations. And, (b) to say that users are seeking experiences not ordinarily available to them, is to say they will choose effects which are unconventional, or deviant; e.g. distortions in space and time, shifts in judgements of the importance and meaning of ordinary events (Becker 1963).

Becker contends that "how a person experiences the effects of a drug greatly depends upon the way others define those effects for him." In other words, the "drug experience" and associated behaviors are intelligible only in an interactionist framework: that is, in a sociological framework as opposed to a biochemical one. Citing Mead, he writes:

> Objects have meaning for the person only as he imputes that meaning to them in the course of his interaction with them. The meaning is not given in the object, but is lodged there as the person acquires a conception of the kind of action that can be taken with, by, toward, and for it. Meaning arises in the course of social interaction, deriving their character from the consensus participants develop about the object in question. (Becker 1963).

For example, "unconventional and deviant" effects of marijuana a limer in San Fernando might have chosen in the 1970s could have included reasonably: "love and togetherness" and "cool"—especially in the face of mounting public and police antagonism, or in a context in which violent "bad john" behavior and unemployment aggravated the responsibilities of increasing age; and "constructive" ideation—or practical means of escaping poverty and self-defeating despair; and a foundation upon which renewed, invigorated personalities might grow. Of course, these have been the very effects which marijuana, in the context of the ganja complex, was reported and observed to have had over the twenty-year (1965 to 1985) period upon many Caribbean users.

Becker's arguments and the field evidence in this book, which adds to his perspective the economic factor of buying and selling which pervades contemporary drug phenomena, imply that marijuana (or drugs) derives symbolic energies from the social milieu in which it was used; and that it was as such a symbol that it had any important effects upon human behavior. Thus marijuana is a cultural good; and ganja, as consumed at least by the core users—unemployed limers turned Rastafari block leaders and Rastafari brethren—was different from the substance (madi-juana) which drives users insane, sends them to sleep, renders them "amotivational," encourages partying and scandal, or causes "psychomotor impairment," flawed judgment, reckless or violent behavior, lowering of body temperature and respiratory depression, apathy and mental slowing, impaired memory and learning (brain damage) and impaired immune response.

Among unemployed San Fernandians, marijuana was the social rearrangement occurring among them—a historical process, described in chapters 1 and *2*—turned into a kind of coin, as it were, which could be passed around in such a way as to define more clearly and expedite these ongoing processes of social rearrangement. Marijuana was a kind of movable storehouse containing these social energies; in this respect, it functioned exactly like money or any other medium of exchange: cowrie shells (Bohannon 1953), kula objects (Malinowski 1939), or cattle (Evans-Pritchard 1943) among many others. Indeed, the descriptions offered by anthropologists of the fascination commonplace objects exert over persons who symbolize with them resemble addicts' descriptions of their favorite drugs.

If marijuana was a cultural good, a produced or manufactured value, then it was the social identity of San Fernandian youth which is the chief instrument in its production. In this view, Rastafari (see chapter 4) represented the accumulation of fixed capital: the religion served as a form of reinvestment of surpluses necessary for improving production, product, and demand. The ritual consumption of its own marijuana on a block concretely reproduced block members as producers of marijuana.

This view of marijuana, as a value created by economic activity on the city blocks (see chapter 3), opened up a fresh perspective on the marijuana economic system, which relates its peculiar functioning, the uniqueness of the forms of social organization required to sell it, and the unique Rastafari development concurrent with it within a single conceptual framework, which is the political economy of drugs.

Chapter 8

The Informal Economy

In this research, ganja was smoked because "it keeps me cool," "it brings togetherness," "it makes me think constructive," and "it makes me see the light." These were properties the substance did not possess before 1968. Before that date, it was called "marijuana" by those of the island's citizens who had heard of it and had the same sinister reputation which films like *Reefer Madness* depicted. By contrast, redolent of antiquity as well as reflecting the complexities of contemporay neocolonialism, ganja revives the ancient Asian ganja complex, adapting it to urgent present-day needs.

Thus, the contemporary ganja acquired its specific beneficial properties from an act of production; and the chief instrument in this productive activity was a social identity. Elements of this social identity were being young, urban, African, unemployed, and marginalized. Such a person could buy a raw vegetable material of variable quality from its growers, if he had the money; and by virtue of *his* possession of it, by virtue of the kind of drama he staged by incorporating it, created a consumer commodity, a cultural good with widely acclaimed educational and therapeutic effects.

This method of production of ganja had become more efficient over the years since 1968, and the quality and reliability of effects of ganja thus produced had improved proportionately, attracting a greater and more varied clientele. These cultural/economic activities had therefore become self-sufficient and self-perpetuating.

The term "mode of production" describes an economic system which is thus able to reproduce itself. In defining "the capitalist mode of production," for example, Karl Marx specified a peculiar system of production, circulation, distribution, consumption, and exchange. He then identified unique forms of social relationships, in this case property relations, which allow the system to function in its peculiar way and then speculated upon the role of political and intellectual life generally, in reproducing the mode of production.

Similarly, the system of production, circulation, distribution, consumption, and exchange which uses ganja as the medium of exchange performs uniquely. The term "precapitalist" is used to capture this unique quality. It encompasses those features which distinguished this system from the mainstream capitalist economy, but suggests the possibility of movement from "precapitalist" to "capitalist," as well as the mutual antagonism between the two systems.

The unique functioning of this economic system was determined by the social relationships of production—involving the block, cultivators, the police—and their continuing evolution in Trinidad's social history. These same social relationships were the key features which distinguished the ganja mode of production from its capitalist counterpart. In this view, Rastafari supplied the "hearts and minds" which operated this peculiar economy.

DISTINGUISHING FEATURES OF THE GANJA MODE OF PRODUCTION

An economic system is distinctive in the way labor is extorted and utilized, and in the way accumulated labor surpluses—or capital—accrues to the controllers of labor and is redistributed by them. In the capitalist or money system, for example, labor is extorted from laborers by appeal to the ideology of the wage. The wage, being the only contract between exploiters of labor and laborers, renders both "free." Tied to one another neither by bonds of personal dependence or fealty nor by the imperatives of a subsistence economy, laborers are "free" to sell their labor to the highest bidder; while the exploiters of labor are free to combine labor and capital in any enterprise, so long as it is the most lucrative. The wage is "freely" and "competitively" negotiated. Thus increments in both freedom and competition are continuously essential, if productivity in this system is to be raised. Many institutions of private and public life in capitalist systems serve to fulfill this condition. Social-productive relations are stamped by ideologies of "freedom" and "competition": laborer competes against laborer, exploiter against exploiter, one class against the other, each thus savoring its "freedom." Capital accumulation in the capitalist system has taken place so calculably that, in its developed forms, the distinction between capital and labor becomes useless both in theory and on the ground.

Feudal society offers an example of yet another kind of mode of production. The exploitation of labor was justified by kinship arrangements, the exchange of military services, and appeals to loyalties of place, religion, language, and custom. Accumulated surplus labor was rendered in kind; the exploiter had rights to a portion of land, or to its produce, or to a fixed number of laborhours in traditional enterprises.

If productivity is to be increased in such a system, the exploiters of labor must aggress against the direct producer or laborer in annexing a greater portion of land or produce or must violate custom, in demanding longer hours or greater effort. The exploiters of labor in this system, unfree to increase productivity without naked aggression, unfree to disengage labor from subsistence activity on ancestral land, are also unfree with respect to accumulated labor, or capital.

The ganja mode of production in Trinidad during this research more resembled the feudal or precapitalist mode, which predates and antecedes it, than the capitalist economy. While the Rastafari block leader (artfully dressed up in "Ethiopian raiment" and appearing as an ancient trader rather than as a modern businessman) had to buy and sell in order to produce values, he entered into unique social-productive relations. In the ganja mode of production, for example, labor was also unfree. It was mobilized and exploited by appeal to religiopolitical sentiments. Associates typically received ganja, clothes, shelter, "I-tal" food, religious and cultural instruction, and generous cash gifts in recompense for their labor. At the same time, the latter was underutilized and geared only toward self-sufficiency. Capital was consequently unfree: it was absorbed, so to speak, in reproducing the social-productive relations which created it, and the latter also determined the distinctive manner in which it is redistributed.

In the ganja mode of production, therefore, labor was controlled, not by the ideology of the wage, but by the very special notion that all participants should "forward ever," meaning by this precept not only the attainment of material self-sufficiency (in the larger urban context of deprivation and increasing povery), but spiritual growth, or becoming more truly and sincerely Rastafari. Gregory stayed with Vim, or Buen Retiro with Botts, because each young man was seeking a certain enlightenment by "going through the stages of the ganja" to "the light." The block leaders Vim and Botts helped to instill this yearning or spiritual quest better than any number of other options open to Buen Retiro and Gregory. Labor was manifestly bound to the exploiters of labor in this religiopolitical activity, and the relation was indissoluble as long as the activity was uninterrupted and advanced.

A brisk wrapper like Buen Retiro on Botts's block could roll forty-seven joints, worth $47, in fifteen minutes. To wrap out a pound in joints, then, took about five hours. To wrap it out in 3-bags, 5-bags, 10-pieces ($3, $5, $10), or ounces took proportionately less time for corresponding decreases in earnings.

On larger San Fernandian blocks, some ten hours had to be spent on this activity every two or three days, or about thirty hours a week. In New York City, where the volume and rate of sales were much higher, large blocks average about a pound a day.

Every two or three days in Trinidad, or at least once a week, the block leader or his delegate had to make a trip to the countryside to purchase marijuana. The trip could take as little as three hours; but usually the block leader spent the entire day visiting many planters, looking for better quality or a bargain, and passed many hours simply cultivating the appearance of leisure and nonchalance, by having a meal or stopping to buy fruits, as a strategem for avoiding police attention and returning home safely with the contraband in tow.

While the block leader was away, other associates were obliged to sell at the block leader's house throughout the day, with the heaviest sales taking place between 3:00 and 10:00 P.M. Sometimes the block leader did not use his home, but shifting locations in the vicinity, as the venue for sales. Block leader also wanted their associates to sell marijuana at dances or other large public gatherings. Few customers, such as workers on the midnight shift or nightclub personnel and patrons, came later than 2:00 or 3:00 A.M., or before 6:00 or 8:00 A.M. A pound of marijuana was sold in two or three days.

In sum, at least 120 hours a week were spent on the block selling marijuana, about 30 hours in wrapping and about 10 hours in buying. A total of 160 hours a week were thus spent on producing two pounds of marijuana on a block in San Fernando in the late 1970s. On Stanley's block or Vim's, where there were four and more associates available, an individual person contributed 27 hours weekly on average; in Navet and La Romaine, where there were nine dreads, 15 hours; with Botts or Matos, even fewer hours are required to attain self-sufficiency in the ganja traffic, leaving associates plenty of time to devote to other pursuits.

Many of those unutilized hours or surpluses are spent, as noted earlier, on the spiritual journey in search of "the light." For example, up to a quarter of each pound of marijuana was consumed by the block leader and his associates: a goodly portion of the product or value in this system was therefore immediately consumed by its producers. Labor in the production of ganja as a consumer good possessed that special skill by which production was possible at all: a particular social identity. In this system, therefore, fixed capital, or the surplus consumed in maintaining, replenishing, and improving the instruments of production, was an ongoing historical process, or the one in which personalities had moved from being petty criminal, street corner limers to Rastafari brethren operating a block. It was this history which had to be accumulated and aggrandized if production was to be sustained or to become more efficient. This "accumulation" was then the purpose of much investment of labor and capital. Other investment was also dictated by pursuit of "the light," such as farms, gardens, flocks of goats and chickens, taxis, and coops, which allowed for further pooling of management skills and labor.

Labor, thus bound, was "unfree" in the economic sense too: it could *not* be transferred to other branches of economic activity, following higher returns of profit. Gregory would not become a commercial farmer hired by Vim. He would do a specific type of agriculture which provided self-sufficiency in order to grow closer to "natural" things and to be confirmed in Rastafari. As his garden grew, his hair grew, and his spirit also. Capital was thus equally constrained: it cannot be "freely" joined to capital and labor for competitive economic aims.

Primacy of Social Relations of Production

The ganja mode of production performed uniquely because the persons engaged in it were united in unique social relationships. For it to continue to perform in this manner, persons had to remain unsyndicated growers, unguilded urban producers, and the police had to continue to act in an uncoordinated fashion if and when they joined the traffic.

Unsyndicated Growers

The cultivators of marijuana had to operate under the constraints they had imposed upon themselves in 1977, when they were observed in rural Trinidad. Typically, this category of persons had become engaged in marijuana cultivation for certain exchange purposes only: to acquire a house and land and to begin some legitimate enterprise which ensured self-employment, social status, moderate income, and self-sufficiency. Growers did not compete with one another to survive, so that the prices they charged for their marijuana were often wildly idiosyncratic, making it worth the buyer's while to shop around. They grew a maximum of 2,000 roots for a couple of seasons, and when they had accumulated about $100,000, went out of business. The early Indian middle-aged growers were replaced eventually by Rastafari brethren, for whom an important and primary aim of cultivation is to have the best-grown marijuana for their personal use, and by younger Indians who have been heavily influenced by the Rastafari.

Thus this type of grower was not responsive economically to increased demand. He did not bring more acreage under cultivation, he did not employ more labor or invest in technological improvement (unless, as in the case of the Rastafari, to improve the quality and enjoyment of the ganja the grower himself smoked), and he did not stay longer in production. If demand had resulted in increased cultivation and quality, as indeed it had, it had done so by stimulating more growers rather than by altering a grower's motivation.

These motivations of cultivators had acted as a curb against their becoming syndicated. If growers had been syndicated, and all cultivation had been brought under oligopolistic control, they would have found themselves the few owners of a huge agribusinesses. They would have dictated all economic conditions in the system, especially with respect to labor and its costs, and they would have been able to coerce labor, by withholding supplies and remuneration or by force. Capital would have accrued to them calculably and manipulably.

Unguilded Urban Producers

A similar result would have occurred if the city blocks had restricted recruitment to their ranks, contained the proliferation of blocks, or even reduced their present number. On the contrary, the emergence of Rastafari was evidence that the very opposite processes were in fact at work. Rastafari had been the means by which greater numbers had become aware of their productive capacity, and by which the social-productive relations on the block had been reproduced. Of course, Rastafari itself persisted because high rates of unemployment and social marginalization affected additional cohorts of youth, or more recruits.

The Police

Finally, the uniqueness of the ganja mode of production depended upon police activity. First, it would have been difficult for planters to become syndicated or producers guilded in the Trinidadian situation (or for that matter, in New York City a few years later) without police consent and active support. An attempt to do so without them would have succeeded only if its authors had produced armed strength which seriously rivaled the police force's.

AN EXEMPLIFYING CASE: CARNIVAL 1979 IN SAN FERNANDO

Proof that the unique features claimed for the ganja economic system did exist, or had existed during the period described, was afforded by the events of the 1979 Carnival in San Fernando, which were introduced in chapter 6.

In July 1978, as part of their DEA-inspired intensification of the war against marijuana, the police introduced light surveillance aircraft; and from July to December, raids by joint army and police units destroyed an unprecedented number of fields. During January 1979, a month before the enormous demand which the Carnival season would generate, the price of ganja had climbed from $300 to $600 per pound. San Fernando blocks were experiencing great difficulty to secure adequate supplies even at that price.

In the first week of January, a violent confrontation had flared up between two blocks. It was the first battle over territory to be fought in the ganja traffic since the very earliest days of use and distribution, when the brethren had been inexperienced in both, younger, and had not converted to Rastafari. One block leader, a Rastafari who was nevertheless heavily connected with *shango* and occult practices, had managed to buy fifteen pounds of mature, well-cured ganja at a bargain price of $350 a pound. He had sent one of his associates further up their street, where another well-known block had been suffering scarcity and had only a very little, low-grade marijuana for sale. Ordinarily, the selling operations would have remained exclusive, and members of either block would have mingled at either location amicably.

The young associate had been repulsed. One of the older members of the ailing block pleaded with the young man. He explained that he had a case in court the following day and needed whatever the block could earn that evening to spend on lawyers and other legal costs in the morning. When the younger man refused to budge, the other slapped him. Soon afterward, the young man, his block leader, and other supporters returned and severely pummeled members of the other block. A day later, the attackers were themselves ambushed at the San Fernando jetty, where they had gone to bathe, and two of them were chopped with cutlasses.

At this juncture, the aggressing block leader committed himself in a fashion which drew sharp censure throughout the network of San Fernandian blocks. He contracted three gangsters or hitmen from Port-of-Spain—three "mafia," as they were called—to retaliate, and paid them a fee of $2,000.

A week later, minutes after the three mafia had returned $1,400 to the block leader and had declined to fulfill the contract, a car pulled up at his house. Among the occupants was a man who bore the block leader a grudge. He had just returned from prison, and had complained that the block leader had framed him and had had him imprisoned in order to steal his girlfriend. The ex-prisoner had heard of the block leader's latest "corruption," or the contract killing of coreligionists, and, on this fateful day, had leapt from from the car brandishing a cutlass. Before escaping, he had badly wounded the block leader and an associate. Both men had to be rushed to the hospital, and in the melee which followed the attack, the fifteen pounds of the "I-riest" (best) ganja at that time circulating in San Fernando had been promptly stolen by an unidentified bystander.

In February, the price of marijuana had risen sharply from $650 to $850 per pound, and more and more block leaders were returning from the countryside empty-handed. There, multiple daily flights of the surveillance aircraft had thoroughly demoralized the growers. In the city, blocks closed, and a count at the end of the month found only forty-two remaining in operation.

Two weeks before Carnival, which began on February 23, ganja was available only at Darius's block. A daily roll-call of the remaining San Fernando blocks could be taken by an observer posted in the roseau bush from which Darius did business. Darius, possessing the capital necessary to buy the available supplies and enjoying the confidence of the planters, had managed to corner the entire San Fernando market, and had stood as the only effective mediator between planters and block leaders. At his block, Darius could be overheard advising his buyers to raise their prices, because he feared that a dark age of scarcity and high prices had begun. In that very week, his recommended price—$1.50 per joint—had become the standard in San Fernando. Smaller joints, containing less than a gram of marijuana, had been rolled; while Darius's favorites among the block leaders benefited from preferential prices and a guaranteed supply.

A week before Carnival, however, Darius was arrested for the eighth time in his marijuana-distributing career. After a weekend in prison, he returned to his block but had to refrain from business. Police squads were patrolling the main road leading from San Fernando to his home in the country continuously. As excitement for Carnival was building in the final days before Jour Ouvert (the start of Carnival at 3:00 A.M. on the Monday before Ash Wednesday), a shipment of what was rumored to be imported "Colombie" (marijuana from Colombia) was released on the city. At $1,200, it had apparently originated on a block in San Juan, a town in the northeast corridor. It had quickly appeared on all the blocks in Port-of-Spain, and block leaders there had diverted a shipment to San Fernando. By the weekend before Carnival, all the remaining blocks in San Fernando, barring a few notable ones, were selling it. The ganja was compressed and brownish in color, quite unlike the fresh stocks usually available.

Many San Fernandians believed that the "imported Colombie" was in fact not imported marijuana at all, but a pressed Trinidadian product which was fetching an exorbitant price. They also believed that the distribution chain, which originated in San Juan, extended eastward to Port-of-Spain, and then as far south as Cedros, was being protected and encouraged by the police. There seemed to have been a battle, therefore, between Darius's "lokey" (local marijuana) and the "police's imported."

On the Saturday before Carnival, a convoy of army trucks and police cars, guided by police helicopters, drove into San Fernando. They stopped first on Coffee Street, where they arrested, chained, handcuffed, and removed the entire personnel of two blocks; they then proceeded to Pleasantville and Navet, where they arrested all the members of blocks they could find. Over 200

Rastafari were imprisoned; none was released until Ash Wednesday, when Carnival was over. The blocks which had been attacked had been the very ones which had continued to sell the supplies they had previously received from Darius! San Fernandians were convinced that that had been the reason for the raids against them.

All the consequences for the ganja mode of production arising from a situation of syndicated supply versus coordinated police activity had already been realized: Darius and the police had dictated prices, labor had been controlled, the large number of blocks had dwindled to a few, and capital flowed to either Darius or the police, in spite of the social arrangements on blocks which constrained its accumulation or outflow, and which had earlier determined its redistribution. Indeed, these social arrangements were visited with violence.

THE INFORMAL ECONOMIC SECTOR

The precapitalist mode of production that developed in Trinidad around the extraction of value from marijuana has remained in a highly unstable state organizationally. While its continued existence has been guaranteed by worsening rates of unemployment and social marginalization, its shape has fluctuated with conditions affecting the supply of ganja, and with changing relationships between the principal actors involved. Nonetheless the emergence of this mode of production has been decisive in Trinidadian and Caribbean sociology. It has altered the understandings of their social terrain which Trinidadians had themselves and, as a result, has forced theorists to reconsider the type of socioeconomic formation Trinidad and Tobago is, the types of social classes there are, and the sorts of changes the formation is likely to undergo.

In the first place, the emergence of this mode of production transports the Trinidadian case outside of its customary social science ambience. It is no longer a quaint, unique, tropical, anglophone meeting place of races, schooled in European traditions, and tucked away in the American underbelly. Instead it joins rank with a legion of populations worldwide under similar pressures of unemployment, migration, and inflation (produced in contexts of increasing industrialization and urbanization) which have developed economic strategies for survival exhibiting features similar to those described in this study. A growing literature has located them throughout Africa and Asia, in both rural and urban areas; in Sicily and southern Italy; in Latin America; and in the ghettos of metropolitan centers. Often these populations are not only large but form national majorities (see preface).

Similar features which these economic strategies share include: an almost complete independence from foreign investment, relatively low labor productivity, and low or limited growth rates. In nearly every country where they exist, these structures are unprotected, unstable, illegal, and harassed by officialdom. Participants have no access to ordinary channels of credit and are subject to all sorts of legal and administrative controls—denial of licenses and slum demolition being ubiquitous. Competition sometimes causes conflict among participants who are already without health or welfare provisions to serve them, and who have no claim to insurance, pensions, or old-age benefits.

At the same time, varieties of a common philosophical orientation and of an ideal of social life are seen to flourish. Participants are proud of skills and learning they have acquired outside the schools, the state-supported churches, and the employee-training programs administered by the official economic and cultural institutions. They are proud of their development of indigenous resources and of the adaptive technologies they have created, which suit the basic needs of the poor, in whose midst they exist. They idealize the strengths of the social networks by which they are supported—family and other small-scale organizational forms—and which are also the primary units in their informal, extralegal economic enterprises.

The worldwide emergence of economic systems or modes of production such as the ones described exhausts the usefulness of the usual approaches to these populations attermpted by social scientists. For those who have labeled them "residual," their majority status in some countries is an embarrassment. Those who have argued that these are populations caught in transition, exhibiting merely features appropriate to an as yet incomplete penetration of capitalist organization, find them strengthened in 1979, or created afresh. Similarly, the proponents of the dual economy, who contrast "modern" versus "traditional" worldviews, cannot account for the novel, contemporary formation of the latter, in nontribal, nonstatic, nontraditional Trinidad and Tobago, especially when the islands were being extensively modernized.

Instead the universality of the phenomena reviewed in this book has suggested a world system approach, which seeks to explore relationships within the capitalist bloc of nations, through which surpluses are extracted from peripheral nations and are accumulated at the centers, or core nations (Wallerstein 1976). In this approach, populations within the capitalist world system are competitively hierarchized, both within nations and in the bloc of nations as a whole. Periphery and core are differentiated, since populations at the core are socially and economically organized to absorb surpluses generated worldwide; while in the peripheral nations, social and economic structures serve to aid in the transfer of surpluses to the core.

In core nations, where conformity and stability are essential for the maintenance of global enterprises, strong social and cultural pressures have developed to link profits to wages. A small dominant population, comprising owners of the means of production, institutes the values of individualism, competition, and the free market within itself, so that members compete with one another to expand production and increase profits. Their competitive urge, enormous profits, the imperatives to find consumers and to maintain stability allows other core populations to be competitively incorporated into wage employment and even ownership of capital. In core nations, therefore, groups compete more or less smoothly with relative success, and rejuvenate in myriad ways the institutions of the free market. The burden of maintaining these privileged populations, however, is borne increasingly by "peripheral" populations at the center and in the peripheral nations themselves.

In the latter, therefore, the makeup of the social formation represents a totally different raison d'être. Populations are also hierarchized in an even fiercer competition, but in order to aid the exploitation and transfer of local resources and values to core countries. Dominant groups or modernizing elites in the typical peripheral nation protect foreign enterprises which manage vital local resources, and their small corps of nonexpatriate or local wage employees. Locally dominant populations, therefore, have no control over production, which is for the most part consumed abroad, yielding profits, further productive capacity, and a greater outlay on wages and labor welfare there. In the business of protection rather than of national husbandry, profits which accrue to them in the form of taxes and other government revenues, political privilege, and brokerage between foreign manufacturing and local consumers or land ownership are jealously guarded. Since there are no social or cultural pressures to increase local production or to develop local values around locally felt needs, the police or army is used to pacify the small labor force and to control those unassimilable by wage employment.

In peripheral nations, the institutions of the free market abort. Competition is not accommodated so comfortably. Guarding few resources which cannot be replenished, dominant elites in peripheral nations begrudge the laboring classes their share, while both elites and working classes are beleaguered by the unanswerable demands of the excluded, who cannot be employed. In this context, liberal sentiments do not take root easily.

Ganja makes men "see the light." In the study of economic systems such as the ganja system, the reasonableness of these assertions concerning the nature of the capitalist world system and of the social classes participating in it can be demonstrated with reference to processual data drawn from everyday life. The degrees of insertion of capitalist structures among populations which cannot all derive benefit from them can be gauged; and a critical point can be determined, on one side of which the insertion is successful and allows for the peaceable reproduction of the world system, while on the other side, the whole system—its social, economic, and cultural institutions—begins to crumble.

Thus in the Trinidadian case under study, the adoption of ganja (which underwrote the rapid growth of the ganja economic system), when taken in the context of soaring prices for all the culturally approved foreign commodities, meant a positive and timely adaptation in working-class household budgets. In the account of the "marijuana" user of chapter 7, the outlays on alcohol and marijuana can be compared. At $100 and more per twenty-six-ounce bottle of imported Scotch whisky—that is, the highly priced varieties which status competition would have compelled the young man to buy—alcohol is many times more expensive. Similarly, the acceptability of Rastafari handmade shoes and sandals, as opposed to Guccis or Famolares (retailing at over $600 a pair) responds to the diminishing value of the worker's dollar. The taste for vegetarian food, and especially those with "folk" credentials, though ignored in "official" diets—eddoes, dasheens, yams, okras, green bananas, and bitter gourds as valued substitutes for imported rice, potatoes, sweet peas, and carrots—has the same pragmatic reference.

In other countries, the subsidies which these economic decisions lend to formal economic activity in peripheral countries, by reconciling comparatively low wages to rising prices, are pervasive in every area of life. Haircuts under mango trees instead of in air-conditioned salons, lunches and snacks served hot to workers by itinerant vendors rather than the company's canteen, cars repaired with old tin cans rather than with the proper imported spare parts, the endless recycling of discarded materials (oil drums, boxes, plastic containers) into consumer articles or pieces of art—all conspire to keep peripheral labor self-reproducing cheaply in comparison to the labor force in core countries. In this manner, the unequal exchange between core and periphery, as represented in differential wage structures, is maintained.

At the same time, these activities and the peculiar frame of mind developed in those who conduct them pose a more serious threat to the continued capitalist insertion than organized wage labor, or the class struggle, as traditionally conceived.

In peripheral countries, the working class, or the classes participating at subordinate levels in wage employment, are small in addition to being poorly paid. As a result, trade union activity has relevance for only a minority of workers. Political parties organized around trade unions are fragmented and lack mass support. At the same time a powerful symbiosis has grown up among poorly paid workers—the majority of those employed—and the unemployed: the production of cheaper, local values to replace imported ones, as in the ganja economy, is helpful in the desperate struggle to survive.

Throughout this study, attention has been drawn to the susceptibility of poorly paid workers to Rastafari and to their willingness to become involved in economic activities modeled upon the ganja system. Where the unemployed often blurred the distinction between themselves and labor by taking up casual, temporary wage employment when available, now many with permanent employment seek out alternative self-employment strategies.

This development rests on a tremendous cultural/motivational reorientation. In the first place, the worker who involves himself in such economic activities, especially if they are illegal, makes equivalent two types of curriculum vitae which are usually kept distinct: on the one hand, progressively accredited disciplines in the workplace, at home, in church, and in other organizations befitting equals; on the other hand, risk of arrest, the venturing of quick losses and profits, and association with unsavory social types.

In the second place, the worker comes to question the desirability of hitherto unquestioned values. Why the air-conditioned salon, why the imported shoes and clothes, why the imported meats, rice, and potatoes? His stock of tastes and consumer expectations therefore undergoes change.

Finally, in self-employment strategies, the qualities of thrift, hard effort, planning, labor management, and innovative thought are abundantly evident. If these economies operate under the constraints of poor returns, low labor productivity, and slow growth rates, this is not on account of faults inherent in them and their operators, but on account of structural and political disadvantages.

In sum, the elements of an anticapitalist, noncompetitive, nonethnic, universalistic and third-worldist, antineocolonialist ideology have assembled around the everyday activities of survival among peripheral populations. Within are the potentials for real development as opposed to modernization: the correct identification of local needs and the creation of strategies and technologies to meet them.

When, in peripheral nations, the tenuously substantiated sociocultural institutions of capitalism are simultaneously challenged, "law and order" remains the only justification for goverment, and the police becomes the most viable governmental agency.

This situation existed during the 1970s, or the period of research, throughout the Caribbean where the police and Rastafari were engaged in a running battle in Barbados, St. Lucia, Dominica, Grenada, and Guyana. In Jamaica, as in the South American nation of Colombia, the ganja traffic, enriched (and exploited) through international export connections, has upset the economic profiles of these countries, placing the political order in an unprecedented state of anxiety.

If the importance of economic systems such as the one described in this book is granted, and if the place of such systems in the capitalist world system is correctly identified, then attention is to be paid to the forms of protest and resistance which are advanced against the aggression directed at them. Vegetarianism, techniques of self-renewal, and global ecological perpectives are viewed as revolutionary praxis, when conformity and "absorption" close other revolutionary options (Breines 1972). In Trinidad, vegetarianism, techniques of self-renewal and the assumption of global ecological commitments are "fighting" matters.

In Trinidad, as in other peripheral-capitalist territories, these concerns are not only ideological, as this study has shown: they involve eminently pragmatic activities which are created to ensure survival—a concrete purpose. Furthermore, they are the rallying point—especially since survival is the issue—for more populations than can be reached by appeals to the "working class" (or to the unemployed, for that matter). In short, these concerns identify a force which is revolutionary almost in spite of itself.

Thus the combination of alternative economy, manned by distinctly organized personnel, fueled by motivations contrary to maximal profit-making and competition, and expressed in terms of religion, tradition, and personal self-renewal, is also imbued with theoretical revolution. While in the core countries with which it is especially concerned, left-wing politics can discover no coherent political formation coalescing around the revolutionary praxis it views as timely, in peripheral territories, the same praxis is the occasion for bloodshed. The chief defect of critical theory therefore resides in its failure to examine capitalism in its global setting, or as a world system.

"Working class politics" and "the proletarian revolution" have also been upstaged by the actual practices of the Trinidadian political actors described in this study. The revolutionary praxis which has emerged around the concrete quest for self-sufficiency and around an ethic of disciplined wants is aimed at the equation of progress with expanded production which "working class politics" has never questioned. Instead, the proletarian disputes only the ownership and control of the expanded production. Outside the confrontation of workers with owners of the means of production, however, is the confrontation of this contradictory system as a whole with the conditions of continued physical survival on this planet. It is in the latter balance that the ideology of infinitely expanding production weighs most ominously; and it is here also that the revolutionary praxis described seeks to make its permanent contribution.

Chapter 9

U.S.–Caribbean Drug Connections

An important aspect of the story of the ganja complex which the previous chapters have reported was its transference across centuries, national boundaries, and racial/ethnic barriers. In particular, it illustrated how busy the interconnections between the islands and nations of the Caribbean Basin and the United States are. Some details of the migration from these countries to the United States were given, as well as many facts about the international distribution and sale of marijuana. In this chapter, a more general treatment of these U.S.–Caribbean drug connections is offered, and arguments are made to support further U.S. intervention, in the form of financial aid for services and basic research.

Since the 1960s, drug trends in America have been inextricably bound up with those in the region. This book has documented how this symbiosis grew with th onset of marijuana use. Beginning first among European American "countercultural" youths, marijuana smoking was next diffused to young Caribbean Africans on the islands, where the experience facilitated transplantation of the Indian ganja complex, stimulated cultivation and Rastafari, and streamlined the drug's international distribution, before it was returned to low-income neighborhoods and immigrant enclaves in major U.S. cities, to be embraced by fresh cohorts of African Americans, Latinos, and European Americans.

In his other works, this researcher shows how those ties were intensified when cocaine hydrochloride powder was introduced. The practice of cocaine smoking may have originated on the islands (Hamid 1992). The emergence of the Colombian cartels was a fateful development in U.S.–Caribbean drug connections. These cocaine distributors launched a full scale campaign to induct the islands and the circum-Caribbean and Latin American nations into cocaine transshipment. The governments and administrations of several islands, including Puerto Rico, the Dominican Republic, and the Bahamas were courted and won over by the Colombians.

One of the most notorious of these cooptations occurred in Haiti. The Haitian military was able to maintain itself in power in 1992 to 1994, surviving an embargo and defying world opinion, because of their drug revenues.

Colonel Manuel Noreiga of Panama, in partnership with Colonel Oliver North and with President George H. Bush's apparent approval, was responsible for much of the cocaine which flooded the streets of North American cities (Cockburn 1989).

Social conditions in the Caribbean will continue to produce fresh generations of youths who will be open to the appeals of migration abroad, drug use and trafficking, and other crime.

Enlightened self-interest, therefore, is a compelling reason the United States should be particularly concerned about drug phenomena in the Caribbean. Like the cocaine-smoking epidemic of 1981 to 1991, future drug fashions may originate on these islands. Rapid assessments of drug trends throughout the hemisphere is thus as important as those undertaken in the continental United States. Indeed the latter alone are misleading, as they are out of context.

There are many areas of U.S.–Caribbean drug connections which are of crucial importance, some of which are described below.

TOURISM

Especially germane to the issues (to be discussed below) of revival of drug practices, AIDS, and crime is the greatly increased tourism linking North America to the islands and nations of the circum-Caribbean. Yearly, several hundred thousand U.S. citizens visit resorts in these locations, some with the express intention of engaging local persons in sex work and drug use. Although the cocaine-smoking epidemic has now subsided, cocaine smoking lingers on in places like Martinique and St. Lucia, and may be waiting to reengage new segments of the U.S. population.

FINANCE AND MONEY LAUNDERING

The ties between the United States and the region's nations are made more inextricable by the extensive financial exchanges between them. For example, the drug trade represents the largest single financial link between Miami and the Caribbean. The Miami banking system is the crucial connection between the financier, the seller, the market, and the offshore centers and tax havens that launder funds. Despite commercial benefits Miami derives from its Caribbean location and Latin population, the city does not have a monopoly on the flow of capital. Miami encounters strong competition from offshore banking centers in the Caribbean which operate primarily as tax havens.

Drug traffickers look for ways to hide and launder the cash they obtain from drug transactions. Some of them, as well as law enforcement officers, have explained how money laundering is carried out, in depositions and testimony in law cases, news stories, and autobiographies. A major purpose of offshore banks is to launder money back into the United States. A typical money-laundering process involves five steps: money is transferred to a secret haven abroad; lawyers create a shell corporation; funds are deposited in the name of a dummy corporation in a cooperative local bank; money is transferred to a larger international bank; and the corporation borrows money from the international bank. In order to stop these operations, the U.S. government requires declaration of sums larger than $10,000 when anyone leaves the country. But drug couriers or other operatives launder money and are not apprehended. Often they are trained accountants and lawyers, who also have the expertise to help their employers invest their revenues in boats, businesses, the stock market, and commercial and residential real estate (Maingot 1988).

Several islands now have established drug relationships with immigrant communities in the United States. This book has described how multiplex these relationships are between Trinidad and the islands of the Lesser Antilles and New York City. Jamaicans also have extensive ties linking their island with communities in the northeast and Florida, and many Jamaican communities rely heavily on their drug distributors, who send food, clothes, shoes, and other necessities to sustain families and whole communities (Gunst 1997). The Dominican Republic has also entered as a major player in cocaine redistribution. Long a nation which maintained extensive return migration links with the United States (Hendricks 1977), especially in such neighborhoods as Washington Heights, the Dominican Republic multiplied its rate of sending migrants in the late 1980s, when the Colombian cartels adopted it as a transshipment depot. Certain towns in the Dominican Republic have been transformed by the influx of drug revenues and the export of young men to communities in New York City, where they serve in the street-level cocaine traffic.

As this book has argued, the rise in drug consumption in the United States occurred simultaneously with the crisis in traditional sectors of Caribbean economies caused by the American-sponsored modernization and development plans (see chapter 1), and the marijuana and drug traffic was the attempt at restitution and repair which the young affected persons on the Caribbean islands had made. The drug trade thus filled an economic vacuum in these countries. Profits from the drug trade, however, are only part of a much larger informal economy in Caribbean countries. Many island economies are heavily dependent on their citizens who work abroad in the immigrant communities.

AIDS

Secondary statistical survey and epidemiological data indicate that the distribution of AIDS cases is not globally uniform: locations within or near the Caribbean Basin have been disproportionately affected by the epidemic, with the highest standardized attack rates per 100,000 population occurring in the Bahamas, Bermuda, and Puerto Rico. Substance abuse has significantly contributed to the epidemiology of AIDS in these areas. Evolving public health policy in the Caribbean has tended to integrate AIDS prevention programs with those aimed at preventing other, more common sexually transmitted diseases, but attention should be paid to specific substance abuse disorders as well (Lange, Contoreggi, and Ball 1991).

Of all reported cases of AIDS in the United States, 38 percent of patients have been black or Latino. In New York City, 45 percent of black or Latino males and 61 percent of black and Latino females identify intravenous drug use as their only risk-related behavior; 77 percent of pediatric AIDS cases are the result of parental IV drug use through perinatal transmission. Drug use is endemic in the poor, inner-city environment, and drug treatment has not always been readily available. Education in inner-city communities has not been culturally specific to the values, norms, or jargon of U.S. or Caribbean people of color (Honey 1988).

In addition, few major changes have been made in the design of national health and social services to accommodate and deal with the potential or existing impact of AIDS. In parts of Africa, the Caribbean, and Latin America, transmission is largely heterosexual, with extensive perinatal transmission. To address the problem of AIDS, primary health care will need to focus on community-based interventions in both developed and developing countries. These interventions will neeed to relate to the characteristics of the groups or communities to which they are directed. The epidemic will significantly impact families and friendship structures (Carballo and Carael 1988).

CRIME

The immigrant communities in Brooklyn and elsewhere are ideal locales for persons pursuing a variety of clandestine purposes to slip into and out of and to operate with impunity.

While the marijuana traffic was conducted relatively peacefully from the 1960s to 1981, rising rates of criminal offending occurred simultaneously with the introduction of cocaine in the early 1980s.

In Jamaica, the postindependence period (after 1962) saw a gradual increase in crime, with violent crimes rising sharply from 1969 to 1976. This resulted in the public calling for strong sanctions. Legislation in the 1970s included (1) the Dangerous Drugs Act, which increased penalties for persons involved in the cultivation, trafficking, and possession of drugs; (2) the Firearms Act, which tightened the issuance of gun licenses; (3) the Gun Court Act, which provides for life imprisonment for any person illegally possessing firearms; and (4) the Juveniles Act, which provides that juveniles over fourteen charged with gun offenses would be processed as adults. Other legislation during this period included the Suppression of Crime Act, which increased police powers in preventing and detecting crime; the Exchange Control Act, which increased penalties for the illicit outflow of currency; the Criminal Justice Reform Act, which increased sentencing options; and the Parole Act, which provides for the introduction of a parole system. In the law enforcement area, the public, particularly the low-income element and those involved in the Rastafarian subculture, views the police as discriminatory in their enforcement of the laws. This perception increases hostility between certain segments of the society and the police, which in turn tends to fuel violent crime. Corrections efforts are beginning to focus on community-based programs as alternatives to punishment, which is increasingly viewed as counterproductive, except where the incapacitation of dangerous and violent offenders is concerned (Allen 1980).

Jamaicans have thus borne the major stigma as Caribbean criminals. In the 1970s and 1980s, as the two political parties in Jamaica sought success in the various elections, politicians depended upon groups of neighborhood thugs, called posses, to keep the loyalty of their followers, to discourage the opposition from mobilizing through acts of terrorism, and to disrupt the actual voting process by stuffing ballot boxes and intimidating voters. But as the politicians, the government, and the country were impoverished further, many of these posses became involved in both marijuana and cocaine trafficking and migrated to the United States.

Although these "political posses" were soon eclipsed in drug distribution by younger Jamaicans, who did not in fact belong to posses or any other type of organization, the idea of an international Jamaican drug distribution conspiracy, executed through ruthless posses who displayed a disregard for life never before encountered in a criminal group, caught the imagination of several law enforcement agencies in the United States. Several, such as the Bureau of Alcohol, Tobacco and Firearms, were rescued from mortal financial straits by the federal funding they received to combat this new foreign scourge. Special units in local precincts throughout the nation were similarly revived.

Following the lead of these agencies, the U.S. Justice Department estimated that

> organized gang activity by criminals from the Caribbean Basin, particularly Jamaican nationals, had become well-established in the United States since their emergence in the mid-1980s. Their presence was now nationwide, with an estimated 30 gangs or "posses" in at least 18 major US cities, with a concentration on the East Coast. They had a reputation for being more violent than other street gangs, having committed an estimated 800 drug-related murders between 1984 and 1987. Although their initial trafficking had been in marijuana, they had been the leaders in orchestrating a quick take-over of a relatively new source of illicit drug revenue: the retail crack cocaine business. They had succeeded in maintaining the entire cocaine smuggling, conversion and subsequent crack manufacturing within their organization, thereby raising profits and lowering the risk of detection (Lyman 1990).

However, the development of blocks, described in chapter 3, portrays the more likely scenario, in which the "criminal groups" so feared by the authorities emerge through trial and error among husbands and wives, other kin, and other quite ordinary people who are unhappy to break the law.

THE WAR ON DRUGS AND FOREIGN POLICY

If the war on drugs in the United States has received mixed evaluations, this book gives ample evidence that in the Caribbean region it was an unmitigated disaster. It has seriously affected U.S. foreign policy in the Caribbean and vice versa, and it has encouraged widescale corruption in the regional police forces.

The activities of the assistant commissioner of police in Trinidad, Randolph Burroughs, were outlined in chapter 5. Trained in the United States and supported by the Drug Enforcement Administration (DEA), Burroughs carried out a relentless campaign against young Rastafari dwelling near the island's rain forests whom he labeled "guerrillas." In reality, they were marijuana growers who had no interest whatsoever in overthrowing the government. Burroughs's Flying Squad murdered thirty-three of them during the 1970s. It was later discovered that in fact Burroughs had been clearing the way for the introduction of cocaine for the Colombian cartels, and he remained to oversee its importation and islandwide distribution. Before he could be charged with these crimes, Burroughs resigned his position and fled to the United States.

> The encouragement of personnel like Burroughs was part of a design by the Drug Enforcement Administration to be more effective in the region, which DEA officers revealed to an investigator in a recent study:

> One strategy for circumventing corruption is for DEA agents to develop special relationships with a few local agents rather than depending on the foreign agency as a whole to conduct investigations. One of the most successful measures has been the creation of elite drug enforcement units composed of local police. DEA agents are active in creating these units, often training them, handpicking their heads, and overseeing their hiring, as well as working closely with them in all aspects of their operations (Nadelmann 1989).

The study, in which data were obtained from 1984 to 1986 from thirty DEA agents, concluded that corruption was not the only hindrance, but that it was an important obstacle to DEA efforts to cripple major drug traffickers in Latin America. Traffickers had been able to elude arrest and conviction by bribing and threatening local officials. DEA agents reported the means they had devised of working around the corruption that infected regional criminal justice agencies; they had pleaded, cajoled, threatened, and tricked their local counterparts into cooperating. Relying both on diplomatic leverage exercised by the U.S. ambassador and on the transnational police subculture, DEA agents had been able to immobilize many trafickers who thought that they had purchased their safety. But efforts to root out corruption in the local police agencies have proven emphemeral (Nadelmann 1989). The author neglected, however, to list the ways in which the DEA agents themselves encouraged corruption or were corrupt personally.

A U.S. Senate Committee on Foreign Relations reviewed past federal policies and practices in the handling of foreign policy and the war on drugs and concluded that the U.S. government had failed to acknowledge or had underestimated the seriousness of the emerging threat to the national security posed by the drug cartels. The drug cartels were so large and so powerful that they had undermined some governments and had taken over others. They worked with revolutionaries and terrorists. Their objectives seriously jeopardized U.S. foreign policy interests and objectives throughout Latin America and the Caribbean. In some instances, U.S. foreign policy considerations had interfered with the United States' ability to fight the war on drugs. The report recommended that the threat posed by the drug cartels be given high priority in the bilateral agenda of the United States with a number of countries including the Bahamas, Haiti, Colombia, Bolivia, and Paraguay (U.S. Senate 1988).

The Caribbean governments see their problems in controlling illicit drug-trafficking operations as difficult because the Caribbean serves as a link between the drug producers in South America and drug users in North America. They have initiated law enforcement measures to combat drug trafficking. They have taken legal and administrative steps to eradicate illicit cultivation of narcotic crops. They have sought to improve international and bilateral attempts to combat drug trafficking and drug abuse. Most Caribbean countries, however, lack trained manpower as well as the technical and economic resources necesary to do battle with sophisticated international drug trafficking groups. They therefore seek technical and financial assistance from the international community.

LEGAL DRUGS

Illicit drugs do not constitute the whole of the drug problem in the Caribbean. There has been growing international concern over many aspects of the use and flow of medicines in developing countries. Factors that have contributed to problems in this area include the marketing and promotional practices of the pharmaceutical companies, rising drug import costs, and the unsuitability or poor quality of available drugs. Many policies have emerged to alleviate such problems, to increase control over multinational drug companies, and to bring about changes in the technology transaction processes and in the pharmaceutical sector. Both the regional cooperation scheme of the Caribbean countries (CARICOM), and the national-level policy of Cuba are efforts to deal with these problems. The CARICOM strategy has significant limitations, primarily due to its voluntary nature and lack of enforcement mechanisms for member countries. On the other hand, the Cuban approach has brought about positive effects and progressive changes, made through political commitment to achieve social benefits and in conjunction with integrated broad reforms of the entire health system within a socialist framework. Policies need to be enforced at the national level and major structural changes are needed in order to adequately meet the health and medical needs of the people (Thrupp 1984).

PREVENTION AND TREATMENT

Providing services is a matter of urgency. To date, treatment facilities and specialists have been cut off from the mainstream of practice being carried out in the United States. Factors that have contributed to the increased availability of cocaine include: (1) proximity to the United States; (2) the use of the islands as a transshipment depot; (3) increased traffic of cocaine through the islands; and (4) the involvement of Bahamians in the transshipment process. Admissions data from the Sandilands Rehabilitation Centre, the island's only psychiatric hospital, show an increase of patients admitted for help with cocaine dependence from 69 in 1983 to 220 in 1984. These figures suggest that cocaine dependence has become a significant problem in the Bahamas. Other

Caribbean nations should begin to implement prevention strategies to avoid the problems the Bahamas is experiencing (Neville and Clark 1985).

Harm reduction messages will have a warm reception among professionals in the treatment establishment, as they are very aware that marijuana smoking was arguably an indigenous harm reductionist strategy, well adapted to Caribbean societies and cultures.

THE FUTURE: HEROIN

In view of the close connections between drug phenomena in the Caribbean and those in the United States, it is foolhardy that there is no coordinated, comprehensive drug-monitoring system for the hemishere. Hemispheric institutions, such as the United Nations Drug Control Programme (UNDCP), should seek to sponsor such a system, with aid from U.S. agencies, such as the National Institute on Drug Abuse (NIDA).

For example, heroin is waiting in the wings. The world production of poppies rose steeply in the 1990s. The size of crops in the traditional growing areas, such as Myanmar, Afghanistan, India, Turkey, the Lebanese Bekaa Valley, and Mexico, has more than doubled. Formerly limited to these geographic areas, large-scale cultivation now engages nations around the globe, such as Kenya, Nigeria, Morocco, the new Commonwealth of Independent States (CIS), Poland, Hungary, Lithuania, the former Yugoslavian Republic, the Ukraine, and the Central Asian Republics (Kazakhstan, Tajikistan, Uzbekistan, Kyrgyzstan, and Turkmenistan).

The watershed, however, may well have been the diversification of the Andean cocaine industry toward the production and marketing of heroin. In the early 1990s, cocaine cartels based in Cali, Colombia, perfected their techniques of heroin extraction and raised its quality to par with the Burmese product. Their cocaine-trafficking networks remain in place to market it. When wholesaling cocaine, they force buyers to accept some heroin too. This heroin may then be transferred to established heroin distribution channels at higher trafficking levels. Just as likely, however, is that it may trickle down the cocaine distribution chain, reaching consumers of all forms of cocaine. For example, Dominicans are selling both drugs from their bodegas.

Increased worldwide heroin production is being matched by a worldwide resurgence in use. Intranasal heroin use, "chasing the dragon" (smoking), and injecting have been observed for the first time in Asian and Eastern European capitals, where use among locals had followed the proliferation of trafficking routes. They grew in many Western European capitals in the 1980s. Popular culture is simultaneously glamorizing heroin. Despite the 1993 heroin overdose deaths of singer Kurt Cobain and actor River Phoenix, a fascination with the drug preoccupies many contemporary Hollywood films, TV movies, documentaries, and tabloid newspapers.

In cities across the United States, potential users can readily buy "Mexican brown tar," "China white," and "Colombian." At a recent meeting in New Orleans of the Community Epidemiology Work Group sponsored by NIDA, representatives from nineteen U.S. cities, Toronto, Mexico, and Paris reported increased purity, availability, and use of heroin. Heroin was their number-one drug of concern. The representative from Jamaica, a medical doctor, privately reported two hospitalizations in that Caribbean nation. Thus, an apparent global ascendancy of heroin use, often in places where it had been formerly absent, contextualizes the increase in use in New York City.

The mention by the Jamaican physician of two cases of heroin injecting is ominous. The Caribbean region has hitherto been innocent of heroin and of drug injecting. The Colombians, however, have used the islands as a transshipment route, and the recent example of Eastern Europe teaches that heroin use typically springs up along such routes. The United States and the islands stand in a mutually threatening relationship, in which harmful drug patterns may again travel to and fro, aggravating a bad situation.

RESEARCH

The Caribbean region can contribute greatly toward understanding the relation between psychoactive men and psychoactive plants. The islands offer a laboratory for the explorations of the impact of different cultures and differential policy on the use of different substances. Research in the region would truly establish drug studies as a multicultural, multinational enterprise. Caribbean islands are small but contain different ethnicities and cultures. Moreover, their drug policies are determined by independent island governments, the United States, Great Britain, France, and Holland.

If heroin consumption climbs in the late 1990s and early 2000s, ethnographic methodologies, tested in the cocaine-smoking epidemic of the 1980s, will be able to assess the development rapidly and accurately. They are an indispensable complement to the usual epidemiological approaches which, by themselves, have often mistaken the extent of use, how users are initiated, how they switch between drugs or use patterns, how much they use, how they quit, who drug distributors are, and how they operate. Thus, although the Drug Abuse Warning Network (DAWN), Drug Use Forecasting (DUF),

National Household Survey of Drug Abuse (NHSDA), and Monitoring the Future (MTF) are valuably affirming the greater availability and consumption of heroin, they have not grasped the characteristics of new users, plumbed the sources of new demand, or tapped into the emergent rituals and norms which are energizing new use patterns.

The principal drawback, however, and the one which an anthropological ethnography rigorously and systematically corrects, is that surveys cannot apprehend the contexts of social life in which drug use and distribution take place, its complexity and situational aspects, and its economic, cultural, and political dimensions. An ethnographic methodology restores this holistic perspective. Ethnographic procedures are also best suited to access and describe populations and social environments which are withdrawn from normal observation and in the investigation of emergent phenomena (Taylor and Bogdan 1984). Research will alert policymakers about the vectors by which heroin use is being diffused to new segments of the population and will advise them of the diverse consequences for communities, households, and individuals.

Glossary

artificial	Recent Rastafari adjective to describe the money culture of Babylon. Refers to money and attitudes and behavior associated with money making, tastes, styles of dress, etc.
Babylon	The ancient biblical city which symbolized the heathen or the ungodly. Rastafari word for the "money" culture and features thought to be intrinsic to it, such as exploitation, oppression, imperialism, racism, unemployment, blasphemy, and ungodliness. It also means the police.
bad john	A character notorious among unemployed youth before the 1960s for his physical courage and his criminal record.
black	In recent Rastafari usage, "true," as in "the blackness of the matter," or "the truth, or crux, of the matter." Hence "blackheart," or a truthful, honest, and aware person.
block	A neighborhood, or the gathering place for (mostly) males in the neighborhood; a place where marijuana is sold; an organization or enterprise selling marijuana and operated by a particular person or block leader (hence, "so and so's block") and his associates. In New York, blocks were renamed "gates."

blockorama	A street fair organized by budding entrepreneurs, popular in Trinidadian cities and towns from 1968 to 1973.
the Bowl	The Naparima Bowl, a concert hall in San Fernando which is also hired out for parties, dances, weddings, and other private celebrations.
Boys' Industrial Home	A borstal, or correctional, center for adolescent offenders.
chalice	A water pipe for smoking marijuana, made of indigenous materials. The hard shell of a mature coconut is cut at the top, and a bowl dug out of hard wood (mora wood, for example) is inserted; a rubber washer is sometimes used to make a snug and watertight fit. On the side of the coconut, a smaller opening is made into which a hollow bamboo tube or a length of rubber hosing is inserted: this serves as the stem or mouthpiece. Before use, the chalice is filled with water. Smoking marijuana through a chalice is thought to clear the head of phlegm.
channa	The Hindi and Trinidadian word for chickpeas, which are served curried or fried.
chilum	A smoking instrument originally imported from India. Now made in Trinidad, it is a conical clay pipe which is cupped in both hands during use.
cigarette papers	Wrappers or leaves in which cigarettes are wrapped. These are imported from abroad and are being replaced by natural tobacco leaves or dried plantain leaves. Scooped-out carrots and corn husks are other substitutes. They remain, however, the most convenient means for making a joint.
coop	A roadside stall, constructed of scrap wood, wire, and corrugated iron, from which cooked foods, fruits, and sundries are sold. Most blocks have one.
Crash Programme	A government employee program designed to alleviate unemployment among the chronically unemployed. A term of employment is usually

	about ten days a month, and jobs are often pointless tasks of road repair and the like.
dealer	A person who sells marijuana.
Democratic Labor Party (DLP)	The political party of Indian professionals, landowners, businessmen, priests, and village bosses; it once enjoyed widespread rural Indian support and formed the opposition in several governments since 1956.
dougla	A person of mixed African and Indian parentage.
dread	A Rastafari brother. As an adjective, it means "terrible" or "horrendous," or terrible and horrendous on account of just convictions. Hence, "going dread," to describe the process of self-questioning, reality testing, and self-affirmation through which one becomes Rastafari.
dreadlocks	Hair grown long and allowed to "knat up," or gather in thick, matted locks.
dunza	Recent Rastafari word meaning money: "done so" or "easy come, easy go."
Ethiopia	The country in the Horn of Africa; Africa; the world before Babylonian corruption; the land to emerge for all mankind after the destruction of Babylon; Zion.
fete	The usual Trinidadian word for a dance or party. A French word (*fête*), it recalls Trinidad's brief period as a French colony and subsequently, the flight to Trinidad of French planters, during periods of unrest in France or during slave revolts, from neighboring French colonies like Martinique and Guadeloupe.
five-bag	About four grams of marijuana packed in a small brown envelope and sold for $5. A five-bag yielded as many as seven or eight thinly wrapped joints or a couple of spliffs (see below).
funk	A bittersweet, deeply felt emotional state. The word refers most often to a cigarette emptied of tobacco at the top into which the butt end of a

	joint is fitted. In this way, all of the joint can be smoked. Cannabinoid oils run down into the remaining tobacco in the cigarette, making it potent also.
funk music	Popular African American music (The Temptations, Lionel Richie, and Marvin Gaye were some of the artists) which was favored by marijuana smokers until 1973, when reggae replaced it.
ganja	Hindi and Sanskrit word for marijuana, which has been adopted throughout the Caribbean. It was introduced, with marijuana itself, by Indians during the East Indian indenture (1937–1911).
gate	*See* block.
guerrilla	Word adopted by Trinidadian newspapers and police to refer mainly to marijuana cultivators who lived in the rain forests. Very few seemed to be active and armed political operatives.
Haile Selassi-I	The Ethiopian emperor who ruled Ethiopia from 1935 to 1976. He is regarded as the true descendant of Solomon and Sheba of the House of David, and hence as the living God, Jah Rastafari.
hashish	A cake prepared from the flowering tips of the marijuana plant which can be added to joints or smoked in a pipe.
head	Being high on marijuana; thus, "to have a head" or "a good head."
herbs	Rastafari word for marijuana.
higgling	"Hustling": hence, "higgler," an entrepreneurial intermediary who buys agricultural produce from growers, or manufactured goods (cigarettes, candles, newspapers, lottery tickets, etc.) from a wholesaler, for resale at retail.
I	A Rastafari word meaning the true "natural," "inner" self, like the Atman in Hindu thought. The adjective, "I-ry," describes things nourishing or pleasing to the "I." "I-tal," a noun, refers to I-ry food. "I-ditation" means contemplation, or thought profitable to "I."

Jah Rastafari	Jahwey or Jehovah. See Haile Selassi-I.
joint	A cigarette made of marijuana.
joy juice	A beverage prepared from the seeds of the datura flower pod, which is said to have powerful hallucinogenic effects. Although the datura grows in Trinidad in the wild, in damp and dark places, it is not widely used as a narcotic by Trinidadians. Some experimentation was noted in the late 1960s and early 1970s, when marijuana was being introduced.
kalli	A Hindi and Sanskrit word for the mature buds of the marijuana plant; any good or potent marijuana.
kaya	The name of a record album by Bob Marley, the most famous Rastafari reggae singer. The lead song on the album is also called "Kaya," and the word means marijuana.
knat-up	*See* dreadlocks.
lime	Recreational gathering of neighborhood friends, who also engaged in economic, political, and cultural exchanges while together. Hence, "to lime" and "liming."
Mandrax	British trade name for Quaaludes.
parlor	The front room of a house which faces the street and which is often converted to a small neighborhood shop from which homemade sweets, snacks, cold drinks, cigarettes, newspapers, and sundries are sold.
People's National Movement (PNM)	Name of the political party which won Trinidad's first general elections in 1956, thus forming the first indigenous government. Until the early 1990s, it won every subsequent general elections.
pot	A word for marijuana in America and Europe.
puja	Hindi and Sanskrit word for a prayer service in honor of a god or goddess, or to give thanks for a boon.
pusher	A person who sells marijuana.

reggae	A form of Jamaican folk music which was developed in the mid-1960s from ska and "rocksteady" antecedents. Rastafari musicians spearheaded the development, and the music emphasizes Rastafari themes, such as ganja use, the worship of Jah Rastafari or Haile Selassi, resistance to Babylon, redemption and repatriation to Africa. The music has been embraced universally by youth cultures.
see de light	An effect of marijuana use in Trinidad, reported after the establishment of regular selling locations or blocks. The phrase refers to the vision of ways out of poverty and unemployment which young Trinidadians say they experienced as they smoked marijuana.
shit-talk	Joking, heckling, word games—which delighted young Trinidadians before they graduated to the more serious, more religious speech of Rastafari.
Special Works Programme	A successor to the Crash Programmes. During the 1970s, the government employed over 49,000 young people annually in this program. Typically, each participant worked for ten days a month. Tasks included removing debris, road repair, or other manual labor.
spliff	A large joint.
ten-piece	Slightly less than half an ounce of marijuana, sold for $10 in a small brown envelope.
think constructive	An effect of marijuana experienced as Trinidadian users were working toward the establishment of blocks.
three-bag	Slightly less than two grams of marijuana, sold for $3 in a small brown envelope.
Youth Training Center	*See* Boys' Industrial Home.
zes' up	Animated or vitalized, full of energy, excitement, and activity.

Bibliography

Abel, E. R.
1980 *Marihuana: The First Twelve Thousand Years*. New York: Plenum.

Adler, Patricia
1985 *Wheeling and Dealing: An Ethnography of an Upper-Level Drug Dealing and Smuggling Community*. New York: Columbia University Press.

Allen, D.
1980 Crime and Treatment in Jamaica. In Rosemary Brana-Shute and Gary Brana-Shute (eds.), *Crime and Punishment in the Caribbean*. Gainesville: University of Florida Center for Latin American Studies, #6, 52–57.

Allum, Desmond
1971 Legality vs. Morality: A Plea for Lt. Raffique Shaw. In D. Lowenthal and L. Comitas, (eds.), *The Aftermath of Sovereignty: West Indian Perspectives*. New York: Anchor Books.

Althusser, Louis, and Etienne, Balibar
1970 *Reading Capital*. London: New Left Books.

Amin, Samir
1974 *Accumulation on a World Scale: A Critique of the Theory of Underdevelopment*. 2 Volumes. New York: Monthly Review Press.

Anderson
1981 *Imagined Communities: Reflections on the Origin and Spread of Nationalism*. New York: Verso.

Andrews, C., and S. Vinkenoog
1967 *The Book of Grass*. New York: Bantam.

Angrosino, Michael
1972 *Outside Is Death: Alcoholism among East Indians in Trinidad and Tobago*. Ann Arbor, Mich.: University Microfilms.

Antonil
1978 *Mama Coca*. London: Hassle Free Press.

Bahadursingh, Krishna
1968 *Trinidad Electoral Politics: The Persistence of the Race Factor*. London: Institute of Race Relations.

Barrett, Leonard E.
1968 *The Rastafarians: A Study of Messianic Cultism in Jamaica* (Caribbean Monograph Series No. 6). Rio Pedras: Institute of Caribbean Studies, University of Puerto Rico.
1977 *The Rastafarians*. Boston: Beason Press.

Becker, Howard S.
1953 Becoming a Marijuana User. *American Journal of Sociology* 59: 235–242.
1967 History, Culture and Subjective Experience: An Exploration of the Social Bases of Drug-Induced Experiences. *Journal of Health and Social Behavior* 8 (3): 163–178.

Bennett, C., L. Osborn, and J. Osborn,
1995 *Green Gold—The Tree of Life: Marijuana in Magic and Religion*. Frazier Park, Calif.: Access Unlimited.

Best, Lloyd
1968 *Externally Propelled Industrialization and Growth in the Caribbean*. Montreal: McGill Center for Developing Areas Studies. 4 volumes (mimeo).
1970 *Black Power and National Reconstruction*. Port-of-Spain
1971 Size and Survival. In N. Girvan and D. Jefferson (eds.), *Readings in the Political Economy of the Caribbean*. Mona, Jamaica: New World.

Bohannon, P.
1955 Some Principles of Exchange and Investment Among the TIV. *American Anthropologist*, 57: 60–70.

Boot, Adrian, and Michael Thomas
1977 *Jamaica: Babylon on a Thin Wire*. New York: Schocken Books.

Boyle, T.C.
1984 *Budding Prospects: A Pastoral*. New York: viking/Penguin.

Brecher, Edward M. (and Editors of *Consumer Reports*)
1972 *Licit & Illicit Drugs: The Consumers' Union Report on Narcotics, Stimulants, Depressants, Inhalants, Hallucinogens, and Marijuana—including Caffeine, Nicotine, and Alcohol*. Boston: Little, Brown.

Breines, P.
1972 *Critical Interruptions*. New York: Herder and Herder.

Brewster, Havelock
1971 *Economic Dependence*. University of London: Institute of Commonwealth Studies (mimeo).

1972 The Growth of Employment Under Expert-Based Underdevelopment: Trinidad. *Social and Economic Studies*, 2 (2): June.

Brewster, Havelock, and Clive Thomas
1967 *The Dynamics of West Indian Economic Integration*. Mona, Jamaica: Institute of Social and Economic Research, University of the West Indies.

Brown, Claude
1971 *Manchild in the Promised Land*. New York: Signet Books.

Campbell, A
1980 *Girls in the Gang: A Report from New York City*. Oxford, U.K.: Basil Blackwell.

Carballo, M., and M. Carael
1988 Impact of AIDS on Social Organization. In Alan Fleming (ed.), *Global Impact of AIDS*. New York: Alan R. Liss.

Chaney, E. and C. Sutton (eds.)
1979 *Special Issue on Caribbean Immigrants to New York City*. New York: International Migration Studies.

Chopra, G., and B. Jandu
1976 Psychoclinical Effects of Long-Term Marijuana Use in 275 Indian Chronic Users: A Comparative Assessment of Effects in Indian and USA Users. *Annals of the New York Academy of Sciences* 282: 95–108.

Cockburn, Leslie
1989 *Out of Control*. New York: Random House.

Codere, Helen
1975 The Social and Cultural Context of Cannabis Use in Rwanda. In V. Rubin (ed.), *Cannabis and Culture*. The Hague: Mouton.

Comitas, Lambros
1973 Occupational Multiplicity in Rural Jamaica. In L. Comitas and D. Lowenthal (eds.), *West Indian Perspectives: Work and Family Life*. 157–173. Garden City, New York: Anchor Press/Doubleday.
1975 The Social Nexus of Ganja in Jamaica. In V. Rubin (ed.), *Cannabis and Culture*. The Hague: Mouton.

Craig, R.
1990 South American Drug Traffic: Domestic Impacts and Foreign Policy Implications. In J. A. Inciardi (ed.), *Handbook of Drug Control in the United States*. Westport, Conn.: Greenwood.

Cronon, Edward D.
1955 *Black Moses: The Story of Marcus Mosiah Garvey and the Universal Negro Improvement Association*. Madison: University of Wisconsin Press.

Crowley, Daniel J.
1957 Plural and Differential Acculturation in Trinidad. *American Anthropologist* 59: 817–824.
1960 Cultural Assimilation in a Multi-Racial Society. In Vera Rubin (ed.), *Social and Cultural Pluralism in the Caribbean. Millwood, New York: Kraus Reprint Company.*

Curtin, Philip
1991 *A Short History of the Caribbean*. London: Nelson.

Demas, William
1965 *The Economics of Development in a Small Country with Special Reference to the Caribbean*. Montreal: McGill University Press.

Despres, Leo
1967 *Cultural Pluralism and Nationalist Politics in British Guiana*. Chicago: Rand McNally.

Dombrowski
1971 Excavations in Ethiopia: Lalibela and Natchabiet Caves, Begemeder Province, Boston: Boston University Ph.D diss.

Drug enforcement Agency
1981 *Drugs of Abuse*. Washington, D.C.: U.S. Department of Justice/Drug Enforcement Agency.

Du Toit, Brian
1975 The History and Ethnographic Setting of Cannabis Sativa in South Africa. In V. Rubin (ed.), *Cannabis and Culture*. The Hague: Mouton.

Edwards, Adolph
1967 *Marcus Garvey, 1887–1943*. London: New Beacon.

Emboden, William J. Jr.
1972 *Narcotic Plants*. New York: Macmillan.

Evans-Pritchard, E. E.
1943 *The Nuer: A Description of the Modes of Livelihood and Political Institutions of a Nilotic People*. Oxford: U.K.: Clarendon Press.

Farrell, Trevor
1974 *The Multi-National Corporation: The Petroleum Industry and Economic Development in Trinidad*. Ph.D dissertation.

Feige, E. L.
1979 *The Irregular Economy: Its Size and Macro-Economic Implications*. Madison: University of Wisconsin Press.

Frank, Andre Gunder
1969 *Capitalism and Underdevelopment in Latin America*. New York: Modern Reader.

Freilich, Morris
1963 The Natural Experiment: Ecology and Culture. *Southwestern Journal of Anthropology* 19: 21–37

Furst, Peter
1986 *The Flesh of the Gods: The Ritualistic Use of Hallucinogens*. New York: Praeger.

Gaughan, J. P., and L. A. Ferman
1987 Towards an Understanding of the Informal Economy. *Annals of the American Academy of Political and Social Sciences* 493: 15–25.

Girvan, Norman
1967 *The Caribbean Bauxite Industry*. Mona, Jamaica: Institute of Social and Economic Research, University of the West Indies.
1970 Multi-National Corporations and Dependent Underdevelopment in Mineral-Export Economies. *Social and Economic Studies* 19 (4), December.

Gitlin, Todd
1987 *The Sixties: Years of Rage, Days of Hope*. New York: Bantam Books.

Goode, Erich
1970 *The Marijuana Smokers*. New York: Basic Books.

Great Britain
1969 *Indian Hemp Drugs Commission, 1893–1894*. Silver Spring, Md.: Thomas Jefferson.

Grinspoon, Lester
1971 *Marijuana Reconsidered*. Cambridge, Mass.: Harvard University Press.

Grinspoon, L. and J. Bakalar
1985 *Cocaine: A Drug and Its social Evolution*. New York: Basic Books

Gunst, Laurie
1997 *Born Fi' Dead*. New York: Henry Holt.

Guttman, P.
1977 The Subterranean Economy. *Financial Analyst's Journal*: 26–34

Hamid, Ansley
1980 A Precapitalist Mode of Production: Ganja and the Rastafarians in San Fernando, Trinidad. Ph.D. Dissertation, Teachers College, Columbia University. (Ann Arbor, Mich: University Microfilms).
1983a "Brooklyn Carnival: From Periphery to Core, Use Value to Commodity." Paper presented at the Colloquium in Applied Anthropology. Teachers College, Columbia University.
1983b "The Grenadian Invasion." Paper presented at the Colloquium in Applied Anthropology. Teachers College, Columbia University.
1991a From Ganja to Crack: Caribbean Participation in the Underground Economy in Brooklyn, 1976–86, Part I. *International Journal of the Addictions* 2(7) 1: 735–744.

1991b From Ganja to Crack: Caribbean Participation in the Underground Economy in Brooklyn, 1976–86, Part II. *International Journal of the Addictions* 26(6) 1: 615–628.

1992a Drugs and Patterns of Opportunity in the Inner City: The Case of Middle-Age, Middle-Income Cocaine Smokers. In A. Harrell and G. Peterson (eds.), *Drugs, Crime and Social Isolation: Barriers to Urban Opportunity*. Washington, D.C.: Urban Institute Press.

1992b The Developmental Cycle of a Drug Epidemic: The Cocaine Smoking Epidemic of 1981–1991. *Journal of Psychoactive Drugs* (special issue: James A. Inciardi, ed.) 24 (4) Oct.–Dec.: 337–349.

1997a The Political Economy of Drugs, Part I: Ganja and Rastafarians in Trinidad and New York. Unpublished manuscript.

1997b The Political Economy of Drugs, Part II: The Cocaine Smoking Epidemic in New York City's Low Income Minority Neighborhoods, 1981–1991. Unpublished manuscript.

1998 *Drugs in America: Sociology, Economics and Politics*. Gaithersburg, Md.: Aspen.

Hamid, A., et. al.

1997 The Heroin Epidemic in New York City: Current Status and Prognoses. *Journal of Psychoactive Drugs*, 29 (4): 375–391.

Hebdige, Gary

1987 *Subculture: The Meaning of Style*. New York: Methuen.

Hendricks, Glenn

1977 *The Dominican Diaspora*. New York: Teachers College Press.

Henry, S.

1988 Can the Hidden Economy Be Revolutionary? Towards a Dialectical Analysis of the Relations Between Formal and Informal Economies. *Social Justice* 15 (3–4): 29–59.

Herodotus

515BC/1954 *The Histories*. Harmondsworth, U.K.: Penguin Books.

Hijuelos, Oscar

1991 *The Mambo Kings Sing Songs of Love*. New York: Harper Perennial.

Honey, Ellen

1988 AIDS and the Inner City: Critical Issues. *Social Casework* 69: (6) 365–370.

Ianni, F. A. J.

1972 *A Family Business*. New York: Mentor Books.

Immigration and Naturalization Service

1970 *Annual Report*. Washington, D.C.: U.S. Department of Justice.

1980 *Annual Report*. Washington, D.C.: U.S. Department of Justice.

Jacques-Garvey, Amy
1963 *Garvey and Garveyism*. Kingston, Jamaica: A. Jacques-Garvey.

James, C. L. R.
1961 *Federation: We Failed Miserably: How and Why*. Port-of-Spain.
1962 *Party Politics in the West Indies*. Port-of-Spain.

Jiminez, J. B.
1989 Cocaine, Informality and the Urban Economy in La Paz, Bolivia. In A. Portes, M. Castells, and L. Benton (eds.), *The Informal Economy: Studies in Advanced and Less Developed Countries*. Baltimore: Johns Hopkins University Press.

Kane, H. H.
1883 *Opium-Smoking in America and China.* New York: Putnam.

Kaplan, J. (ed.)
1969 Marijuana: Report of the Indian Hemp Drugs Commission, 1893–1894. Silver Spring, Md.: Thomas Jefferson.

Kasinitz, Phillip
1992 *Caribbean Migration to New York.* Newark, N.J.: Rutgers University Press.

Katzin, M. F.
1959 The Jamaican Country Higgler. *Social and Economic Studies* 8 (5). Mona, Jamaica: University of the West Indies, Institute of Social and Economic Research.

Klass, Morton
1960 East and West Indian: Cultural Complexity in Trinidad. In Vera Rubin (ed.), *Social and Cultural Pluralism in the Caribbean*. Millwood, New York: Kraus Reprint Company.
1961 *East Indians in Trinidad: A Study in Cultural Persistence*. New York: Columbia University Press.

Kolanski, L., and W. Moore
1971 Effects of Marijuana on Adolescents and Young Adults. *Journal of the American Medical Association* 216: 486–492.

Koslofski, Joanne
1981 Going Foreign: The Causes of Jamaican Emigration. *NACLA* Vol. XV (1) Jan.–Feb.

Lange, Robert W., Carlo S. Contoreggi, and John C. Ball
1991 The Interface of Drugs and AIDS in the Caribbean Region. *AIDS and Public Policy Journal* 6 (3): 121–124.

Levy, R.
1957 *The Social Structure of Islam*. Cambridge: Cambridge University Press.

Lewis, Oscar
1968 The Culture of Poverty. In D. Moynihan (ed.), *On Understanding Poverty: Perspectives from the Social Sciences*. New York: Basic Books.

Lewis, Sir W. Arthur
1950 The Industrialization of the British West Indies. *Caribbean Economic Review*, May.

Li, Hui-Lin
1975 The Origin and Use of Cannabis in Eastern Asia: Their Linguistic-Cultural Implications. In V. Rubin (ed.), *Cannabis and Culture*. The Hague: Mouton.

Liebow, Elliott
1967 *Tally's Corner: A Study of Negro Streetcorner Men*. Boston: Little, Brown.

Light, Ivan Hubert
1972 *Ethnic Enterprise in America: Business and Welfare among Chinese, Japanese and Blacks*. Berkeley: University of California Press.

Long, Norman
1984 *Miners, Peasants and Entrepreneurs: Regional Development in the Central Highlands of Peru*. Manchester, U.K.: Institute for African Studies, University of Zambia/University of Manchester University Press.

Ludlow, Fitzhugh
1857/1975 *The Hasheesh Eater*. San Francisco: Level Press.

Maingot, A. P.
1988 Laundering the Gains of the Drug Trade: Miami and Caribbean Tax Havens. *Journal of InterAmerican Studies and World Affairs* 30 (2 & 3), (summer/fall): 167–187.

Malik, Yogendra C.
1971 *East Indians in Trinidad: A Study in Minority Politics*. London: Oxford University Press for the Institute of Race Relations.

Malinowski, Bronislaw
1922 *Argonausts of the Western Pacific*. London: Routledge & Kegan Paul.

Malowist, M.
1972 *Croissance et Regression en Europe, X1Ve–XV11e Siècles: Récueil D'Articles*. Paris: A. Colin

Mattera, P.
1985 *Off the Books: The Rise of the Underground Economy*. London: Pluto Press.

Mazumdar, Dipak
1975 The Informal Economic Sector. *International Bank of Reconstruction and Development Staff Working Paper No. 211*. Washington, D.C.: IBFD.

McCrohan, K. F., and J. D. Smith

1986 A Consumer Expenditure Approach to Estimating the Size of the Underground Economy. *Journal of Marketing* 50: 48–60.

Meillassoux, Claude

1981 *Maidens, Meals and Money: Capitalism and the Domestic Community*. Cambridge: Cambridge University Press.

Morales, Edmundo

1989 *White Gold Rush in Peru*. Tucson: University of Arizona Press.

Myerhoff, Barbara

1974 *The Peyote Hunt: The Secred Journey of the Huichol Indians*. Ithaca: New York: Cornell University Press.

New York Police Department

1944 *An American Dilemma: The Negro Problem and Modern Democracy*. New York: Random House.

Morton, Sarah (ed.)

1916 *John Morton of Trinidad: Journals, Letters and Papers*. Toronto: Westminster.

Nadelmann, Ethan

1989 Drug Prohibition in the United States: Costs, Consequences and Alternatives. *Science*: 939–947.

1990 The DEA in Latin America: Dealing with Institutionalized Corruption. *Journal of InterAmerican Studies and World Affairs* 29 (4): 1–39.

1993 *Cops Across Borders*. University Park: Pennsylvania State University Press.

Nahas, Gabriel

1975 *Marijuana: The Deceptive Weed*. New York: Raven Press.

Nettleford, Rex

1972 *Identity, Race and Protest in Jamaica*. New York: William Morrow.

Neville, Michael, and Nelson Clark

1985 Drug Abuse in the Bahamas. *Journal of Substance Abuse Treatment* 2 (3): 195–197.

New World Associates

1971 The Long-Term Economic, Political and Cultural Programme for Guyana. In N. Girvan and O. Jefferson (eds.), *Readings in the Political Economy of the Caribbean*. Mona, Jamaica: New World.

New York Police Department

1985 Rasta Crime. a Confidential report. *Caribbean Revew* 14: 12–15; 39–40.

Niehoff, Arthur, and Juanita Niehoff

1960 *East Indians in the West Indies*. Milwaukee: Milwaukee Public Museum.

Owen, Joseph

1976 *Dread*. Kingston, Jamaica: Sangster.

Oxaal, Ivar
1971 *Race and Revolutionary Consciousness*. London: Schenkman Publishing.

Palgi, Phyliss
1975 The Traditional Role and Symbolism of Hashish among Moroccan Jews in Israel and the Effect of Acculturation. In V. Rubin (ed.), *Cannabis and Culture*. The Hague: Mouton.

Parry, S.
1968 *History of the West Indies*. Mona, Jamaica: University of the West Indies Press.

Patterson, H. Orlando
1964 Ras Tafari: Cult of Outcasts. *New Society* (3): 15–17.

Portes, Alejandro
1978 The Informal Sector and The World Economy: Notes on the Structure of Subsidized Labor. Paper presented at Duke University (mimeo).

Portes, Alejandro, and Saskia Sassen-Koob
1987 Making It Underground: A Comparative Material on the Informal Sector in Western Market Economies. *American Journal of Sociology* 9 (3): 30–61.

Post., Ken
1978 *Arise Ye Starvelings: The Jamaican Labor Riot of 1938 and Its Aftermath*. The Hague: Martinus Nijhoff.

Robinson, Victor
1925 An *Essay on Hasheesh, Historical and Experimental.* New York: E. H. Ringer

Rubin, Vera (ed.)
1975 *Cannabis and Culture*. The Hague: Mouton.

Rubin, Vera, and Lambros Comitas
1969 *Ganja in Jamaica: The Effects of Chronic Marihuana Use*. New York: Anchor Books.

Rubin, Vera, and Marisa Zavalloni
1969 *We Wish To Be Looked Upon*. New York: Teachers College Press.

Ryan, Selwyn Douglas
1972 *Race and Nationalism in Trinidad and Tobago: A Study of Decolonization in a Multi-Racial Society*. Toronto: University of Toronto Press.

Sassen-Koob, Saskia
1989 New York City's Informal Economy. In A. Portes, M. Castells, and L. Benton (eds.), *The Informal Economy: Studies in Advanced and Less Developed Countries*. Baltimore: Johns Hopkins University Press.
1991 The Informal Economy. In H. Mollenkopf and M. Castells (eds.), *Dual City: Restructuring New York*. New York: Russell Sage Foundation.

Schneider, Jane, Peter Schneider, and Edward Hansen
1972 Modernization and Development: The Role of Regional Elites and Non-Corporate Groups in the European Mediterranean. *Comparative Studies in Society and History*. 4(3): 328–350.

Schultes, Richard Evan
1975 An Overview of Hallucinogens in the Western Hemisphere. In P. T. Furst (ed.), *Flesh of the Gods: The Ritual Use of Hallucinogens*. New York: Praeger.

Scott, Garvin
1986 *Report of Narcotics.* Port-of-Spain, Trinidad: Government Printing Office.

Sherlock, Phillip
1966 *A Short History of the Caribbean*. New York: Praeger.

Sherman-Peter, A. M.
1987 Coordinated Countermeasures of Caribbean Countries and Territories against the Illicit Drug Traffic: Recent Developments and Prospects, *Bulletin on Narcotics* 39 (1): 69–78.

Simpson, George E.
1955 Political Cultism in West Kingston, Jamaica. *Social and Economic Studies,* University of the West Indies 5 (2): 133–149.

Smith, M. G., R. Augier, and Rex Nettleford
1960 *The Rastafari in Kingston, Jamaica*. Mona: Institute of Social and Economic Research, University of the West Indies.

Smith, Michael G.
1960 Social and Cultural Pluralism in the Caribbean. In Vera Rubin (ed.), *Social and Cultural Pluralism in the Caribbean. Annals of the New York Academy of Sciences* 83: 763–785.
1965 *The Plural Society in the British West Indies.* Berkeley: University of California Press.

Solomon, David (ed.)
1966 *The Marihuana Papers*. New York: Bobbs-Merrill.

Taylor, S. J. and R. Bogdan
1984 *Introduction to Qualitative Research Methods: The Search for Meanings*. (2nd ed.) New York: Wiley-Interscience.

Thomas, Clive
1965 *Monetary and Financial Arrangements in a Dependent Monetary Economy*. Mona, Jamaica: Institute of Social and Economic Research, University of the West Indies.

Thomas-Hope, E.
1976 The Adaptation of Migrants from the English-speaking Caribbean in Selected Urban Centers of Britain and North America. Amsterdam: Paper presented to the Annual Meetings of the Society of Applied Anthropology.

Thrupp, Lori-Ann

1984 Technology Policy and Planning in the Third World Pharmaceutical Sector: The Cuban and Caribbean Community Approaches. *International Journal of Health Services* 14 (2): 189–216.)

U.S. Senate Committee on Foreign Relations

1988 Drugs, Law Enforcement, and Foreign Policy, Washington, D.C.

van de Merwe, Nicholaas J.

1975 Cannabis Smoking in 13th–14th Century Ethiopia: Chemical Evidence. In V. Rubin (ed.), *Cannabis and Culture*. The Hague: Mouton.

Wallerstein, Immanuel

1974 *The Modern World System*. New York: Academic Press.

Weller, Judith Ann

1972 *East Indian Indenture to Trinidad* (Caribbean Monograph Series No. 4). Rio Pedras: University of Puerto Rico Institute of Caribbean Studies.

Whyte, William W.

1955 *Street Corner Society*. Chicago: University of Chicago Press.

Williams, Eric E.

1955a *The Economic Problems of Trinidad and Tobago*. Public Affairs Pamphlet No. 1. Port-of-Spain.

1955b *My Relations with the Caribbean Commission, 1943–1955*. Port-of-Spain.

1955c *Constitution Reform in Trinidad and Tobago*. Public Affairs Pamphlet No. 2. Port-of-Spain.

1957 Race Relations in a Caribbean Society. In Vera Rubin (ed.), *Caribbean Studies: A Symposium*. Kingston, Jamaica.

1960a *The Approach to Independence*. Port-of-Spain.

1960b *Capitalism and Slavery*. London: Andre Deutsch.

1964 Trinidad and Tobago: International Perspectives. *Freedomways* 4 (3): Summer.

1970 *From Columbus to Castro: A History of the Caribbean*. New York: Morrow.

Williams, Terry

1989 *Cocaine Kids*. Orange, N.J.: Addison-Wesley.

1992 *Crackhouse: Notes from the End of the Line*. New York: Addison-Wesley.

Yawney, Carole

1969 Drinking Patterns and Alcoholism in Trinidad. In Frances Henry (ed.), *McGill Studies in Caribbean Anthropology*. Montreal: McGill University for Developing Area Studies.

Zimmer, Lynn
1987 Operation Pressure Point: The Disruption of the Street-Level Drug Trade on New York's Lower East side. *American Journal of Police* 9 (1): 43–74.

Zinberg, Norman
1984 *Drug, Set and Setting: The Social Bases of Controlled Drug Use*. New Haven, Conn.: Yale University Press.

Index

About the Author

Ansley Hamid is associate professor of anthropology at John Jay College of Criminal Justice in New York. Born in Trinidad and Tobago, he studied at the London School of Economics and at Teachers College, Columbia University, where he earned his doctorate in anthropology and education in 1980. He has taught previously in Trinidad, Britain, and Nigeria. Since 1976, he has conducted research funded by the Ford Foundation, the Harry Frank Guggenheim Foundation, the Social Science Research Council, and the National Institute on Drug Abuse on the use and distribution of marijuana, cocaine, and heroin in the Caribbean and the United States. He has written extensively on these topics and is the author of *Drugs in America: Sociology, Economics and Politics* (Aspen 1998).